Short Bike Rides®

in
Western Washington

Help Us Keep
This Guide Up to Date

Every effort has been made by the author and editors to make this guide as accurate and useful as possible. However, many things can change after a guide is published—establishments close, phone numbers change, facilities come under new management, and so on.

We would love to hear from you concerning your experiences with this guide and how you feel it could be made better and be kept up to date. While we may not be able to respond to all comments and suggestions, we'll take them to heart, and we'll also make certain to share them with the author. Please send your comments and suggestions to the following address:

The Globe Pequot Press
Reader Response/Editorial
Department
P.O. Box 480
Guilford, CT 06437

Or you may e-mail us at:

editorial@globe-pequot.com

Thanks for your input, and happy travels!

SHORT BIKE RIDES® SERIES

Short Bike Rides®

Third Edition

BY
JUDY WAGONFELD

The Globe Pequot Press

Guilford, Connecticut

Cover design: Saralyn D'Amato-Twomey
Cover photograph: West Stock
Map design: Erin Hernandez
Interior photos provided by the author.

Library of Congress Cataloging-in-Publication Data

Wagonfeld, Judy
    Short bike rides in western Washington / by Judy Wagonfeld.
— 3rd ed.
        p.   cm.   — (Short bike rides series)
    ISBN 0-7627-0435-7
    1. Bicycle touring—Washington (State), Western Guide-
books. 2. Washington (State), Western Guidebooks. I. Title. II.
Series.
GV1045.5.W22W34   2000
796.6'4'09797—dc21   99–37534
                                                      CIP

Manufactured in the United States of America
Third Edition/Third Printing

Acknowledgments

Cycling and researching this book's routes brought me into contact with innumerable enthusiastic and friendly people. It gave me great faith in humanity. Every person I dealt with, whether alone or representing an agency, delighted in assisting someone writing a bicycle book—often wanting to provide information far in excess of my requests. Most people seemed awestruck that I actually rode all the routes.

Though it is impossible to thank everyone individually, some need singling out. Those who suggested routes, places to include, or changes, I value greatly. I appreciate the encouragement and support afforded to me. I want to thank the Tacoma Wheelmen and Ellensburg Bicycle Club for supporting bicycling through group rides, several of which I have adapted in this book. My cycling partner and husband, Jim, deserves special hugs for his incredible patience while I collected information and dictated mileage as we rode, and for tolerating my late nights at the computer. Heaps of thanks to Dennis Coello for getting me into this and pushing me on. Lastly, immeasurable gratitude to my dear friends Val O'Shea and Tracy Eaton. Not only did they cycle with me, they spent Sunday afternoons whipping up delicious grub while the computer held me captive.

To everyone, *Salude!*

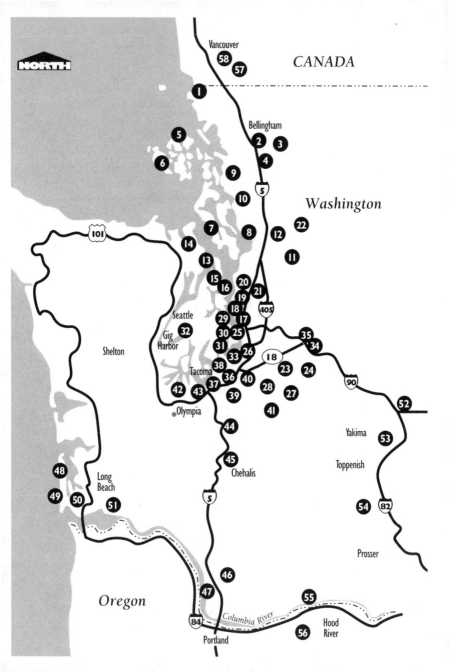

Contents

King County

Pierce County

Multnomah County, Oregon

Canada

Introduction

If I were editing a thesaurus, coffee and gray would be synonyms for Pacific Northwest. No place has better espresso or wetter weather. A Seattle paper surveyed what locals like best and least about their town. Topping both lists was rain. Figure that out.

If Northwesterners don't bike in the mist and rain, they don't bike. Seasoned bicyclists leave bike racks atop cars year-round, ready at any sign of decent weather. Once, I sought sun on a California bike trip. When torrents burst from the sky, we Northwesterners slithered expertly into our rain gear while a Bostonian gaped. Peering wistfully for the van that had driven off with less hearty souls, she donned an inadequate yellow poncho—no rain pants. We rode in a deluge, 60 miles to a Bodega Bay hotel and slid into the hot tub to the applause of the twenty vanners, swelling our friend's pride. For us, another rainy day. . . .

Think of rain as refreshing. (Buy that and you'll buy a bridge!) I've rusted and grown moss a few times. But it's a small price to pay for the rare, dry, brilliant sunny days. Our swiftly changing weather assures that no mountain view, no sunrise, and no sunset look the same twice; it makes the gray tolerable.

There's no better way to experience a place, whether urban or rural, than by bike. People trust bicyclists and volunteer friendship. Each ride evokes an area's flavor. Some destinations are reached quickly; other rides require overnight stays. Link several for a weekend getaway.

To simplify your excursion planning, the Eats, Sleeps, and Bikes sections list reliable and sampled spots.

And now a few words of wisdom:

• **Better safe than sorry.** Ben Franklin's "An ounce of prevention is worth a pound of cure" holds true for bicycle safety. Most of us feel invincible, but even Superman checked for kryptonite.

• **Directions** Although some routes appear as complicated as toy directions on Christmas Eve, don't be scared off. The Northwest, notorious for street-name changes and curves, challenges map readers, but most turns flow along. As much as possible, the rides avoid main thoroughfares. Watch for landmarks and street signs; odometers remain an imperfect tool.

• **Dogs!** Soaring along, I'm often oblivious to the territorial, snarling dog salivating behind the next hedge. Canine instincts scream, "Chase that moving object! Get it off the property!" I'm an innocent bicyclist savoring the countryside. Doesn't this mongrel get it? Heck, no. Anything moving is potential prey. And what is my natural reaction? Fight or flight.

Both choices challenge "man's best friend." Teeth bared, ears back, growling; he races at the speed of light. What's a cyclist to do? The impossible—*stop and freeze*. I dismount and avoid eye contact. He stops. Praying for mercy, I will my quavering legs to walk slowly out of Marmaduke's territory and thank some higher being for a reprieve. Though this has always worked for me, there are out-of-control dogs. Mace or Cap-Stun sounds good, but by the time you grab it, the dog's upon you. Mailmen say the sprays may not work. Picking up a rock makes dogs retreat, provided they have experience being stoned. Crossing the road may help, but forget out-racing a dog's acceleration and endurance; it doesn't work.

If attacked, play dead; crouch down in a ball, remain quiet, and cover your face. Passivity works as the best tactic to defuse aggression. Doggie thinks he's boss and trots off. Once freezing works for you, Pavlov's patterned response takes over.

• **Helmets** I'm giving an order: *Wear one!* I've heard every excuse— after all, I'm a parent. "They're too expensive, they mess my hair, they make me sweat, I like the feel of the wind, the chin strap bugs me," and last but not least, "no one else wears one." I locked my kids' bikes up for a year until they snapped on helmets.

How could I live with myself if my child was one of the 1,000 unhelmeted bicyclists who die yearly from head injuries? Or what if

I became disabled because I liked the feel of the wind? Helmets approved by the American National Standards Institute (ANSI) and the Snell Memorial Foundation cut the risk of riders' head injuries by 85 to 88 percent. Enough said.

• **Urban riding** Mountain or cross bikes negotiate city traffic, streets, and curbs best. Kevlar tires protect from glass and urban hazards. Carry a solid lock and use it. Ride with an "attitude"—a right to the streets. Watch for traffic, people, and opening car doors. Hitting a door at even 10 miles per hour spells disaster.

• **Sharing the road** You know the gorilla jokes; ditto for vehicles—move out of their way. Protect yourself and improve cyclists' images. Ride on the right, single file—and remember:

Motorists are not clairvoyant, so signal.

Get off the road to stop.

Watch for drain grate demons. Signal to veer around them.

Be wimpy. For left turns in heavy traffic, dismount in the right lane and walk across.

Be seen. Use reflectors, lights, and vests at dusk and night.

"Get off the road you . . ." Ignore it. No hand signals here; 2,000-pound vehicles outweigh your puny bike.

• **Riding in the rain** Pump your brakes, wear rain gear, oil your bike frequently, and slow down. Smile; it could be snowing.

• **Clothing** Neon is best; it helps motorists find you. Padded bike shorts and pants protect your bum, though not your pocketbook. Rain gear (preferably breathable) is a must; sweating inside it equalizes outside wetness. Cycling gloves pad your hands and, in case the sun comes out, form the telltale triangular bicyclist's tan.

Wicking fabrics such as Capilene or Coolmax wick moisture away from your body to keep you dry. Odors follow, giving garments a distinctive aroma that makes them easy to locate. Bike shirts with pockets let you stash keys and keep handkerchiefs handy—unless you prefer your sleeve. Besides, they look cool.

• **Food** The reason I ride. Current science emphasizes high carbohydrate fuel, and I must admit it works. Save the gorp, chocolate, peanut butter, salami, cheese, or cookies until later. While cycling, their fat lies undigested, like Grandma's pot roast. Instead, haul fruit and whole-grain bread or bagels. Throw in an energy bar (those congealed slabs of unidentifiable content) and a sports energy drink. I was a skeptic of this plan, but a 6,000-foot Norwegian mountain pass convinced me. Those drinks are like a shot of adrenalin. On a casual ride you can temper this purity at gourmet spots. Skip alcohol; no riding and imbibing.

Above all, have a great time, stay safe, and keep healthy.

Whatcom County: Birch Bay
Semi-ah-moo Point & Birch Bay Loop

Distance & Rating:	21.5 miles; moderate
Surface & Traffic:	Paved roads, bike lanes, bike paths; light traffic
Highlights:	Semi-ah-moo, Drayton Harbor, Birch Bay, Mount Baker and Olympic Mountain views
Eats:	Stars (fine dining), Packers Pub, Pierside (casual), Seaside Coffee Bar
Sleeps:	The Inn at Semi-ah-moo (800) 770–7992; www.semiahmoo.com
Etc.:	Beach, golf, sailing, kayaking

Reaching into Semi-ah-moo Bay, this stunning peninsula of rocky and sandy shorelines provides a study in contrasts; an elegant resort, gated developments, and a golf course line the north and west while a proliferation of trailer parks, apartments, and boxy cottages battle for space on Birch Bay—in clear view (and smell) of Arco Refinery. Here, the real estate maxim of "area, area, area" is starkly clear.

Birch Bay State Park offers camping and standard park amenities. But Semi-ah-moo State Park and Spit can't be beat. On this windswept coastal beach, the gray-frame, classic park headquarters appear to step out from a Norman Rockwell painting. Drayton Harbor nestles peacefully as a healthy estuary serving up meals to shorebirds and waterfowl. At low tide it's a wet, muddy moonscape strewn with boulders. At high tide water laps peacefully against the shores. Bald eagles rest in tree snags. Geese in V-formation slice the sky. Beaches lure visitors to endless walking and kid-like squishing in the sand.

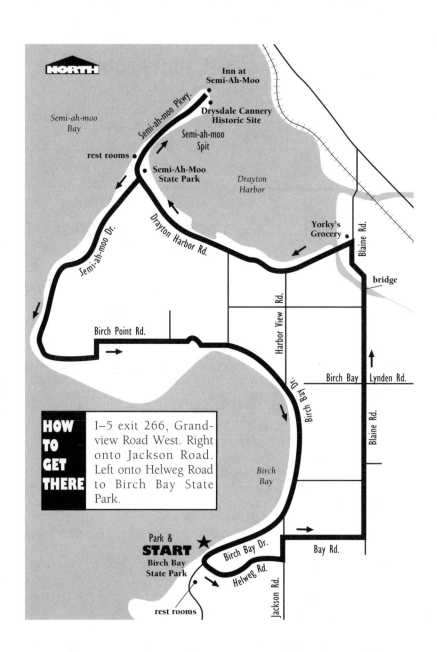

Explore the upscale Inn at Semi-ah-moo. It costs nothing to look; however, if you want a tasty, expensive lunch, this is the place. Inside, near Packers Pub, old photos depict the past. From the pub or outside decks, look across the Georgia Strait for the Point Roberts. Although part of the United States, this peninsula, which juts south into the sea, can be reached only from Canada.

Out back, abandoned canneries and remnants of the 1870 sawmill and shingle company remain. The 1891 Drysdale Cannery processed 36,000 cases a year but upped that significantly in the early 1900s when the Alaska Packers Association bought it and installed a Seattle company's new invention known as the "Iron Chink." Where cannery girls in black-and-white uniforms and long leather aprons worked, machines stepped in; however, when a 1934 edict outlawed traps that had enabled each fisherman to haul in 50,000 fish a year, the cannery had nothing to can and closed.

The old buildings and pilings function as a historical park surrounding a marine deck that offers orca-seeking cruises and charters. When the peaceful Coast Salish of the Semi-ah-moo tribes inhabited this land, they needed no charters to find wildlife. Their era ended in the 1850s as folk swept up in the Fraser River gold fever barged in and built Semi-ah-moo City.

Two pointers concerning this route: (1) In low-lying areas take ROAD CLOSED signs with a grain of salt. Roads get flooded and closed, but somehow the signs remain long past drying out. Ask at Yorky's for current conditions. (2) Do not shortcut across busy Harbor View Road. This is a nasty, well-traveled road bordered by RV parks, food stops, and the massive Wet & Wild Waterpark (a big sign says PULL TABS INSIDE).

DIRECTIONS
FOR
THE RIDE

0.0 Birch Bay State Park—Helweg Road.
1.0 Left onto Jackson Road.
1.2 Right onto Bay Road.
2.2 Left onto Blaine Road; curves left after bridge.
5.9 Left onto Drayton Harbor Road at Yorky's Grocery.

6.8 Right onto Drayton Harbor Road at the Harbor View Road junction.

9.1 Right onto Semi-ah-moo Parkway. Bike lane or paved path.

9.5 Semi-ah-moo Park. Paved path.

10.8 The Inn at Semi-ah-moo. Marina, services, bike rental. Back-track.

12.5 Right onto Semi-ah-moo Drive bike lane. Merges with road later.

15.2 Semi-ah-moo Drive becomes Birch Point Road.

18.7 Pass Harbor View Road. Bike lane in 0.5 miles.

20.0 Veer right to Birch Bay State Park.

21.5 Parking and picnic area.

Whatcom County: Bellingham
Interurban Trail, Larrabee State Park, Historic Fairhaven

Distance & Rating:	19.5 miles; easy (except Arroyo Park)
Surface & Traffic:	Includes bike lanes, paved paths, dirt trails; brief segments of heavy traffic, rest little or none, mountain bike needed
Highlights:	Historic Bellingham, Larrabee State Park, Arroyo Park, Historic Fairhaven, Boulevard Park
Eats:	Bellingham: Pacific Café, Pepper Sisters Southwest Cuisine, Il Fiasco Cucina Italiana, Manninos, The Bagelry, Café La Gente; Fairhaven: Village Books and Colophon Cafe
Sleeps:	Anderson Creek Lodge (360) 966–0598, andersoncreek@compuserve.com; Big Trees Bed and Breakfast (800) 647–2850, www.nas.com/bigtrees/; Schnauzer Crossing B&B Inn, (800) 562–2808, www.schnauzercrossing.com; A Secret Garden (360) 671–5327; Bellingham-Whatcom Visitor's Bureau (800) 487–2032 or www.bellingham.org/accommgif.html; Whatcom County B&B Guild (12 members) (360) 378–3030 or www.bellingham.org/traveldir
Bikes:	Old Town Cycles & Café, Kulshan Cycles, Fairhaven Bike and Mountain Sports

Bellingham seems like a baby Chicago. Adjacent to a bay, it sports massive industry, a university, culture, good food, sculpture, extensive parks, spacious old mansions, students, working folk, and wealth. Mount Baker, rising 10,778 feet amid the North Cascades, looms to the east. Rugged hills and channeled glacial valleys descend to Bellingham Bay's rocky shores. Beyond, the San Juan Archipelago (172 islands) lures the adventurous soul.

Of course, Bellingham is a pip-squeak next to Chicago. After all, Mrs. O'Leary had burned Chicago down when Bellingham settlers were wielding the first ax. In fact, it wasn't until 1852 that Lummi Indians led Henry Roder and Russell Peabody to Whatcom Creek and the water to run their future timber mill. Commemorating this "co-operation," an odd totem mast arises from a boat bearing painted figures of early settlers. Dedicated in 1952, it is displayed outside the sheriff's office.

Unlike Chicago, which sprawled across Illinois' flat plains, Bellingham began as four shoreline towns; Fairhaven, Sehome, Whatcom, and Bellingham. Separated by thick forests and capital "H" hills, the townships merged into Bellingham in 1902. Coal, timber, a brewery, fishing, canneries, a shipping port (at first for Alaska Gold Rush gamblers), and shipbuilding drove the economy. When Western Washington University expanded on Sehome Hill, it brought a change to the face of Whatcom County. Art and culture seeped in. Environmental concerns challenged industrial-centered policies and promoted alternative transportation. Bike lanes, paths, and racks abound. No one cares if you wear rancid bike clothing.

Downtown Bellingham's character reads more Main Street, U.S.A., than big city. Late-nineteenth- and early-twentieth-century Victorian buildings remain. Some serve their original purpose, such as the Feed and Seed store where laborers haul sacks, its fading green walls and red letters bespeaking of a past era. Across the street the funky Bagelry is jam-packed with university types. The sole match with the farm crowd is the blue jeans. Tevas, Birkenstocks, body piercings, message T-shirts, cappuccinos, veggie bagel

6

sandwiches, and the Northwest's latest addiction to fresh juices separate the bagel eaters from the wheat workers. Vintage wood tables and chairs rest on worn wood floors; shabby barstools form a ragged queue along a newspaper-strewn window counter. The masses hang out, reading alternative magazines and textbooks, perusing bulletin boards and posters, and pecking at laptop computers. The bagels meet strict New York standards: heavy doughy insides and crunchy outsides. Even the bialys, with resplendent crisp onion centers, could pass muster in Brooklyn.

For Italian imbibing of espresso, grilled paninis, or the usual breakfast carb array, settle in at Cafe la Gente (Cornwall and Magnolia). Done up in slick black with green accents, it opens to an outside cafe via windowed garage doors. Not quite Milan but nice. Around the corner on Magnolia, grab reading material at the well-stocked International News Stand.

From the 1880s to 1930s, electric rails dominated Whatcom County's transportation scene. The Interurban Line (1912 to 1930) clicked along a flat path above Chuckanut Drive. As automobiles flourished, the line was abandoned. In 1987 it was dedicated as the Interurban Trail, a public use, unpaved path for walkers, runners, and cyclists. From the bus depot (the Interurban Line's terminal), you pass Pepper Sisters and the Brenthaven Company, Northwest producers of top-quality packs, luggage, computer gear, briefcases, etc. In the park above the shore, check out Tom McClelland's 1978 *Conference Table*, a humorous public artwork sculpted in rusting steel. Three sets of figures say, "Yes," "No," and "N/A," perhaps replicating Bellingham's industrial conferences and deals.

Pass Fairhaven, waiting for your leisurely exploration on the return. Just beyond the Fairhaven Rose Garden and Hosteling International, a post bears a sign that pleads, PLEASE DO NOT PICK ROSES. A brief jaunt on Chuckanut Drive's shoulder leads to the Interurban trailhead and smooth sailing—except for one gravel ravine. Lock up and hike Larrabee State Park's rocky cliffside, where blue herons, eagles, and ducks feed as kayakers glide gracefully in the gray mist.

Backtracking on the Interurban, check carefully for the single-track route to Arroyo Park. Unless you're a loony, macho expert, walk the steep switchbacks down to Chuckanut Creek. After Samish Way push up the dirt-trail steps to the flat trail through forests and swampy wetlands scattered with yellow-flowered skunk cabbage on the way to Fairhaven Park.

Gifted by the Larrabee family, the park is the jewel of South Bellingham. Designed in 1910 by the Olmsted brothers, sons of the architect of New York City's Central Park, it includes a rose test garden, pavilion, pastoral grassy fields, Padden Creek, and winding trails. Slip off the Interurban–Lower Padden Creek Trail to roam its rolling terrain that evokes visions of George Seurat's *Sunday Afternoon on the Island of La Grande Jatte*—women in ankle-length bustle dresses and hats, parasols overhead, and Sunday-best–dressed men strolling on broad lawns. Don't miss the ornate red-and-white entry gate on Chuckanut Drive.

Back on the trail, thick forests line Padden Creek. Exiting, ride up Harris Street to Historic Fairhaven. Billed in 1889 as the "next Chicago," it drew investors by the boatload and arose like dandelions gone awry. Thirty-five hotels and boardinghouses were so chock-full that men slept in tents and haphazard driftwood shelters. McKenzie Avenue emerged as the red-light district; an invasion of gamblers and prostitutes (many as young as thirteen) filled more than thirty saloons and bordellos. Amid this, weekly cattle drives charged up muddy Harris Street to the 10th Street slaughterhouse. At present, a more pristine Fairhaven of brick and stone storefronts lures the Cruise Terminal crowds and tourists.

Needless to say, vittles abound. Village Books and The Colophon Cafe are an extravaganza that feeds the stomach and soul. Upstairs a snack bar awaits; downstairs sample the full-meal deal—calories to suit any tastes, espresso, and decadent desserts. Two expansive levels teem with books and magazines; top-notch travel and art sections can't be beat. Staff members stock shelves of personal favorites, tacking up comment cards. Brick walls, wood shelves, carpet, classical music, lighting, and author readings invite long stays. Their *Chuckanut Reader* newsletter is far from junk mail; get on the mailing list. Plan time for an unrushed visit. Then stop at the Brenthaven shop on 10th Street. Their exceptionally well-designed, lightweight but sturdy packs, briefcases, wallets, luggage, and accessories will tempt you to haul out the credit card.

On Memorial Day Weekend a Fairhaven festival and "Dancing in the Streets" culminates "Ski to Sea." This seven-leg marathon of team stamina includes cross-country and downhill skiing, running, biking, canoeing/kayaking, mountain biking, and sea-kayaking. Just the thought is exhausting; head back downtown to rest.

At dinner replenish with top fusion cuisine at the Pacific Café, where an oriental motif creates a serene atomosphere. The food's spicing of fresh items lingers on your taste buds—carrot-caraway soup, salmon in mango salsa, roast duck shiitake. Yum. Pepper Sisters dishes up new Southwest delights in an energetic bistro. Vivid paintings complement the hot yellow, orange, red, and aqua decor. Chipoltes, enchiladas, eggplant tostada, microbrews on tap, fish specials, all fresh and cooked in an open kitchen. Delicious and filling. If pasta calls your name, Il Fiasco is the answer. Though the space is country chic, the food is worthy of slicker Italian decor. Penne with chicken and Gorgonzola tidbits, veal dishes, and flavorful soups go well with the crusty bread. Enough on food. Go cycle.

DIRECTIONS

FOR

THE RIDE

0.0 South on Railroad Avenue from Bus Depot. The Bagelry.

0.3 Left onto West Chestnut Street.

0.4 Right onto North State Street. Old Town Cycles.

1.7 Bike lane begins. *Conference Table* sculpture.

2.5 Veer left onto 11th Street.

2.6 Veer left onto Finnegan Way.

2.7 Veer right onto 12th Street. Fairhaven Historical District.

3.0 Fairhaven B&B. Stoplight. Veer left onto Chuckanut Drive.

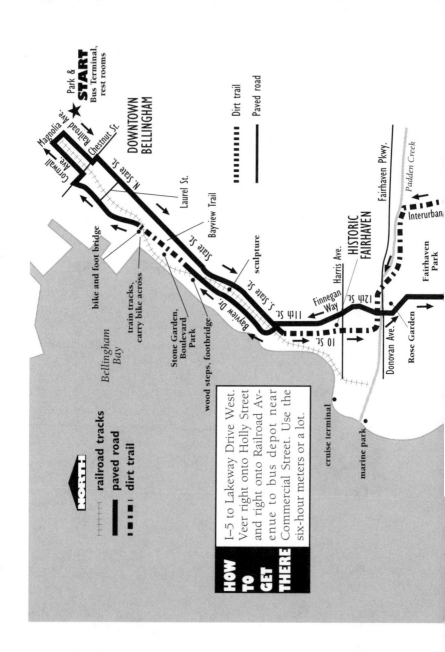

NORTH

railroad tracks
paved road
dirt trail

Park &
START
Bus Terminal,
rest rooms

Magnolia

Cornwall Ave.

Railroad Ave.

Chestnut St.

**DOWNTOWN
BELLINGHAM**

N. State St.

Laurel St.

Bayview Trail

State St.

bike and foot bridge

train tracks,
carry bike across

Stone Garden,
Boulevard Park

wood steps, footbridge

*Bellingham
Bay*

Bayview Dr.

sculpture

S. State St.

11th St.

Finnegan
Way

Harris Ave.

12th St.

10 St.

**HISTORIC
FAIRHAVEN**

Donovan Ave.

Rose Garden

Fairhaven
Park

Fairhaven Pkwy.

Padden Creek

Interurban

cruise terminal

marine park

Dirt trail

Paved road

**HOW
TO
GET
THERE**

I–5 to Lakeway Drive West.
Veer right onto Holly Street
and right onto Railroad Avenue to bus depot near
Commercial Street. Use the
six-hour meters or a lot.

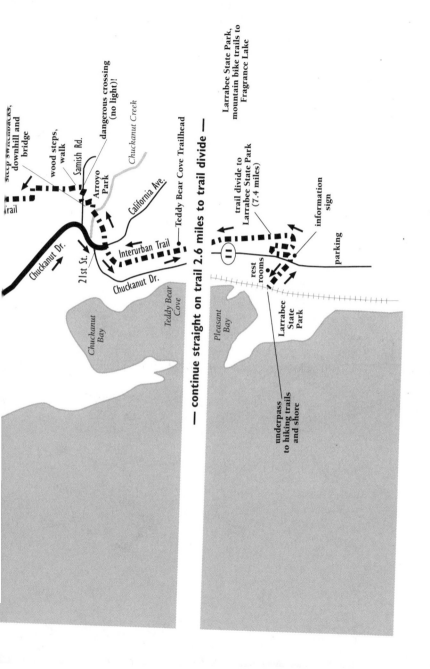

Steep switchbacks,
downhill and
bridge

wood steps,
walk

dangerous crossing
(no light)!

Samish Rd.

Chuckanut Creek

Arroyo
Park

Trail

California Ave.

Chuckanut Dr.

21st St.

Teddy Bear Cove Trailhead

Interurban Trail

Chuckanut Dr.

Larrabee State Park,
mountain bike trails to
Fragrance Lake

trail divide to
Larrabee State Park
(7.4 miles)

information
sign

parking

rest
rooms

Chuckanut Bay

Teddy Bear
Cove

Pleasant
Bay

Larrabee
State Park

underpass
to hiking trails
and shore

— continue straight on trail 2.6 miles to trail divide —

4.3 Left onto 21st Street/California Street. Up steep hill to Interurban Trail on right.

4.8 Teddy Bear Cove trailhead.

7.4 Veer right and downhill as trail divides.

7.5 Cross Chuckanut Drive to Larrabee State Park. Downhill.

7.7 Lock bike. Walk to rocky shoreline. Return to Interurban Trail.

11.8 Cross California Street onto the single-track trail.

12.2 Trail switchbacks down to Chuckanut Creek. Caution: walk!

12.8 Cross wood bridge. Left on trail up to Old Samish Road.

13.6 Cross road and walk bike up trail's steps to the top.

14.8 Veer left, past apartments to Fairhaven Park.

15.8 Follow main wide dirt trail straight. Pass creek and go under Chuckanut Drive.

16.8 Exit trail at 10th and Donovan Streets. Right onto Harris Street. Fairhaven.

17.0 Backtrack to 10th Street. Right and onto gravel trail.

17.5 Left into park across RR tracks.

17.8 Right across RR tracks at end of fence near rest rooms. Carry bike. Caution!

18.9 Cross trail bridge. Trail ends at Laurel Street. Continue straight through alley.

19.0 Right onto Chestnut Street and quick left onto Cornwall Avenue. Kulshan Cycles.

19.1 Cafe la Gente. Right onto Magnolia Street. Newsstand.

Whatcom County: Bellingham
Railroad Trail/Lake Whatcom Loop

Distance & Rating:	17.6+ miles; moderate
Surface & Traffic:	Mixed surfaces; light traffic
Highlights:	Railroad Trail, Bloedel Donovan Park, Whatcom Falls Park, Connelly Creek Trail, Western Washington University, outdoor sculptures, Sehome Hill Arboretum, Whatcom County Museum
Eats, Sleeps, Etc.:	See Ride 1

Greenways are generally leftovers. Like vegetables rejected by children, they were once undesirable plots—difficult building sites, hard-to-fill swamps, far from city centers, abandoned industrial quagmires, water and power management sites. With luck or by fate, however, these "undesirables" become choice morsels of land when in public hands.

During 1945 the city of Bellingham snapped up sixty-five such acres on Sehome Hill for a pittance: $508.00 in unpaid taxes. A far cry from the 1990 $7-million Bellingham Greenway Levy that is now being used to purchase land and build a trail system. A work in progress, it can be disjointed; trails may end abruptly in steps or require crossing busy streets. Use care, watching for the dirt and gravel trails marked by yellow-ringed, brown wood posts.

The Railroad Trail cruises the abandoned route that served the Bloedel-Donovan Mill on Lake Whatcom. In 1946 the defunct twelve-acre waterfront site was donated to the city. If you bring children, consider riding the Railroad Trail both ways and recreating (swimming, fishing, boating, play lots) at the park for an easy day.

Nearby is the 241-acre Whatcom Falls Park, replete with dense forests, waterfalls, and trails. A Juvenile Fishing Pond (for age fourteen and under only), surrounded by native grasses and rising cliffs, feeds diverse waterfowl. Upstream, at the Falls, the 1939 Works Progress Administration stone-and-iron bridge stands as a prime specimen of that era. Across it the trail wends to a spectacular whirlpool that cascades down rock walls. A wood bridge crosses to a wide path that leads to Bayview Cemetery, a historic public burial ground.

Cutting west, cycle down through a suburban development and pick up the trail near Civic Stadium. Next is a mundane stretch of street cycling leading to the Connelly Creek Trail, a gorgeous single track beneath shimmering alders. Emerge to Joe's Garden, a prolific mind-boggling flower and crop display.

Western Washington University (WWU) has the toughest admission requirements in the state and a minuscule transfer rate. It's no wonder. The striking Sehome Hill campus enjoys prime views, is near terrific outdoor resources, and is in a medium-sized city. Eons ahead of their time in 1957, WWU's Board of Trustees committed to include artworks in new construction budgets. What has emerged is an unrivaled campus collection of contemporary outdoor sculpture and the excellent Western Art Gallery. The sculptures create a motif linking the quadrangle of stately brown-brick, ivy-covered, and stained-glass-windowed historic buildings with the plant-filled rocky berms of the red-brick and concrete plaza that meanders among the ultramodern architecture. Connecting the old (North) and new (South) campuses is Red Square, a gathering spot reminiscent of European brick plazas built around a central fountain.

Designed by international, national, and regional artists, the twenty-four outdoor sculptures are major works of art. They focus on such issues as the relationship of nature and culture, human scale, types of narration, personal perceptions, and spiritual dynamics. Grab a map at the campus Visitor's Center and explore. Among them, there's *Wright's Triangle* by Richard Serra (one of his New York

City plaza works was removed due to pressure from irritated citizens), addressing confrontation, enclosure, action, and intellectual thinking. Red Square's *Skyviewing Sculpture*, in painted steel by Isamu Noguchi, invites you in to view the sky, creating a union of the forces of man and nature. *For Handel*, by Mark di Suvero, is composed of red-painted steel that seems to draw the viewer up to float above the Performing Arts Center plaza and recital hall below. At the library don't miss Richard Beyer's oddly gentle *The Man Who Used To Hunt Cougars for Bounty*. Sculpted of granite on this site, it portrays the union of man and cougar, a haunting relationship between the hunt and the hunted.

WWU's campus evokes a sense of humanization that makes it work. Plazas fill with lounging students, paths with the hustle-bustle of class-break scurrying, and bicycles seem as insidious as trees. It's truly an ideal environment—immersion in nature, art, and learning. Leaving this speck of nirvana, head to downtown's reality. On the way note the North Garden Inn, a charming Queen Anne Victorian on the National Register.

But there's more. A visit to Bellingham would be incomplete without a stop at the Whatcom Museum in old City Hall. Nearby, the renovated ornate, Moorish-Spanish–style Mount Baker Theater showcases a fine example of vaudeville-era palaces. Its 110-foot lighted tower glitters spectacularly at night. A brief downtown loop passes additional public art, the Children's Museum, and the creekside reclamation project at Maritime Heritage Park.

DIRECTIONS
FOR
THE RIDE

0.0 Bus Terminal on Railroad Avenue. Cross Champion and York Streets.

0.2 Veer right onto trail. Cross Whatcom Creek.

0.3 Cross Ohio Street onto Franklin Street.

0.7 Right onto Carolina Street. Cross Grant Street.

1.0 Cross James Street. Caution!

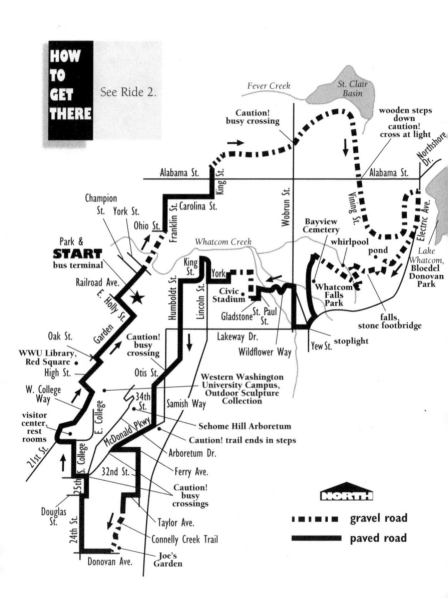

HOW TO GET THERE

See Ride 2.

Fever Creek

St. Clair Basin

Caution! busy crossing

wooden steps down caution! cross at light

Northshore Dr.

Alabama St.

King St.

Carolina St.

Franklin St.

Champion St.   York St.

Ohio St.

Wobrun St.

Vining St.

Alabama St.

Electric Ave.

Park & **START** bus terminal

Railroad Ave.

E. Holly St.

Garden

Whatcom Creek

Bayview Cemetery

whirlpool

pond

Lake Whatcom, Bloedel Donovan Park

King St.   York

Civic Stadium

Gladstone   St. Paul St.

Whatcom Falls Park

falls, stone footbridge

Humboldt St.

Lincoln St.

Oak St.

WWU Library, Red Square

High St.

W. College Way

Caution! busy crossing

Otis St.

Lakeway Dr.

Wildflower Way

Yew St.   stoplight

Western Washington University Campus, Outdoor Sculpture Collection

visitor center, rest rooms

21st St.

E. College

34th St.

Samish Way

Sehome Hill Arboretum

Caution! trail ends in steps

McDonald Pkwy

25th St.   S. College

32nd St.

Arboretum Dr.

Ferry Ave.

Caution! busy crossings

Douglas St.

24th St.

Taylor Ave.

Connelly Creek Trail

Joe's Garden

Donovan Ave.

NORTH

▪ ▬ ▪ ▬ ▪ ▬ gravel road

▬▬▬▬▬ paved road

1.1	Left onto King Street.
1.4	Right onto gravel bike trail.
2.5	Cross Woburn Street.
2.9	St. Clair Basin and Fever Creek.
3.6	Caution! Wooden steps to Alabama Street. Busy crossing.
4.4	Veer left as trail splits.
5.0	Exit trail right onto Electric Avenue/Northshore Drive shoulder.
5.1	Left into Bloedel Donovan Park to Lake Whatcom. Left from parking lot to dirt trail.
5.8	Cross Electric Avenue. Left onto trail. Whatcom Falls Park.
6.2	Right around Juvenile Fishing Pond.
6.3	Footbridge on right. Left onto trail into parking area.
6.6	Follow path downhill on right and cross WPA stone bridge. Falls below.
6.7	Veer left at end of bridge.
6.8	Whirlpool Loop sign. Caution! Slippery downhill to fence above whirlpool. Go left and right over wood bridge, following broad gravel trail that veers right.
7.4	Left into Bayview Cemetery.
7.6	Right from cemetery onto Lakeway Drive.
7.7	Cross Yew Street at stoplight.
7.8	Right onto Woburn Street. Downhill.
7.9	Left onto Wildflower Way. Wind downhill past homes.
8.2	Cross footbridge over creek at end of cul-de-sac.
8.3	Curve left onto St. Paul Street and quick right onto Gladstone. Short climb.
8.5	Right onto side road of Civic Stadium and quick right onto single-track trail.
9.5	Exit along bottom edge of athletic field.
9.7	Left onto Moore Street. Quick rights onto York and Lincoln Streets.

10.0 Go under I–5 onto Meador Avenue.

10.2 Left onto King Street.

10.4 Right onto York Street.

10.6 Left onto Humboldt Street.

11.2 Veer right onto Otis Street.

11.4 Cross Samish Way. Caution! No stoplight. Uphill.

11.8 Left onto 34th Street, continuing onto trail at end.

12.5 Caution! Steps. Right onto McDonald Parkway's bike lane.

12.7 Sharp left onto Ferry Avenue. Caution crossing.

12.9 Right onto 32nd Street.

13.2 Right onto Taylor Avenue.

13.3 Left onto Connelly Creek Trail. Dirt single track.

14.3 Exit through Joe's Garden.

14.4 Right onto Donovan Avenue. Bike lane.

14.6 Right onto 24th Street.

14.8 Right onto Douglas Avenue and quick left onto 25th Street.

15.0 Left onto McDonald Parkway. Caution at crossing.
Option: Straight across and uphill to loop Sehome Hill Arboretum.

15.1 Right onto South College Drive.

15.5 Left onto East College Way at Visitor's Center. Pick up map.

15.6 Right onto 21st Street and veer right onto brick path to university plazas. Sculptures.

15.8 Western Gallery and Fine Arts Building. Red Square.

16.1 Left onto path along Wilson Library at grassy Commons.

16.2 Performing Arts Center Plaza, bookstore, and food shops across High Street (bikes, pedestrians, and buses only). Sculptures and views. Juice bar.

16.5 Left downhill onto Oak Street.

16.6 Right onto Garden Street. North Garden Inn.

17.2 Left onto East Holly Street.

17.5 Right onto Railroad Avenue. The Bagelry.

17.6 Bus Depot and return to start.

Option: Downtown Tour (about 2 miles)

0.0   Left onto Champion Street, right onto Commercial Street, left onto Lottie Street, right at City Hall and through lot, left along Whatcom Creek (trail) to Maritime Heritage Park.

1.0   Cross Holly Street onto Central Avenue, left onto Chestnut Street, left onto Bay Street, left onto Prospect Street to Whatcom Museum.

2.0   Right onto Flora Street, right onto Grande Avenue, veer left onto Magnolia Street, left onto Railroad Avenue to end.

Whatcom County: Bellingham
Lake Padden Park

Distance & Rating:	2.8 miles, easy, good for children
Surface & Traffic:	Hard-packed dirt and gravel, no cars (A/T bike required)
Highlights:	Lake Padden, Lake Padden Park
Eats:	Picnic

Listening to lapping water as you circle Lake Padden on this hard-packed, wide path adds to a delightful ride. Shaded trails are perfect for a hot summer day.

Circle the lake counterclockwise, always veering left at path junctions. To the right more technical mountain biking paths climb through hilly forests if you want to try them out. When you come to a T-intersection on the trail, make a sharp left; you'll see an information board and a grassy lakeside and beach. Summers, this is the spot to swim or rent a boat. Along the lake piers extend into the water for wildlife viewing. Choose one for a quiet lunch.

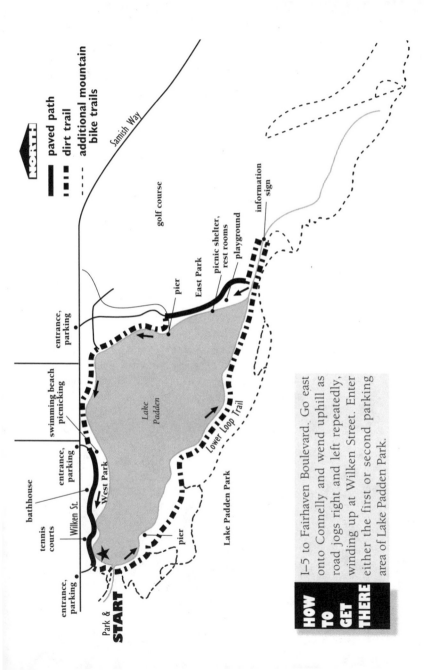

NORTH

- —— paved path
- ▬▬▬ dirt trail
- ▬ ▬ ▬ additional mountain bike trails

Samish Way

golf course

entrance, parking

pier

East Park

picnic shelter, rest rooms

playground

information sign

swimming beach picnicking

entrance, parking

bathhouse

tennis courts

Wilken St.

West Park

entrance, parking

Park & START

Lake Padden

pier

Lower Loop Trail

Lake Padden Park

HOW TO GET THERE

I-5 to Fairhaven Boulevard. Go east onto Connelly and wend uphill as road jogs right and left repeatedly, winding up at Wilken Street. Enter either the first or second parking area of Lake Padden Park.

San Juan County: Orcas Island
East Orcas, West Orcas Loops

Distance & Rating:	East Horseshoe, 20 miles; West Horseshoe, 20.2 miles; dessert-worthy hills
Surface & Traffic:	Paved roads, few bike lanes; light to moderate depending on season
Highlights:	Eastsound Village, Moran State Park, Mount Constitution, Orcas Island Artworks, Obstruction Pass, Doe Bay, West Sound, Deer Harbor
Eats:	Eastsound: Bilbo's Festivo Restaurant, Comet Cafe, La Famiglia, Owl's Bagel Cafe, Teezer's Cookies; Olga: Olga Café
Sleeps:	Orcas Island Info (360) 376–2273; www.thesanjuans.com; Eastsound: Outlook Inn & Restaurant, Kangaroo House, Smuggler's Villa; East side: Doe Bay Village, Sand Dollar Inn, Rosario Resort, Spring Bay Inn; West central: WindSong B&B, Turtleback Inn; West Sound: Chestnut Hill Inn, Deer Harbor Inn & Restaurant
Bikes:	Eastsound: Wildlife Cycles (360) 376–4708, Ferry Landing: Dolphin Bay Bicycles (360) 376–4157
Etc.:	Kayaking at Doe Bay (360) 376–2291; taxi from ferry (360) 376–TAXI

Though a challenging pedal, Orcas's charms entice even novice cyclists. Beware: Stunning views and the laid-back life may incite love. Even if it's just a crush, once you reach this magical island, you won't want to rush off.

The jewel of Orcas, Moran State Park, lies on East Horseshoe. Owner Robert Moran, a successful Seattle mayor and industrialist, donated its 5,000 acres at his death. Moran, told during his thirties that he had only a short time to live, retired to Orcas to die peacefully. Stubbornly and vigorously, he lived to his mid-eighties at Rosario, his home since 1904. Now a resort and historic landmark, it is well worth a 3.5-mile hilly separate or side trip.

Moran State Park includes lakes, a mountain, terrific hiking, and tough biking. Off-season (September 15 to May 15), trails open to mountain bikes. One easy trail circles Cascade Lake, where in summers a stand rents paddle or row boats. If you plan on grinding or hiking up Mount Constitution, stock up on water. The road climbs in switchbacks to the 2,409 foot summit (less the 700 feet already climbed). Breathtaking views replenish dwindling energy. The FALSE SUMMIT sign (sorry) means the top is near. From the parking lot head up to the real summit. Climb the medieval-looking stone tower, designed as a fire lookout. Payback comes in magnificent views and the screaming descent.

Olga Café and Orcas Island Artworks (Co-Op) represent the island's essence. Tasty food (served daily 10:00 A.M. to 6:00 P.M.) and artisans' pottery, wood, jewelry, and woven items replenish your tummy and soul—but diminish your funds. Beyond Olga cycle along Buck Bay to Obstruction Pass Trailhead for a 0.5-mile hike to the beach and the upscale Spring Bay Inn (rates include daily kayaking). As an option visit Doe Bay Resort, a sixties counterculture remnant that exemplifies "laid-back." Scattered across a stunning ravine, it is better visited than described. Bring tie-dye and Birkenstocks. For upper-body action take a short kayak trip into Doe Bay, where seals pop up but disappear if you meet their eyes. Waterfowl abound on windswept, miniature, rocky islands—a wildlife bonanza.

Backtrack to Eastsound Village, which retains much of its 1880 island-center character. Scattered eateries, shops, and markets supply island residents and visitors. Darvill's, a superb print and high-quality book vendor, makes you long for old-fashioned book shops. Glimpses of the past are evident at Emmanuel Episcopal Church (1886) and Historical Museum, a hand-hewn, dovetailed log cabin. Bask in the sun at Comet Cafe, sipping top-quality espresso and munching a chocolate-coated cookie; or lunch on specialty soups, pizza, and bread—healthy fare dispensed by sixties knock-off kids. Teezer's whips up yummy moist oatmeal chocolate chip delights. No matter what you nibble, save room for Bilbo's Festivo—Mexican fare with a special flare. Their enchiladas verdes are lip-smacking good. The sensuous pleasure of hot, ice-cream–stuffed sopapillas, slathered in praline sauce, requires immediate confession.

West Sound, once home to the Elelung Indian village, supplied bountiful fish, deer, small mammals, berries, and wild plants. Residents fashioned cedar logs into shelters and canoes, bark into clothing and diapers. Destroyed by an 1856 Haida Indian raid, the village never recovered. Massacre Bay memorializes the slaughter.

Deer Harbor, the hot sunset viewing spot, sits on a finger-like peninsula forming West Sound and reached by cycling an idyllic shore. Pick up picnic pasta and salad fixings at the Bounty Market or grab a table at Hemingway's by the Sea or the Deer Harbor Inn (restaurant) and pottery shop.

Crow Valley Road runs up the West Horseshoe along sprawling, verdant pastures speckled with grazing sheep and cattle. Halfway up is the Turtleback Farm Inn, a gutted and restored farmhouse owned by Susan Fletcher, daughter of Buster Crabbe (of Olympic medal and Tarzan fame). With husband Bill and a shaggy black dog named Vicar, they offer luxurious (but not soundproofed) rooms and gourmet breakfasts.

Hyperactive, power-thighed cyclists might add the West Beach loop—see map. Though plagued by steep hills, there's interesting stuff here: an 1895 apple packing house built with 20-inch lower walls to ensure coolness, a cemetery, the Pottery Studio, and the Look Out Mountain trailhead.

On the basic route don't miss Tony Howe's gargantuan wind sculptures dangling from roadside trees on Horseshoe Highway. Hike up to his huge, grassy hilltop sculpture garden and gallery. For a flat, Eastsound Village tour, pedal up North Beach Road (see map), past Kangaroo House B&B and Smuggler's Villa, to a striking pocket-sized beach. Unfortunately, most shoreline rests in private hands—enjoy this teeny bit.

To East Horseshoe and Moran State Park

0.0 Eastsound Village at Horseshoe Highway and North Beach Road; go left onto Horseshoe Highway.

0.3 Crescent Beach. Oyster Beds. Kayak rental.

1.0 Right at T-intersection, following Horseshoe Highway.

4.2 Uphill mile ends. Pass Rosario Road. Moran State Park.

5.2 Cascade Lake. Campgrounds.

6.0 Straight to Olga.
Option: Left to Mount Constitution. Little Summit (2,040 feet), False Summit (2.4 miles), Summit (2,409 feet). Caution on the screeching downhill. Left to Olga.

7.8 Olga and Olga Café. Left onto Point Lawrence Road (3.1 miles to Doe Bay Village from Olga).

8.3 Right to Obstruction Pass Trailhead and Spring Bay Inn.

9.0 Right onto dirt road to trailhead. Pass Spring Bay Inn gates.

10.0 Parking lot trailhead. 0.5-mile hike to beach. Backtrack.

20.0 Return to Eastsound Village.

To West Horseshoe and Deer Harbor

0.0 Begin at Eastsound Village. Head toward the ferry on Horseshoe Highway.

0.2 Left at T-intersection as Horseshoe Highway turns left.

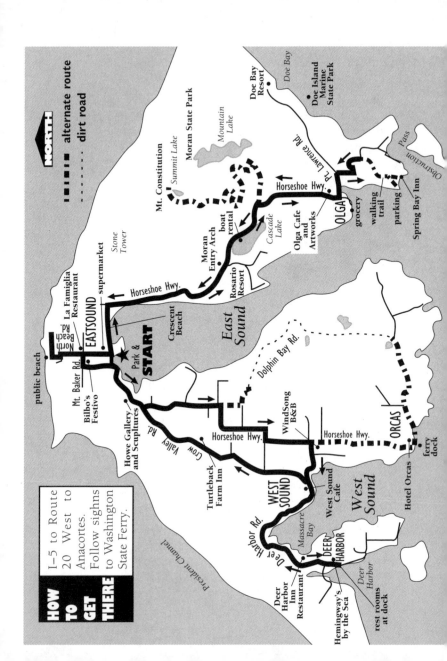

1.5 Veer left following Horseshoe Highway at the Y-intersection.
5.8 Right onto Deer Harbor Road to West Sound. WindSong B&B.
6.6 Pass Crow Valley Road. Westsound Cafe & Grill.
10.2 Deer Harbor Inn Restaurant.
10.6 Deer Harbor Village and cafes. Rest rooms at dock. Backtrack.
14.6 Left onto Crow Valley Road.
16.4 Turtleback Inn.
18.2 Pass West Beach Road.
18.8 Left onto Horseshoe Highway. Caution! Hanging sculptures.
19.8 Curve right on Horseshoe Highway into Eastsound Village.
20.2 Return to start.

San Juan County:
San Juan Island
American Camp and Roche Harbor Loops

Distance & Rating:	Loop 1, 30 miles, steep hills; Loop 2, 16 miles, moderate hills
Surface & Traffic:	Smooth to rough roads; traffic heavy in summer
Highlights:	Loop 1—Friday Harbor, Whale Museum, Pig War Museum, Roche Harbor Resort, Mausoleum and cemetery, San Juan Island Historical Park and English Camp, San Juan Park, Lime Kiln Lighthouse and Whale Watch Park, views; Loop 2—False Bay, American Camp National Historic Park, Pickett's Monument, lighthouse
Eats:	Madelyn's Bagel bakery, Springtree Cafe, Duck Soup Inn, Friday Harbor House Dining, Roche Harbor
Sleeps:	B&B Association of San Juan Island Reservation Hotline—short-notice bookings only (360) 378–3030 or www.san-juan-island.net; Roche Harbor: Hotel de Haro; Friday Harbor: Harrison House, Panacea, Westwinds, Orcinus Inn
Bikes:	Island Bicycles in Friday Harbor (360) 378–4941
Etc.:	San Juan Excursions (360) 378–6675 or www.watchwhales.com

San Juan Island's terrain varies from flat to rocky marine bluffs, a cyclist's paradise of extensive shoreline and panoramic views. Multiple lakes and wetlands harbor wildlife. Abundant deer wander meadows, cattle graze lush fields, and orca surface in Haro Strait. Near the ferry Friday Harbor has ready access to shops, food, and museums.

Early Spanish explorers, mindful of San Juan Island's strategic location, named and claimed this prime real estate. British settlers renamed it Bellevue Island. U.S. pioneers restored the original name but almost created a war.

After the 1846 Oregon Territory Treaty with the British, U.S. officials realized they had overlooked vague language referring to the "worthless" islands in the Sound. Meanwhile, the British set up shop, tapping into rich fur, fish, timber, and grazing potential. The Americans, assuming ownership, grabbed the island's southern end. Tempers flared. Meanwhile, a British pig regularly destroyed American Lyle Cutler's potato patch. Cutler shot it, bringing tensions to a head. The American Camp's General Pickett failed to resolve the issue. President Buchanan dispensed an envoy who negotiated temporary joint ownership until, in 1872, a German arbitrator ruled in favor of the United States, kicking the British out. Both camps later became historic parks. Keith Murray's *The Pig War* details this diplomatic mess.

At British Camp, multiple-trunked, massive maples dwarf white clapboard buildings. The blockhouse, symbol of occupation, was never used against the Americans, but it kept the northern Indians away. Enclosed in a white picket fence, sculpted gardens form a maze. Fortunately for later generations, when the Brits departed in 1872, the Crook family settled here. Because James Crook treasured the grassy, waterfront site, he cared for it until his death in 1967 (at the age of ninety-three). At that time the land received public park designation.

At American Camp a Visitor Center leads to an interpretive walk that begins with General Pickett's home. Situated on a grassy rise, it remains as the only remnant of the fenced compound. Outside, the plain Laundress' Quarters remains. A prized job for a senior enlisted man's wife, this position earned extra rations for the family and kept a woman around as a "stabilizing effect on men at a frontier military outpost."

At the cove's marina, kayakers and divers suit up while couch potatoes look on or gaze at distant mountains. Don't miss the weird Mausoleum burial park. Grab a brochure at the Hotel de Haro. Trails lead to the forested workers' cemetery, presently under research and repair by locals.

San Juan County Park, the only public campsite, boasts million-dollar waterfront views across Smallpox Bay. Legend has it that smallpox-afflicted Indians cooled their fevers here, only to die of pneumonia. Just south, Lime Kiln State Park is also known as "Whale Watch Park." Whale hopefuls disperse on the rocky cliffs, binoculars and cameras pointed as the graceful orca surface for air. A resident pod regularly entertains. Multiple companies run kayaking and boat trips to get up close and personal.

Loop 1

0.0 Begin at Spring and First Streets.
0.1 Right onto Second Street.
0.3 Veer left onto Guard Street.
0.4 Right onto Tucker Avenue—becomes Roche Harbor Road. Pig War Museum.
5.2 Duck Soup Inn Restaurant.
6.4 Llama farm.
8.3 Right at T-intersection to remain on Roche Harbor Road.
9.6 Roche Harbor arch. Main road to resort. Exit on narrow road past hotel.
Option: 3-mile Mausoleum visit. Left at arch, uphill onto private road. Cemetery on right. At Mausoleum sign, walk or ride up dirt road.
12.2 Veer right onto West Valley Road.
13.5 Right to British Camp. 0.3 miles gravel road.

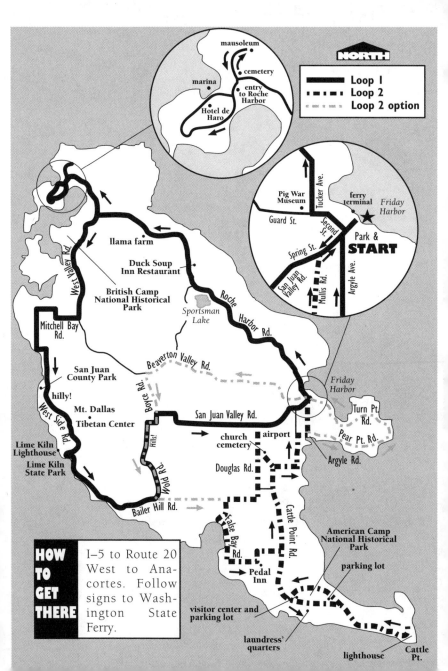

NORTH

Loop 1
Loop 2
Loop 2 option

mausoleum
cemetery
marina
entry to Roche Harbor
Hotel de Haro

Pig War Museum
Tucker Ave.
ferry terminal
Friday Harbor
Guard St.
Second St.
Spring St.
Park & **START**
San Juan Valley Rd.
Mullis Rd.
Argyle Ave.

West Valley Rd.
llama farm
Duck Soup Inn Restaurant
British Camp National Historical Park
Sportsman Lake
Roche Harbor Rd.
Mitchell Bay Rd.
Beaverton Valley Rd.
San Juan County Park
Boyce Rd.
San Juan Valley Rd.
Friday Harbor
Turn Pt. Rd.
hilly!
West Side Rd.
Mt. Dallas
Tibetan Center
Wold Rd.
Hills!
church cemetery
airport
Pear Pt. Rd.
Argyle Rd.
Lime Kiln Lighthouse
Lime Kiln State Park
Douglas Rd.
Bailer Hill Rd.
False Bay Rd.
Pedal Inn
Cattle Point Rd.
American Camp National Historical Park
parking lot
visitor center and parking lot
laundress' quarters
lighthouse
Cattle Pt.

HOW TO GET THERE I–5 to Route 20 West to Anacortes. Follow signs to Washington State Ferry.

15.0 Right onto Mitchell Bay Road.

16.4 Veer left onto West Side Road (turns into Bailer Hill Road).

18.2 Straight at Sunset Point Road.

18.5 San Juan County Park.

20.8 Lime Kiln State Park. AKA Whale Watch Park.

23.8 Left onto Wold Road.

26.4 Right onto San Juan Valley Road.

30.0 Return to start at Spring and First Streets.

Loop 2

0.0 Spring and First Streets. Head up Spring Street.
Option: To add 9 hilly miles, head out Beaverton Valley Road, left onto Boyce Road, which becomes Wold Road, left onto Bailer Hill Road, right onto False Bay Road, joining basic route.

1.0 Veer left as Spring becomes San Juan Valley Road.

1.6 Left onto Douglas Road.

3.3 Right as Douglas turns, becoming Bailer Hill Road.

4.0 Left onto False Bay Road. Dirt and gravel. Farm, False Bay.

5.8 Left at curve. Paving resumes.

6.5 Pedal Inn Bicycle Camp.

7.4 Right onto Cattle Point Road.

8.7 Right at American Camp entrance. Gravel road to Visitor Center; path from lot heads to historic area. Continue to second lot and road.

10.0 Left onto Pickett's Lane (or right to beach).

10.1 Left onto Cattle Point Road out of park. Forested; no views.
Option: Right on paved road 2.2 miles to Cattle Point Lighthouse. Wide open views. Backtrack.

11.7 Left at curve as road becomes Argyle Road.

14.7 Right as Argyle turns before airport. Straight is Mullis Road, flatter route to town.

Option: 4.3 hilly miles looping Pear Point and Turn Point Roads. 1,200-foot gravel stretch at gravel pit. Splendid views. See map.

15.4 Curve left uphill. Right onto Cormorant to Isis Bakery (open on Tuesdays and Wednesdays only).

15.7 Right onto Spring Street (from either Mullis or Argyle).

16.0 Return to start.

7 Island County: Whidbey Island
Keystone/Ebey's Landing Loop

Distance & Rating:	35 miles; easy to difficult
Surface & Traffic:	Paved road; minimal traffic except Route 20
Highlights:	Admiralty Bay, Rhododendron State Park (May), Captain Whidbey Inn, Fort Ebey and Fort Casey State Parks, Coupeville Arts Center (360) 678–3396
Eats:	Langley: Raven Cafe, Star Bistro, Inn at Langley, Cafe Langley; Coupeville: Captain Whidbey Restaurant; Coupeville Dock: market, restaurant, kayak rentals
Sleeps:	For Whidbey information www.whidbeyisland.com or call (800) 880–0886; Langley: The Dove House, Eagle's Nest, Lone Lake Cottage & Breakfast, Log Castle, Inn at Langley; Coupeville: Anchorage Inn B&B, Compass Rose, Captain Whidbey Inn, Inn at Penn Cove, Old Morris Farm; Keystone Ferry area: Fort Casey Inn, The Colonel Crocket Farm B&B
Bikes:	Langley: The Pedaler (360) 321–5040; Coupeville: All Island Bicycles (360) 678–3351
Etc.:	Parks, camping (360) 675–7665 or (360) 331–4559; bird-watching; (August) Coupeville Arts & Craft Festival (360) 678–3396

When is an island not an island? This isn't a trick question; rather, it's a query concerning atmosphere. Mapped as a peninsula, this "island" was "discovered" in 1792 by Captain Joseph Whidbey. In his honor Captain George Vancouver christened it "Whidbey" and the passage, "Deception Pass," because Whidbey saw through the "deception."

Whidbey's 45-mile length and 212 square miles exude a blend of developed mainland and rural character. Within its six towns and Naval Air Station, more than 60,000 people reside here. Nestled in a mountain rain shadow, Whidbey Island basks in less than 25 inches of rain annually. That, and accessibility by two ferry routes and one bridge, makes this the state's fastest growing county. At the same time it remains a great vacation getaway.

Threatened by creeping development, central-islanders, in 1978, established Ebey's Landing National Historic Reserve, 22 square miles designed to foster sensible relationships between people and land. It mandates farmland, avoids intrusive ridge or shore changes, preserves historic buildings, and allows public access without violating private rights—a tall order, but it's working. And the reserve offers top cycling to boot.

The reserve's west-side, windswept spit, anchored by the Keystone Ferry Dock, is one of the two state marine parks that lure divers to a rich underworld and landlubbers to remarkable rocky tide pools. Ferries, crisply painted white, green, and red, glide against the view, feeding photo hounds' hunger in both misty fog and brilliant sunsets. The adjacent Fort Casey State Park's jetty lighthouse gleams in the sun. Fort Casey, one of the "Triangle of Fire" forts protecting Puget Sound and the Bremerton Naval Yard, displays classic World War I–era coastal fortifications. Its 180-degree view encompasses sprawling green lawns, sandy beaches, white-capped blue water, dark green Olympic forests, and the mountains' icy peaks, together forming dazzling bands as if color slashes across a Rothko minimalist painting. Luck may add a crimson sunset.

Admiralty Bay and nearby brackish-water Crockett Lake host resident and migratory birds. Even a brief stop rewards with marsh and red-tailed hawks, herons, swans, pintails, teals, mallards, and sand-pipers. Across the reserve, gray whales travel through Saratoga Passage, unfortunately not on a predictable schedule. On the plateau the colonial-style Old Morris Farm Inn nestles among English gardens and agricultural fields. Owner Marilyn Randock (not a cyclist), who rises with the roosters but remains in her bathrobe at 9:00 A.M., whips up full farm breakfasts bent on inhibiting vigorous cycling. Peek at the impeccably decorated rooms, cheery parlors, sunny decks, and spa.

Coupeville, the island's first city (1852) nestles on serene Penn Cove. Reached only by sea, it was dubbed the "City of Sea Captains." Its historic Victorian buildings suggest lazy garden-guild afternoons where captains' wives sipped tea. The cove's all-weather anchorage allowed brisk trading of wool, lumber, crops, and apples. As roads developed, Penn Cove converted to pleasure crafts and oyster production. Take a self-guided tour at the Historical Museum, Alexander Blockhouse, and the scenic 1901 Wharf.

As in all villages along the Cascade Loop, tourist shops abound. Sprouting from one genetic pool, they pop up like toast in La Conner, Mt. Vernon, Winthrop, (frontier theme) or Leavenworth (Swiss Alps theme). It's all souvenir "stuff," known in Yiddish as *tchotchke*. At Nautical 'N' Nice, fishnets frame ship clocks, nautical wear, and Northwest paraphernalia. A haughty sign warns, NO PHOTOGRAPHS. NO NOTEPADS OR PENS OR NOTE TAKING. WE CONSIDER THESE ACTIONS THIEVERY. It's no joke; lift a camera and the clerks flock like vultures.

For a quiet lunch grab picnic fixings in Coupeville. Or try the enchanting Captain Whidbey Inn. Built in 1907 of madroña logs, it remains family-run, preserved (except for added roads and indoor plumbing), and filled with smoky aromas. The intimate restaurant, cozy bar, creaking floorboards, quaint rooms (don't get one above the noisy bar) with featherbeds, and cushy fireside chairs ooze serenity. Originally, guests arrived by paddle-wheel steamer for a pampered rest and meals of local seafood and the inn's garden produce.

On Admiralty Inlet, gorgeous Fort Ebey State Park evolved from an abandoned bluff-top World War II encampment. South of the park, Isaac Ebey settled Ebey's Prairie, where friends and relatives cut and sold oak and fir, trading for vittles at Ebey's Landing until they cultivated potatoes, oats, and wheat and raised sheep. Davis Blockhouse provided refuge for pioneers during Indian attacks though Ebey was beheaded in a reprisal attack. Nearby, the Sunnyside Cemetery weaves its own saga.

Adjacent Hill Road (aptly named) climbs to an eagle-watching cliff. End in a welcome downhill glide.

DIRECTIONS
FOR
THE RIDE

0.0 Keystone Ferry parking lot. Right onto Keystone Road/Route 20.

1.0 Left at T-intersection as Keystone Road turns.

1.3 Right onto Wanamaker Road. Uphill.

3.5 Cross Route 525/20—caution. Becomes Race Road. Uphill.

6.0 Pass Welcher Road. Race becomes Harrington Road.

7.0 Left onto Morris Road. The Old Morris Farm Inn.

7.5 Left at T-intersection onto Route 20's wide shoulder; caution.

8.9 Right onto Patmore Road. Rhododendron County Park.

10.5 Right at T-intersectiononto Fort Casey Road.

12.2 Right at T-intersectiononto Terry Road and right onto Route 20.

14.4 Cross Route 20 just before it veers right. Go left onto NE Parker Road.

16.7 Downhill to Coupeville. Right onto NE Gould Street, veering left onto NE Front Street.

17.1 Left onto NW Alexander Street. Museum. Public dock. Alexander Blockhouse.

17.2 Right onto NW Coveland Street to intersection at Coupeville City Park.

17.4 Left onto NW Madrona Way. Uphill.

20.0 Captain Whidbey Inn on right.

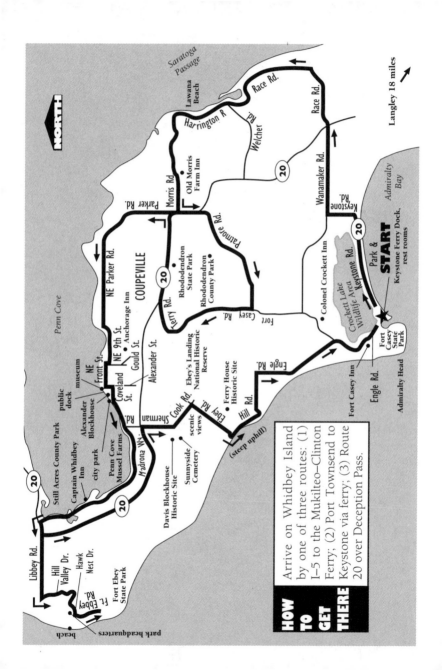

NORTH

Saratoga Passage

Langley 18 miles

Lawana Beach

Race Rd.

Race Rd.

Harrington R

Welcher Rd.

Penn Cove

Old Morris Farm Inn

Morris Rd.

Parker Rd.

20

Wanamaker Rd.

NE Parker Rd.

COUPEVILLE

Patmore Rd.

Keystone Rd.

20

Admiralty Bay

NE 9th St.
Anchorage Inn

Gould St.

Ferry Rd.

Rhododendron State Park

Rhododendron County Park

Colonel Crockett Inn

START

Keystone Ferry Dock, rest rooms

museum

NE Front St.

Alexander St.

Fort Casey Rd.

Crockett Lake Wildlife Area

Keystone Rd.

public dock

Loveland St.

Alexander Blockhouse

Ebey's Landing National Historic Reserve

Park & rest rooms

Penn Cove Mussel Farms

Captain Whidbey Inn

Still Acres County Park

city park

Sherman Rd.

Cook Rd.

Ferry House Historic Site

Engle Rd.

Fort Casey Inn

Fort Casey State Park

20

Madrona Wy.

scenic views

Ebey Rd.

Hill Rd.

Engle Rd.

Admiralty Head

20

Davis Blockhouse Historic Site

Sunnyside Cemetery

(steep uphill)

Libbey Rd.

Hill Valley Dr.

Hawk Nest Dr.

Ft. Ebey Rd.

Fort Ebey State Park

beach

park headquarters

HOW TO GET THERE Arrive on Whidbey Island by one of three routes: (1) I-5 to the Mukilteo-Clinton Ferry; (2) Port Townsend to Keystone via ferry; (3) Route 20 over Deception Pass.

21.0 Left at T-intersectiononto Route 20. Immediate right onto Libbey Road.

23.5 Left onto Hill Valley Drive. Park sign.

24.0 Right onto park road at barrier (unmarked Hawk Nest Drive). Downhill.

24.4 Left to Fort. Hilly. Backtrack. Pass headquarters to beach. Backtrack.

26.4 Right onto Libbey Road.

27.0 Right onto Route 20. Wide shoulder, heavy traffic.

29.0 Right onto Sherman Road. Cemetery and blockhouse.   •

29.3 Veer left onto Cook Road.

29.7 Veer right onto Ebey Road. Views! Follow switchbacks to the bay.

31.0 Uphill on Hill Road and curve left.

32.0 Right onto Engle Road.

34.0 Fort Casey. Fort Casey Inn.

35.0 Keystone Ferry parking lot.

8 Skagit County: La Conner
Fir Island Loop

Distance & Rating:	24.0 miles, 13.7-mile option; easy
Surface & Traffic:	Flat paved road; two easy hills
Highlights:	La Conner, farms, wetlands, B&Bs, museum, Fir Island, Wildlife Game Range
Eats:	Palmer's Restaurant, Wild Iris, Andiamo, Calico Cupboard & Bakery, Cascade Candy
Bikes:	Bike Hotline (360) 428–9487
Sleeps:	Hotel Planter, The Heron in La Conner, Katy's Inn, La Conner Country Inn, White Swan Guest House, Wild Iris Inn, Rainbow Inn
Etc.:	Museum of Northwest Art, (360) 466–4446; Skagit County Historical Museum, (360) 466–3365; Skagit Valley Tulip Festival (April), (360) 428–5959; Mount Vernon Chamber of Commerce, (360) 428–8347; La Conner Chamber of Commerce, (888) 642–9284, www.laconner-chamber.com

Let's make one thing clear. The April Skagit Valley Tulip Festival weekend is not the time to bicycle here—unless you're a carbon monoxide fan. Several hundred thousand visitors descend on these two-lane roads to ogle tulips, daffodils, and irises. Like a rainbow quilt, these brilliant red, yellow, pink, blue, and white fields refresh one's view of simple pleasures. To the Dutch immigrants, however, it's not mere aesthetics. Arriving after World War II, they transformed a modest local flower industry to a $12 million a year extravaganza.

Okay, you work weekdays yet lust after a colorful antidote to winter's gray. So, go. Cycle single file, stick to bike lanes or the white line, and get off the road for photos. You won't be alone; rainfall of only 15 inches and an average temperature of 57°F offer unbeatable bicycling. Grab a chewy, firm bagel at the Bagel House; nowhere else can you get a schmear of Oreo (yes!) cream cheese. Owner Bob Zuidema, an avid fisherman, trades bagels for fish photos. Plaster yours amid his motley collection while getting jump-started by Fidalgo Island coffee.

Head out to rural Fir Island, smack in the middle of a floodplain. Though "reclaimed" from wetland status by dikes and drainage, Fir Island floods every 2.2 years—a fact evident from how homes sit high. Larry Kunzler, author of *The Disaster Waiting To Happen*, explains the valley lives on borrowed time. He quotes a *Skagit Valley Herald* editorial: ". . . a 100-year flood would rampage through the valley, destroy salt water dikes and roar through the town of La Conner." Get out the ark; but remember, what's bad for people can be luxurious for trumpeter swans, bald eagles, herons, ducks, and geese. In fact, wildlife flourishes in the prime wetland nesting and feeding sites of the Wildlife Game Range.

One-third of the population raises flowers, vegetables, berries, mint, and seeds. Farmers mark fields peas, potatoes, and so forth to help naive city folk. Massive combines harvest crops and migrant laborers pick berries and flowers. A Victorian farmhouse, now the White Swan Guest House B&B, nestles amid a spectacular English garden. Host Peter Goldfarb caters to visitors desiring a peaceful haven for resting, reading, and healthy grub—yogurt, fruit, and muffins—rather than the ubiquitous fatty B&B breakfasts. Goldfarb's three dogs meander about, seeking friends to lick.

Cascade Loop tourists flock to La Conner's idyllic river setting; it makes for the ultimate day trip, chock full of quaint shops, antiques, historic architecture, and museums. A steady stream of buses and cars dispense the plump and polyestered who grab a tulip screened T-shirt, kitchen towel, cup, key chain, wind sock, or hand-crafted teddy bear. Worn from decision making, they plop down at a waterfront restaurant or stroll outside with a mid-afternoon waffle cone (no food or drinks allowed in the store!). As six o'clock approaches, shops close and tourists retreat like the surf at low tide.

Until smallpox hit, Native Americans fished and gathered food on these lush acres. Waning tribes ceded chunks of land to Governor Isaac Stevens in the late 1800s, retaining only two small reservations away from white folk. La Conner, named for Louisa Ann Conner, the wife of a town father and the first non-Indian woman to live here, drew canneries, farmers, artists, and writers to its bustling waterfront village. As a rural refuge, it inspired Northwest art—subtle, muted abstractions of nature created by Morris Graves, Mark Tobey, and Guy Anderson. Here, Tom Robbins' wild, irreverent ideas fed novels such as *Another Roadside Attraction*.

Check out the historic hill homes, Historical Museum, Rainbow Bridge, and Museum of Northwest Art. Dine at one of La Conner's excellent bistro restaurants (Palmer's, Wild Iris, or Andiamo) tucked between the antiques and cutesy shops. Pick up a visitor's map and take a stroll.

Optional or Separate Reservation Loop

Entering the Swinomish Reservation for this optional loop, don't miss the simple white church. Outside, a folksy carved and painted crèche sits kitty-corner from a unique blue totem the height of a telephone pole. Rolling hills traverse dense forests of fir and massive, multiple-trunked maples, branched like umbrellas overhead. Needless to say, the Skagit Indian tribe camped, fished, and hunted along the Skagit River eons before the "first settlers" cut trees for cabins on Fidalgo Island in 1856–59. Presently, the tribe operates a lumber mill, casinos, and multiple small businesses. Mountain and valley views abound as you pass expensive-view homes or littered yards and crumbling shacks.

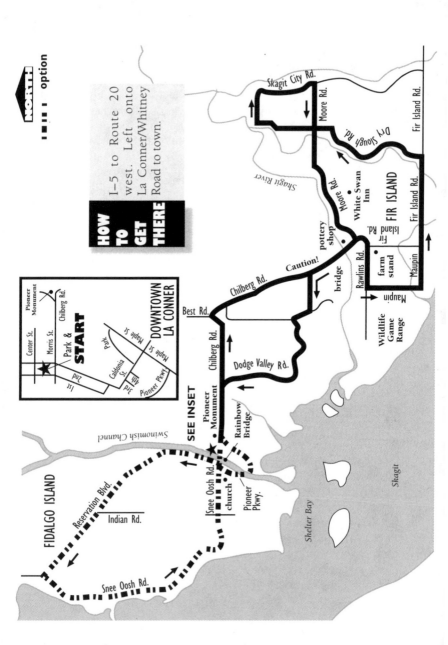

NORTH

▬ ▬ ▬ option

HOW TO GET THERE

I–5 to Route 20 west. Left onto La Conner/Whitney Road to town.

DOWNTOWN LA CONNER

Pioneer Monument

Center St.

Morris St.

Chilberg Rd.

START

Park &

1st

2nd

3rd

4th

Caledonia St.

Park

Maple St.

Maple St.

Pioneer Pkwy.

SEE INSET

Pioneer Monument

Rainbow Bridge

Swinomish Channel

FIDALGO ISLAND

Reservation Blvd.

Indian Rd.

Snee Oosh Rd.

church

Pioneer Pkwy.

Shelter Bay

Skagit

Best Rd.

Chilberg Rd.

Dodge Valley Rd.

Chilberg Rd.

Caution!

pottery shop

bridge

Rawlins Rd.

farm stand

Maupin

Wildlife Game Range

Maupin

Fir Island Rd.

Fir Island Rd.

FIR ISLAND

White Swan Inn

Moore Rd.

Moore Rd.

Dry Slough Rd.

Skagit River

Skagit City Rd.

Fir Island Rd.

DIRECTIONS
FOR
THE RIDE

0.0 North 2nd and Center Streets.

0.1 Left onto Morris Street; becomes Chilberg Road at Pioneer Monument. Wide shoulder.

2.8 Right at BEST ROAD sign, staying on Chilberg Road.

5.4 Pleasant Ridge Pottery. Uphill across Skagit River bridge.

5.8 Right at T-intersection onto Fir Island Road.

6.3 Right before farmstand onto Rawlins Road. Skagit Wildlife Game Range.

7.0 Left onto Maupin Road. Cross Brown's Slough and curve left.

8.8 Veer right onto Fir Island Road. Wide shoulder.

10.4 Left onto Dry Slough Road. Cross Polson and Moore Roads.

14.0 Curve right following Dry Slough Road. Note dikes.

15.6 Right onto Moore Road and cross Dry Slough Road.

17.4 White Swan Guest House. English Gardens.

18.2 Right onto Chilberg Road. Cross bridge.

19.2 Left onto Dodge Valley Road. Caution! Veer left at Y-intersection.

22.8 Left onto Chilberg Road; becomes Morris Street. Rainbow Inn.

24.0 Right onto North 2nd Street to Center Street.

Optional or Separate Reservation Loop

13.5 miles, moderate ride

0.0 Park near North 2nd and Center Streets.

0.1 Right onto Morris Street and left onto North 1st Street.

0.2 Right onto North 2nd Street at Town Hall, curving left onto Caldonia Street.

0.6 Right onto Maple Street/Pioneer Parkway. Pioneer Park. Rainbow Bridge.

1.5 Pass Snee Oosh Road, church, and blue totem, continuing onto Reservation Boulevard.

3.5 Pass Indian Road.

6.0 Left at Y-intersection onto Snee Oosh Road.

9.5 Veer left as Snee Oosh Road curves.

11.7 Right onto Reservation Road/Pioneer Parkway. Cross Rainbow Bridge.

13.7 La Conner.

Skagit County: Bow
Valley Loop

Distance & Rating:	20 miles; flat, easy
Surface & Traffic:	Paved road; few cars
Highlights:	Expansive views of farm buildings, crops, mountains, art colony
Eats, Bikes:	See Ride 8; Rhododendron Café

Hovering over vast fields dotted with black and white cows, the morning mist seems a protective cover. Melding into the gray clouds wrapping intermittent segments of the steep Cascade foothills, it forms a panorama replicated in the well-known Northwest prints of Gary Markgraf. In fact, his work has become part of the language; as in, when viewing these fog-ensconced scenes, fans say, "It's a Markgraf," as though he envisioned the scene and it materialized.

Sliced by the winding Samish River, this flat floodplain produces potatoes, vegetables, and flowers. In spring vast stretches of tilled dirt contrast with rustic red barns, sleek silos, and white farmhouses. Crumbling weathered barns reveal the rain's rotting effect on wood. Blueberry bushes blossom in delicate pinks. Color is abundant, not to mention the immense spring tulip displays. In rain-saturated pastures, horses frolic and llamas munch, their thick fur matted and wet. Tractors drop mud on the roads. Cows drop chips. Late summer and autumn row crops blossom: purple potato-plant flowers, tall corn stalks, pea patches, ripe berries, orange pumpkins, green zucchini, and yellow squash. When the sun burns off the fog, the valley sparkles in new dimensions.

Stop at Edison, in the throes of conversion from pure farm town to artists colony. The Edison Eye and Samishg Studios display the creative work of locals; artists open their studios on weekends. If you time the ride right, eat at the Rhododendron Café, an informal spot that cooks up high-quality fare.

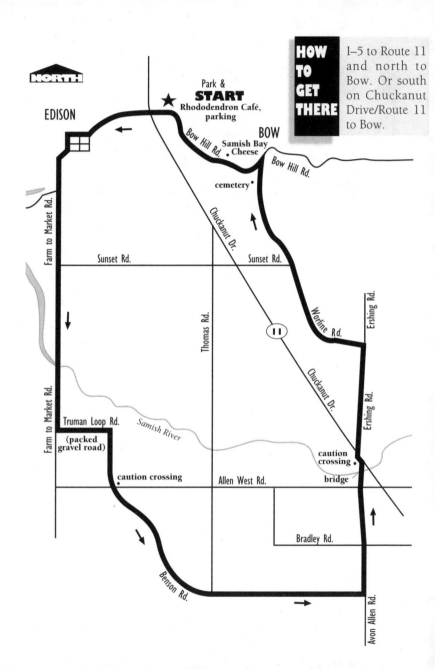

DIRECTIONS
FOR
THE RIDE

0.0 West on Bow Hill Road from Route 11/Chuckanut Drive.

1.1 Edison. Samish Studio. Edison Studio.

1.2 Veer right, then left onto Farm To Market Road.

4.8 Left onto Truman Loop Road. Packed gravel. Follow curves.

6.0 Cross Allen West Road to Benson Road.Caution!

9.8 Left onto Avon Allen Road.

11.2 Cross Samish River, jog left onto Route 11. Immediate right onto Ershing Road. Caution!

15.2 Left onto Worline Road.

18.0 Left onto Bow Hill Road. Cemetery to left.

20.0 Return to start. Rhododendron Café and Rhody Gallery, Gifts, & Espresso.

Skagit County: Bow
Padilla Bay Shore Trail

Distance and Rating:	3.3 miles; easy; good for kids
Surface & Traffic:	Packed gravel; wide bike lane on road
Highlights:	Padilla Bay, Breazeale Interpretive Center, Upland Trail, Bay View State Park, picturesque farms—bring binoculars!
Eats, Sleeps:	See Ride 8; picnic
Note:	Waterfowl hunters may be near trail October through January

Meandering, ribbon-like tributaries of the Skagit River once fed the vast mudflats and sea-grass meadows of Padilla Bay Estuary. As settlers arrived in the late 1800s, they tamed these "purposeless" branches to flow toward Skagit Bay dikes, reclaiming fertile soil for "productive" use. What seemed logical to the settlers we now know to be harmful to the diverse plants and creatures that depend on the estuary for sustenance. Despite the alterations in terrain, the remaining sloughs and the Swinomish Channel dump enough water into the estuary to maintain a relatively pristine environment.

The Braezeale Interpretive Center tells what to look for. Borrow a guidebook. Tidal swings determine what you'll view. At high tide, eelgrass, mammals, and birds predominate; look for great blue herons, harbor seals, and river otters. Low tide reveals sea grass, mudflats, crabs, clams, and tide pools.

Fulfilling Edna Breazeale's dream that children should learn "that it wasn't all people and houses," this National Reserve was established in 1987. Jump-started by Breazeale's donation of her family's sixty-four-acre farm, the reserve draws hordes. Visitors receive a reality-based education that we are part of nature.

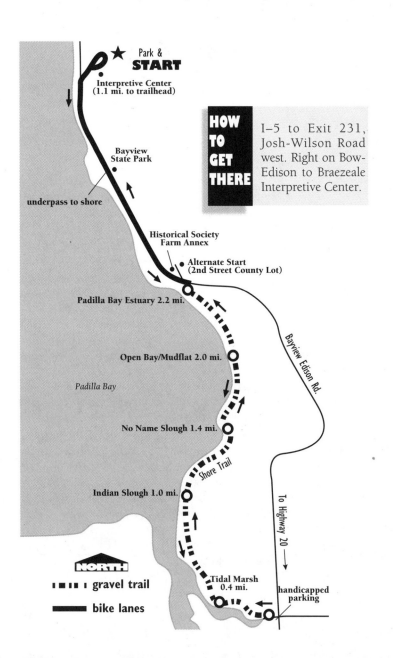

Park &
START

★

Interpretive Center
(1.1 mi. to trailhead)

HOW TO GET THERE — I–5 to Exit 231, Josh-Wilson Road west. Right on Bow-Edison to Braezeale Interpretive Center.

Bayview
State Park

underpass to shore

Historical Society
Farm Annex

Alternate Start
(2nd Street County Lot)

Padilla Bay Estuary 2.2 mi.

Open Bay/Mudflat 2.0 mi.

Padilla Bay

No Name Slough 1.4 mi.

Shore Trail

Indian Slough 1.0 mi.

Bayview Edison Rd.

To Highway 20

Tidal Marsh
0.4 mi.

handicapped
parking

NORTH

▪ ▪ ▪ gravel trail

━━ bike lanes

Snohomish County: Snohomish

Centennial Trail

Distance & Rating:	7.4 path and 7.6 dirt single track (mountain bike required)
Surface & Traffic:	Paved and dirt; no cars, one busy crossing
Highlights:	Snohomish, farmlands, wetlands, woodlands, wildlife
Eats:	Picnic or Historic Snohomish
Etc.:	Trail information, Snohomish Parks & Recreation (425) 339–1208

Visionaries dream big—sometimes making miracles. When the Snohomish-Arlington Trail Coalition (SATC) formed in 1988, they aimed to convert the Burlington-Northern tracks to recreational use. Their idea caught like wildfire, becoming reality in just three years. Eventually, the Centennial Trail will stretch from British Columbia to Oregon. Toward the end of 2000, construction of 10.3 new paved miles will reach Arlington, with another 10 miles north and a stretch south to Duvall planned for two years later.

The paved trail begins 2 miles north of Historic Snohomish, heading north through fertile farmland. Dairy and produce farmers proudly maintain picturesque farms here. One sign declares, NO UDDER BUSINESS IS BETTER THAN DAIRY and describes "Miss Sadie's" yearly production: 27,500 pounds of milk and 110,212 pounds of butter. Another cow, "Rose," the first officially named bovine in Snohomish County, bore twenty-three offspring who followed in her milky footsteps. From the early settlers' back porches, dairying, massive creameries, cheese factories, and condensaries evolved in the late 1800s.

Nomadic Native Americans once hunted, fished, and traded here, later forming villages and tribal societies. Non-native settlers arrived in the 1850s, drained the swamps, and subsistence homesteaded until recognition of the vast timber and mining resources in the 1860s and 1870s. The 1880s brought the railroad, boosting incomes of timber, silver, and precious metal industries. At Machias a renovated depot (rest rooms) and park offer a perfect picnic and turnaround point for tiring munchkins.

After Machias the paving leads to Hartford, where the county is negotiating further land purchases and right-of-ways. Continuing to the dirt (future paved) trailhead requires 1.5 miles of road cycling to the easy single track that runs about 7.5 miles to Quilceda Creek, where a bridge is needed. Building it and paving the railroad bed—a long-adopted equestrian trail—are planned for 2000, when wetlands disputes are resolved. Meanwhile, expect to get muddy.

After cycling stroll Historic Snohomish, "The Antique Capital of the Northwest," and favorite spot for hot-air ballooning and parachuting. Though tourists on the Cascade Loop zoom in like homing pigeons, the Snohomish River and turn-of-the-century architecture are worth perusing. A casual cycle up and down Avenues A through E passes Victorian homes, cottages, the Blackman Historic Museum, and "Soap Suds Row," where townswomen laundered for loggers and millworkers. Pick up a tour map at the Chamber of Commerce.

DIRECTIONS
FOR
THE RIDE

0.0   Trailhead of paved path. Maple Avenue and Three Lakes Road.

4.7   Machias. Rest rooms. Park.

7.4   20th Street NE. Hartford/Lake Stevens. Paved path ends. Backtrack.

Road link to dirt-trail section (1.5 miles). Left onto 20th Street NE, right onto 131st Avenue NE, straight at Y-intersection onto Old Hartford Drive. Curve left onto 36th Street NE and right onto 127th Avenue East. Use Route 92 underpass to cross.

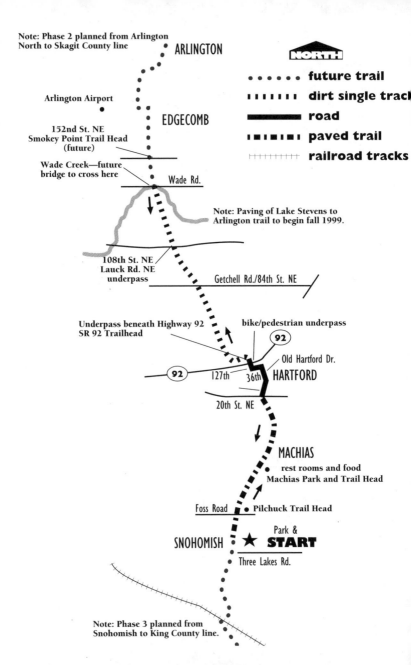

Note: Phase 2 planned from Arlington
North to Skagit County line

ARLINGTON

NORTH

• • • • • **future trail**
▪ ▪ ▪ ▪ ▪ ▪ **dirt single track**
▬▬▬▬▬ **road**
▪▬▪▬▪▬▪ **paved trail**
┼┼┼┼┼┼┼ **railroad tracks**

Arlington Airport

EDGECOMB

152nd St. NE
Smokey Point Trail Head
(future)

Wade Creek—future
bridge to cross here

Wade Rd.

Note: Paving of Lake Stevens to
Arlington trail to begin fall 1999.

108th St. NE
Lauck Rd. NE
underpass

Getchell Rd./84th St. NE

Underpass beneath Highway 92
SR 92 Trailhead

bike/pedestrian underpass

92

Old Hartford Dr.

92   127th   36th   **HARTFORD**

20th St. NE

MACHIAS

rest rooms and food
Machias Park and Trail Head

Foss Road   • Pilchuck Trail Head

SNOHOMISH   ★   Park &
START

Three Lakes Rd.

Note: Phase 3 planned from
Snohomish to King County line.

Option

0.0   Trailhead of dirt path/future paved Centennial Trail.

2.8   Getchell Road/84th Street NE.

5.9   Lauck Road/108th Street underpass.

8.5   End. Quilceda Creek near Wade Road. Bridge planned.

17.7 Arlington (after bridge and paving complete).

HOW TO GET THERE I–5 to Highway 2 east. Right to Route 9/Business Highway 2; follow left into Snohomish. Left to 2nd Street and left to Maple Avenue. In 2 miles at Three Lakes Road (68th Street SE), park near the trailhead.

Snohomish County: Everett
Smith Island Loop

Distance & Rating:	2.2 or 4+ miles; easy; good for kids
Surface & Traffic:	Paved path, dirt trail (mountain bike required); no traffic except 1 mile on full loop
Highlights:	Spencer Bridge and Island Wildlife Refuge estuary, Langus Riverfront Park, Snohomish River, Steamboat Slough
Eats:	See Ride 11; picnic

If you're lucky on this jaunt, you'll spot a big old sturgeon hooked on a hopeful's line. Even if you aren't so fortunate, this ride is fine—safe and flat. Paved paths, easy dirt trails, and Spencer Island Reserve provide a day's activity. Bring a picnic and bike lock.

Smith Island brims with wildlife, unhampered by the wastewater treatment plant and distant colossal log and sawdust piles. Hunks of driftwood on sandy shores contrast with the island's center, a marshy woods chock-full of alders, cottonwoods, blackberry vines, grasses, wild crimson roses, and yellow monkshead. Shorebirds, waterfowl, and forest birds abound. On the island's southern tip, benches offer bird-watching and photo ops.

At 1.5 miles choose one of three options: (1) Spencer Island hike—see below (no bikes on island); (2) gravel road left, back to the start; (3) proceed straight for 1 mile to end of paved path and backtrack or continue on the dirt single track, turning left at the first junction across fields to a gravel road and bridge (12th Street) over I-5. If you follow the latter option, turn left at the T-intersection, heading to Langus Riverfront Park (1 mile of road traffic). Paving of

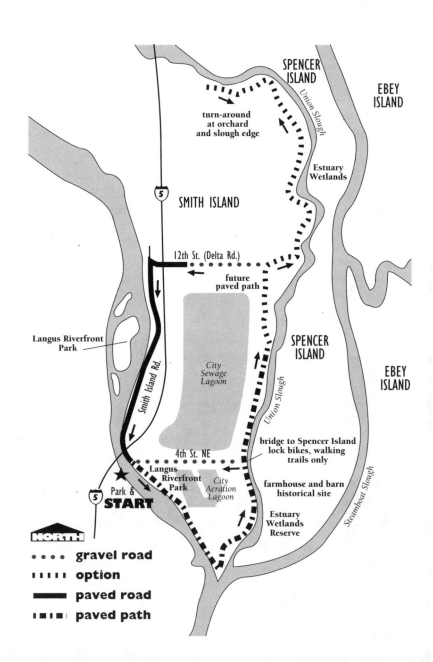

SPENCER ISLAND

EBEY ISLAND

Union Slough

turn-around at orchard and slough edge

Estuary Wetlands

(5) SMITH ISLAND

12th St. (Delta Rd.)

future paved path

Langus Riverfront Park

Smith Island Rd.

City Sewage Lagoon

SPENCER ISLAND

EBEY ISLAND

Union Slough

4th St. NE

bridge to Spencer Island lock bikes, walking trails only

Langus Riverfront Park

City Aeration Lagoon

farmhouse and barn historical site

Steamboat Slough

(5) Park & START

Estuary Wetlands Reserve

NORTH

• • • **gravel road**

ı ı ı ı ı **option**

▬▬ **paved road**

▰ ▰ ▰ ▰ **paved path**

the entire loop is planned. For additional dirt-track miles, instead of a left from the single track, veer right for an up-and-back ride along the slough (4–6 miles).

Whatever you do, don't miss serene twelve-acre Spencer Island, an estuary with 3–4 miles of barked trails and wooden walkways. Acquired by the county in 1989, it opened to the public in 1996. A crumbling barn and rusting farm machinery remain, remnants of 1920s rugged dairy farm life. Dikes, culverts, and tide gates, which allowed farming of the rich floodplain soil, now are manipulated to accommodate waterfowl, fish, and small mammals. The island's muddy sloughs and fresh-water marshes abound with reeds, sedges, rushes, and cattails. Plaques detail historical and environmental tidbits.

To investigate, lock bikes at the 1914 Spencer Bridge. Originally a counterbalanced opening bridge, it served Ebey Island. After the 1990 floods destroyed Spencer's original bridge, this abandoned bascule (French for "weighing scales") "Jacknife Bridge" was towed here. Check the photos set into the bridge's center struts.

DIRECTIONS
FOR
THE RIDE

0.0 Begin at end of parking area under I–5 at the trail map.
0.8 Tip of island.
1.5 Spencer Bridge. Left onto gravel road or straight on paved and dirt trail for 4-mile loop.
2.2 Return to start.

HOW TO GET THERE

I–5 to Exit 195/E Marine View Drive. Go north onto Route 529. Exit to 28th Street NE. Right to 35th Avenue NE/Smith-Spencer Island Access. Left to Ross Avenue. Right to Langus Riverfront Park.

Jefferson County:
Quimper Peninsula
Marrowstone Island

Distance & Rating:	20+ miles; easy; good for kids
Surface & Traffic:	Paved; few cars
Highlights:	Fort Flagler, rural road, beaches, views
Eats:	Picnic (supplies at Hadlock shops)
Sleeps:	The Ecologic Place, Fort Flagler camping
Etc.:	Kayaking, cultural events in Port Townsend (15 miles), Fort Worden Events (360) 385–4730, Olympic Music Festival (360) 732–4000 or (360) 527–8839, Centrum Summer Festivals (800) 733–3608

Gawking at the panoramic Olympic Mountain and serene bay vista at the start of this ride, you'll be struck by the ease of finding such a stunning Northwest retreat. And this is only the parking lot!

Islands are meant for relaxing and savoring: therefore, this ride's low mileage allows beachcombing, bird-watching, and lazy meanderings through gorgeous Fort Flagler, unmarred by traffic.

Leaving the parking area, turn right up Indian Island's Flagler Road for 0.5 mile to the first Jefferson County Park. Consider hiking or beachcombing its expansive sand spits and marshes at the ride's end. A mountain bike or car is needed to negotiate the steep gravel road. For now continue straight, gliding downhill and crossing Kilisut Harbor's marshy terminus to the WELCOME TO MARROWSTONE sign. To the right a short climb up Robbins Road reveals Cascade Mountain views before gliding down to flat East Marrowstone Road.

Small-acreage farms and expansive lawned, beachfront homes blend into cedar forests along the Admiralty Inlet shore.

Near Second View Cemetery a previously logged open space affords glorious marine and Mount Baker views. Visit the second Jefferson County Park, a tiny gem complete with rest rooms, to the right on East Beach Road. Its sandy driftwood beach, used by horseback riders, lures you to spectacular views—but enough comment. Too many superlatives here may diminish your own sense of discovery. From the park follow East Beach Road.

Fort Flagler State Park encompasses Marrowstone Island's north end. In simpler militaristic times Fort Flagler, along with Fort Casey (Seattle) and Fort Worden (Port Townsend), formed a "Triangle of Fire" to prevent invasion of Puget Sound and to protect Bremerton Naval Yards. Used for training during both world wars, at present its windswept hills, wooded acres, well-maintained gray and yellow barracks (one is a youth hostel) and striking officer homes compose a picturesque retreat with panoramic views.

A maze of paths wends beneath massive cedar trees and along awesome cliffs and banks. At the first intersection you must choose: straight, right, or left. Right leads to the gun emplacements, a beach trail (superb photo ops), blackberry thickets, bunkers, Cascades and snow-topped Mount Baker views. Unbelievable! Straight heads to Marrowstone Point Park Headquarters and interpretive displays. Follow signs to a cliff above a rocky shore. A steep one-lane road leads to the lighthouse, now a fisheries research laboratory area. Wetland marshes and extensive beaches provide a natural habitat for marine and bird life. This is an idyllic picnic spot. Left from the intersection takes you through wooded park roads to the bayside and scenic viewpoints of the Olympic Mountains and Port Townsend.

Backtrack to the park's entrance, re-riding Flagler Road past the town of Nordland on Kilisut Bay, which comprises a country grocery store, a post office, and an oyster farm. Curve right at the triangle intersection to the start.

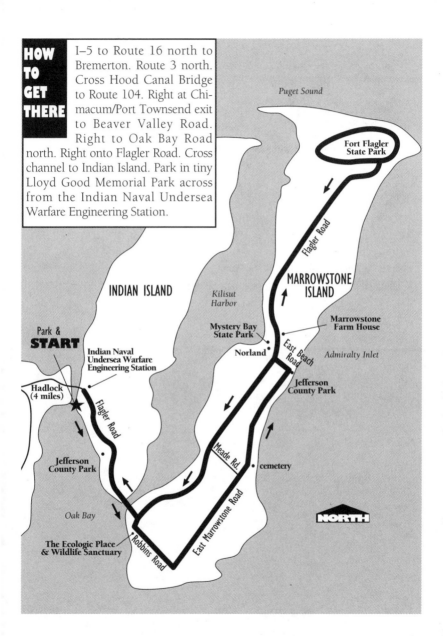

HOW TO GET THERE

I–5 to Route 16 north to Bremerton. Route 3 north. Cross Hood Canal Bridge to Route 104. Right at Chimacum/Port Townsend exit to Beaver Valley Road. Right to Oak Bay Road north. Right onto Flagler Road. Cross channel to Indian Island. Park in tiny Lloyd Good Memorial Park across from the Indian Naval Undersea Warfare Engineering Station.

Puget Sound

Fort Flagler State Park

Flagler Road

MARROWSTONE ISLAND

INDIAN ISLAND

Kilisut Harbor

Mystery Bay State Park

Marrowstone Farm House

Park & **START**

Indian Naval Undersea Warfare Engineering Station

Norland

East Beach Road

Admiralty Inlet

Hadlock (4 miles)

Flagler Road

Jefferson County Park

Jefferson County Park

Meade Rd.

cemetery

Oak Bay

The Ecologic Place & Wildlife Sanctuary

Robbins Road

East Marrowstone Road

NORTH

DIRECTIONS
FOR
THE RIDE

0.0 Right from the parking area onto Indian Island's Flagler Road.

0.5 Jefferson County Park.

1.1 Cross Kilisut Harbor to Marrowstone Island.

1.4 Right onto Robbins Road; curve left.

2.0 Left onto East Marrowstone Road. Admiralty Inlet shore. The Ecological Place.

5.0 Pass Meade Road and Second View Cemetery.

5.6 Right onto East Beach Road to Jefferson County Park.

5.8 Straight on East Beach Road from Jefferson County Park.

6.0 Right onto Flagler Road. Mystery Bay State Park. Marrowstone Farm House.

8.2 Enter Fort Flagler State Park.

13.2 Return to park entrance onto Flagler Road.

15.4 Pass East Beach Road.

18.6 Right curve at the triangle intersection.

20.0 Return to starting point.

Jefferson County: Quimper Peninsula
Fort Worden/Port Townsend

Distance & Rating:	24 miles; not for the faint-hearted—rolling hills, steep pitches
Surface & Traffic:	Paved, some rough road; few cars except on weekends
Highlights:	Fort Worden State Park, rural backroad solitude, Port Townsend historic homes, fabulous views, Chetemoka Park
Eats:	Downtown—Picnic fixings at The Wine Seller; Belmont, Lonny's Restaurant, Silverwater Café, Salal Café (breakfast); Uptown—Coho Café, Blackberries at Fort Worden
Sleeps:	Downtown: Palace Hotel, Ravenscroft, Heritage House, Lizzie's; Uptown: James House, Starrett Mansion, Quimper Inn, Fort Worden Olympic Hostel
Etc.:	See Ride 13

Just try rolling through Fort Worden and not thinking of Richard Gere marching and shouting "Yes, Sir!" in the basic training scene of *An Officer and a Gentleman*, filmed on this lovely spot. Or of him sweeping Debra Winger off her feet to wedded bliss. Well, that might not happen to you here, but you can sure enjoy the spectacular setting. Fort Worden, built at the turn of the century as a harbor defense, functions today as a site for camps, accommodations, and public events.

Nearby Port Townsend, named by Captain George Vancouver for his buddy the Marquis of Townshend, remains charming despite its high tourist quotient. On your way into town, pick up historic site maps at the Information Center. Save time to wander.

Though this is a road ride, it quickly enters rural areas. Stretches of bumpy, partly gravel roads might be negotiated more comfortably and with less teeth-clattering (not to mention your butt) on a mountain bike. Begin at Fort Worden State Park's huge center field that is surrounded by streets named for past presidents; pick your favorite. Head right onto W Street, past the Army Cemetery, and glide downhill on San Juan Avenue to spectacular views.

Traffic picks up along Hastings Avenue's rolling hills. After a sand and gravel pit, a turn onto Cape George Way leads to Cape George Road, a curving, steep hill. Near the crest, re-hydrate with water at the fire station (rest rooms available if you ask). A reprieve of gently rolling hills ends in a downhill glide past Beckett Point; and then (sorry!) a climb to a high logged and reforested plateau where you get peek-a-boo magnificent vistas.

At 9.0 miles comes a true test of nerves. Thrill-seekers get an exhilarating high while thrill-avoiding types will white-knuckle it down the screeching, gut-wrenching 2.0-mile descent, clinging viciously to their brakes. What a ride! Regain your composure on Discovery Road, where stately poplars line a golf course–manicured green that seems ridiculous in this rural setting. On the uphill red-barked madrona trees displace poplars. Isolated farms, their fences carving patchwork squares from rounded hillsides, dot acreage logged long ago.

After a bridge over what appears to be an old railroad bed, you escape traffic by cycling Jacob Miller Road. There, a sprawling Victorian farmhouse with wraparound porches bears a sign reading ARCADIA B&B. A CLOSED—DO NOT DISTURB sign hangs on the fence of what appears to be a peaceful retreat (at one time home base of Seattle's wild "Flying Karamazovs"). Jacob Miller Road bends around the Arcadia property and is relatively flat until the final uphill to Hastings Avenue.

The downhill cruise on Hastings Avenue reveals stunning views of the Cascade Mountains. When you hit Lawrence Street, you might want to take a break in the Uptown Business Street district; sample a coffee or explore the craft shops. In this area up on the bluff above downtown Port Townsend are a slew of meticulously restored, elegant, late-nineteenth-century homes. Consider cycling a self-designed tour of this charming neighborhood. Don't miss the James House B&B on Washington Street, a historic home with a view that in 1973 became the Northwest's first bed and breakfast.

Dominating the hill is the red and white Jefferson County Courthouse, with its 100-foot clock tower and turrets. Around the corner, across from a park, visit the Hastings House B&B, whose claim to fame is that the German consul once roomed there. Fly downhill on Washington Street, following the series of turns in the directions (required as no left to Water Street is allowed). Off Kearney Street, if you are a bird-watcher, take a brief side-trip to the Kah-Tai Lagoon.

In historic "downtown" Port Townsend, lock up and browse the restaurant menus, prolific bookstores, kite shops, art galleries, and gift shops. Sip an espresso and try Bread and Roses Bakery's (Quincy Street) yummy baguettes and macaroons. Munching customers also laud the moist, fruity bread pudding.

After your fill of food and wandering, head back to Fort Worden State Park, wending along the shoreline. Squeeze around the sides of the Fort Worden gate at the end of Walnut Street and head for Point Wilson, a blow-your-mind piece of real estate that's tough to leave. There you'll see the Marine Science Center and Lighthouse. Backtrack from the spit to the parking lot. Then you can go home and rent *An Officer and a Gentleman*.

DIRECTIONS
FOR
THE RIDE

0.0 Right onto W Street from Fort Worden State Park.

0.2 Right onto Spruce Street. Army Cemetery.

0.3 Left curve onto Admiralty Avenue.

0.4 Right onto San Juan Avenue at the T-intersection.

0.5 Left curve onto 49th Street. North Beach Park to the right.

1.7 Left onto Cook Avenue at the stop sign.

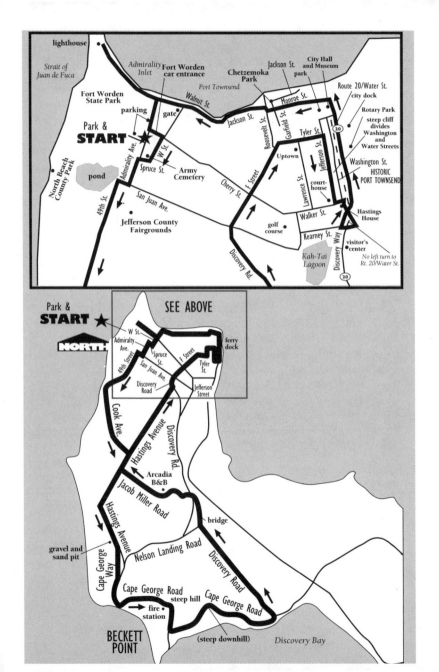

lighthouse

Strait of Juan de Fuca

Admirality Inlet **Fort Worden** car entrance

Chetzemoka Park

Jackson St. park

City Hall and Museum

Route 20/Water St. city dock

Port Townsend

Fort Worden State Park

Walnut St.

Monroe St.

Rotary Park

parking

gate

Jackson St.

Garfield St.

Roosevelt St.

Tyler St.

steep cliff divides Washington and Water Streets

Park & START

W St.

Washington St. HISTORIC PORT TOWNSEND

Admiralty Ave.

Spruce St.

Army Cemetery

Uptown

Jefferson St.

North Beach County Park

pond

Cherry St.

F Street

Lawrence St.

courthouse

Hastings House

49th St.

San Juan Ave.

Walker St.

visitor's center

Jefferson County Fairgrounds

golf course

Kearney St.

Discovery Way

No left turn to Rt. 20/Water St.

Discovery Rd.

Kah-Tai Lagoon

Park & START

NORTH

SEE ABOVE

W St.

ferry dock

Admiralty Ave.

Spruce St.

F Street

49th Street

San Juan Ave.

Tyler St.

Discovery Road

Jefferson Street

Cook Ave.

Hastings Avenue

Discovery Rd.

Arcadia B&B

Jacob Miller Road

bridge

Hastings Avenue

Nelson Landing Road

Discovery Road

gravel and sand pit

Cape George Way

Cape George Road

steep hill

Cape George Road

fire station

(steep downhill)

Discovery Bay

BECKETT POINT

3.3 Right onto Hastings Road at the T-intersection.

5.8 Right onto Cape George Way after sand and gravel pit.

5.9 Right onto Cape George Road at the T-intersection.

7.2 Crest. Fire station.

8.7 Left curve, avoiding Beckett Point on right.

9.0 Big downhill.

11.0 Left onto Discovery Road at the stop sign and hill's bottom.

13.2 Pass Nelson Landing Road and a bridge.

13.4 Left onto Jacob Miller Road. Arcadia.

13.5 Right as Jacob Miller Road bends right around Arcadia.

15.4 Right onto Hastings Avenue.

17.0 Left onto Discovery Road at the T-intersection. Downhill.

17.2 Cross San Juan Avenue. Discovery Road becomes F Street.

17.8 F Street curves into Tyler Street. Uphill.

18.2 Cross Lawrence Street (Uptown Business Street).

18.3 Right onto Jefferson Street. Jefferson County Courthouse.

18.6 Left onto Walker. Hastings House B&B. Park.

18.7 Right onto Washington Street. Downhill.

HOW TO GET THERE By car: (1) I–5 to Route 16 North. At Bremerton take Route 3 to Route 104. Cross the Hood Canal Bridge to Highway 101 North. Change to Route 20 to Port Townsend and signs to Fort Worden State Park; or (2) Bainbridge Ferry from Seattle's waterfront. Cross Bainbridge Island to Route 3 North and then Route 104. Take 101 North and Route 20 to Port Townsend.

By car and ferry: I–5 to Mukilteo. Ferry to Clinton on Whidbey Island. Drive across Route 525 to Keystone. Ferry to Port Townsend (can leave car at Keystone); or (2) Route 20 from the Skagit Valley across Deception Pass and south to Keystone where you can pick up ferry.

18.9 Curve right onto Route 20/Water Street. (No left turn across Water Street.)

19.0 Left onto Kearney Street (Kah-Tai Lagoon), quick left onto Washington Street, and veer right onto Water Street. Historic Port Townsend.

20.0 Left onto Monroe Street. City Hall and Museum.

20.4 Option: Right on Garfield Street 1 block to Chetzemoka Park.

20.5 Right onto Roosevelt Street.

20.6 Left onto Jackson Street at the T-intersection.

21.0 Right curve onto Walnut Street.

21.3 Closed park gate. Slip around edge.

22.6 Straight to Point Wilson. Marine Science Center and Lighthouse.

24.0 Backtrack and return to the parking lot.

Kitsap County: I

Chief Sealth (a.k.a. Chief ⁚
Loop

Neverthel ness a of ⁚

Distance & Rating:	30+ miles; mode⁚ flat stretches, one⁚ ⁚⁚⁚
Surface & Traffic:	Paved; light to moderate
Highlights:	Historic Poulsbo, Port Gamble, Suquamish Museum, Chief Sealth grave and totem, views
Eats:	Judith's Tearooms and Rose Cafe, Poulsbo Smokehouse, Caffe Parousia, Checkers, Liberty Bay Bakery & Café
Sleeps:	Manor Farm Inn, Edgewater Beach B&B, Foxbridge B&B, Murphy House
Etc.:	Festivals (360) 779–4848; Chamber of Commerce (360) 779–4848, www.poulsbo.net; Liberty Bay Books, Marine Science Center

"Every part of this earth is sacred to my people. Every shining pine needle, every sandy shorey. . . . The earth is not his [white man's] brother, but his enemy. . . . His appetite will devour the earth and leave behind only a desert. . . . We will consider your offer to go to the reservation. . . . It matters little where we pass the remnant of our days. . . . If we sell you our land, love it as we've loved it. . . ."

So spoke Kitsap Peninsula's Chief Sealth to Governor Issac Stevens. Or at least so we thought, until a modern writer's poignant embellishments, geared to a television documentary, were revealed.

s, the speech captures the spirit, frustrations, and sad-
e end of a life in harmony with the land and the beginning
e of conquering its resources.

Though invaded by late-eighteenth-century industry, Kitsap Peninsula retains a charming rural and marine beauty. Coves tucked into steep, banked shorelines, lush forests, fertile valleys, and mountain views lured mid-1800s Scandinavian fishermen, loggers, and farmers, most migrating from other United States territory.

Poulsbo, their home and our ride's origin, hugs an exquisite harbor. It's known as "Little Norway" because 90 percent of the residents were of Norwegian background. Norwegian remained the common language until World War II, when naval shipyards brought diverse labor forces, diluting the Norwegian population. Proud ethnic roots still evidence themselves in architecture, murals, folk art, food, and the Norwegian National Holiday Festival in May. Not replicated in Poulsbo are the demonic trolls that adorn Norway's village streets; immigrants left them behind in favor of American style storefronts.

Starting at Waterfront Park, head right onto Front Street past Sluys Bakery (makers of Poulsbo Bread). Warning! This is not a health-food store; they bake whole-grain rolls, but specialize in fatty, fried donuts, sugary sweet rolls, and rich frosted cakes. Pick up a snack or haul fruit from home. Outside of town provisions are limited. Save your appetite for lunch at Judith's Tearooms (Scandinavian delicacies and nouvelle salads), the New Day Seafood Eatery (fish and chips), or picnic with a foamy espresso and smoked salmon from the Poulsbo Smokehouse.

Getting back to the riding at hand, climb to East Fjord Avenue to an immaculate residential stretch edging Liberty Bay. Framed above are the snowcapped Olympic Mountains. Along here Lomolo Smokehouse is worth a stop to inhale smoky aromas and chat with owner Ron. Ask about the "pen from Lyle" for a good story.

After Lomolo Market enter wooded, rolling terrain where you travel, indecipherably, in and out of the Port Madison Indian

Reservation. Deeded to the Suquamish tribe in the January 1855 Treaty of Point Elliot, it is a scattered patchwork of land. Across Route 305 (caution!) climb Totten Road NE through cool, shaded woods that seem like a cavernous retreat. At Suquamish Way, unless you're pressed for time, take the side trip to the Suquamish Museum. Stick to the wide but bumpy shoulder.

On the outskirts of Suquamish, watch for Division Street to visit the Old Man House City Park. Originally the Suquamish tribe's longhouse, it's now a secluded spot on a sandy, shell-studded beach (rest room). Historical information helps you imagine the longhouse, its curling smoke carrying the pungent odors of smoked fish. Relax against a hunk of driftwood; screeching seagulls and lapping water provide a quick cure for city stress.

Returning to reality, pump uphill to rejoin the route. Glide downhill, braking just before Main Street to view the outstanding Chief Sealth and Kitsap Totem. Elegantly carved and painted in striking grays and earth tones, the totem, cut from a thousand-year-old tree, dominates its triangular park. At its top is a spectacular eagle. Uphill, visit St. Peter's Catholic Mission and graveyard where Chief Sealth's (1786–1866) grave lies on a prominent knoll. Beneath an Indian canoe canopy, it is marked by a Christian tombstone, indicative of the white settlers' influence upon the Chief's heritage.

The pocket-sized town of Suquamish is located on a tranquil waterfront. In rough-hewn cedar-shingled buildings near the dock, stop in at the tribal art gallery (sign says OPEN 12–5 MAYBE) and local cafe. In August during Chief Seattle Days, the town's crowded celebrations include a drum and dance program, princess crowning, salmon bake, and canoe races. A marker proclaims Chief Sealth FRIEND, COUNSELOR AND PROTECTOR OF THE PIONEERS. To demonstrate their joy in his co-operation, the pioneers honored him by naming their city Seattle.

Use caution on shoulderless Augusta Avenue, where traffic rushes by. In late summer, munch on sweet, succulent blackberries from heavily laden roadside thickets. At the Route 104 stoplight, a gas station/market bears whimsical, massive wood sculptures (chain-saw carved, it seems). On Route 104 avail yourself of the wide shoulder. On this uphill, streams of cars whiz by as if entering the Indy 500. Caution! Heading to Port Gamble, traffic thins as you pass a bark dust processing plant from which rich cedar aromas emanate.

Port Gamble is a former company lumber town imbued with quintessential tranquillity. Founded by Andrew Pope and Frederic Talbot in 1853, it was, until 1996, the oldest working mill town in the United States. Modeled after their Maine hometown, it bears meticulously maintained New England–style architectural delights. Note the brown 1856 Thompson House, the sole continuously occupied home in this picture-perfect town.

Two time-worn, green, wood water towers dominate the town's entrance before the unique Of Sea & Shore Museum (free), the Port Gamble Historical Museum, and The General Store (cookies). A yellow frame building, which imparts the warm, mellow feel of age, holds a post office, rest rooms, and artifacts along wainscoted walls. Across the street on the cliff's edge, Pope and Talbot's offices once presided over the sprawling lumberyard. Only the rising steam and humming machinery hinted of the mill below.

The hilltop cemetery, enclosed by a white picket fence and surrounded by sloping farmland, has stunning 360-degree views. The bluff overlooks Hood Canal and the infamous mile-long Hood Canal Bridge that collapsed in 1979 when buffeted by 100-mile-per-hour winds. The stunning scenery makes a divine picnic spot; wander among the Scandinavian grave markers for a bit of history.

On Route 104 old clear-cuts provide evidence of Port Gamble's hungry mill (everything can't be picturesque). After the Salisbury County Park turnoff, traffic heading to the Hood Canal Bridge picks up. For a brief traffic respite, detour onto Faulker Road and cut across Route 3 to Big Valley Road (Manor Farm Inn sign) before Kitsap Memorial State Park.

In this narrow bucolic valley, the charming Manor Farm Inn is a working farm B&B and top-notch restaurant. Sublimely peaceful and upscale, it is a popular getaway retreat for a biking weekend (you have to reserve when you're born, however!). Its white stucco buildings, surrounded by floral gardens, trellises, pastures, and orchards, have appeared in the Eddie Bauer catalogue.

Across Bond Road (heavy traffic—caution!), Little Valley Road is a narrow, winding affair that ascends a short, steep hill. Walking may be required. The payback comes as you soar down to cross Route 305 and enter Poulsbo. Lunchtime.

Saunter through thriving tourist shops and a crowded marina—a sharp contrast with Indian ways. In this era of environmental concern, it brings to mind Native American Martha George's comments from the Suquamish Museum video, *Come Forth Laughing*, "You want to leave things as they are and just take what you need. Don't be wasteful, that's what the elders taught."

Optional Visit to Suquamish Indian Museum (2.5-mile round-trip)

A right onto Suquamish Way heads downhill to a peaceful shorefront museum that brings Native American culture to life. Outside, carved canoes edge the parking lot. Inside, an atmosphere penetrated by the aromas of cedar and smoked fish enhances The Eyes of Chief Seattle exhibit and *Come Forth Laughing*, a heart-moving video (you must ask to have it run). Depicting tribal traditions and transitions to contemporary life, it describes the massive attempt at assimilation that removed Native American children to boarding schools in Tacoma and Everett, where many died from whooping cough, measles, and other epidemics. Later, the experiment obviously a failure, students attended local schools with white children. After your visit attack the steep exit, backtracking to Suquamish Road.

DIRECTIONS
FOR
THE RIDE

0.0 Right from Waterfront Park onto Front Street. Sluys Bakery.

0.2 Left curve uphill onto Hostmark Street. Marine Science Center. Murphy House B&B.

0.3 Right onto East Fjord Avenue. Liberty Bay.

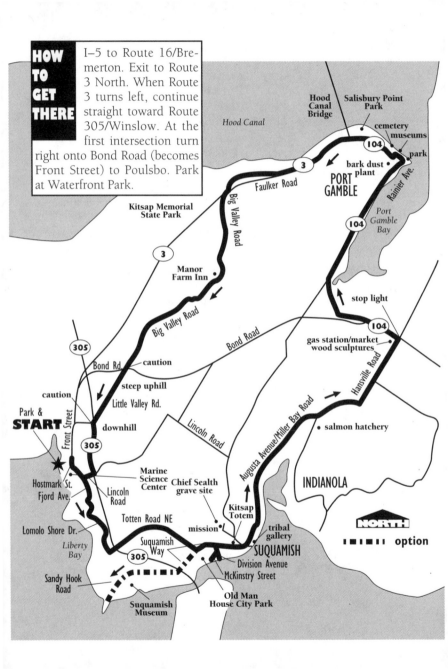

HOW TO GET THERE

I–5 to Route 16/Bremerton. Exit to Route 3 North. When Route 3 turns left, continue straight toward Route 305/Winslow. At the first intersection turn right onto Bond Road (becomes Front Street) to Poulsbo. Park at Waterfront Park.

Hood Canal

Hood Canal Bridge

Salisbury Point Park

cemetery
museums
park

3

104

bark dust plant

PORT GAMBLE

Faulker Road

Rainier Ave.

Kitsap Memorial State Park

Big Valley Road

104

Port Gamble Bay

3

Manor Farm Inn

Big Valley Road

stop light

305

Bond Road

104

gas station/market
wood sculptures

Bond Rd.   caution

caution

steep uphill

Little Valley Rd.

Hansville Road

Park &
START

Front Street

downhill

305

Lincoln Road

Augusta Avenue/Miller Bay Road

salmon hatchery

Hostmark St.
Fjord Ave.

Lincoln Road

Marine Science Center

Chief Sealth grave site

INDIANOLA

Totten Road NE

Kitsap Totem

mission

NORTH

Lomolo Shore Dr.

Liberty Bay

305

Suquamish Way

tribal gallery

■ ▪ ■ ▪ ■ option

SUQUAMISH

Sandy Hook Road

Division Avenue
McKinstry Street

Old Man House City Park

Suquamish Museum

1.5 Lomolo Smokehouse. Fjord becomes Lomolo Shore Drive.

2.5 Left curve following Lomolo Shore Drive. Port Madison Indian Reservation.

2.8 Cross Route 305 onto Totten Road NE. Uphill.

5.0 Left (or see Option below) onto Suquamish Way.

6.0 Suquamish city limits.

7.0 Right onto Division Avenue. Downhill curve onto McKinstry Street.

7.3 Old Man House City Park. Backtrack uphill.

7.6 Right onto Suquamish Way. Downhill.

7.8 Left at the Chief Sealth and Kitsap Totem.

8.0 St. Peter's Catholic Mission and Chief Sealth grave site.

8.2 Return to Suquamish Way. Tribal Art Gallery. Chief Sealth marker.

8.3 Left curve onto Augusta Avenue (no shoulder); becomes Miller Bay Road.

10.8 Pass Indianola intersection. Tribal Grover Salmon Hatchery.

12.0 Miller Bay Road becomes Hansville Road.

14.2 Left onto unmarked Route 104 (shoulder) to the Hood Canal Bridge.

15.0 Right curve at the Y-intersection, staying with Route 104.

18.4 Right onto Rainer Avenue NE and Port Gamble. Of Sea & Shore Museum. Historical Museum. Lumber Mill (closed 1995).

18.7 Left along NE Walker Street and park to the cemetery.

19.0 Straight downhill onto Olympic Avenue and right onto Route 104.

20.0 Pass Salisbury County Park entrance.

21.2 Pass Hood Canal Bridge. Straight onto Route 3.

22.5 Right onto Faulker Road. Foxbridge & Edgewater B&Bs.

23.5 Right, rejoining Route 3 south for 0.25 mile.

23.7 Left onto Big Valley Road before Kitsap Memorial State Park.

25.0 Manor Farm Inn.

27.0 Cross Bond Road to Little Valley Road. Steep uphill and downhill.

27.5 Left onto Route 305 to Poulsbo. (Walk to stoplight if heavy traffic.) Shopping center.

28.7 Right at second light onto Lincoln Road (ignore signs to historic town).

29.2 Right curve as Lincoln Avenue joins Hostmarket Street.

29.5 Right curve onto Front Street.

30.0 Return to Waterfront Park.

Option to Suquamish Museum

0.0 Right onto Suquamish Way.

0.1 Right onto Route 305.

0.2 Left across Route 305 onto Sandy Hook Road. Follow signs.

1.2 Museum. Backtrack.

2.5 Suquamish Way; pick up basic directions.

Kitsap County: Islands
Bainbridge Island Loop

Distance & Rating:	30 to 40 miles, or less as desired; this ride's nickname, "Chilly Hilly," says it all.
Surface & Traffic:	Paved; varies with roads, mostly light
Highlights:	Rural roads, views, artsy shops, Bloedel Reserve
Eats:	Pegasus Espresso, Bainbridge Bakers, Eagle Harbor Books & Café, Ruby's, Café Nola, New Rose Café, Bainbridge Bakers, Blue Water Diner, Europa West Take-Out
Sleeps:	The Buchanan Inn, The Beach Cottage, Bainbridge House, Captain's House B&B, Monarch Manor Estates, Island Country Inn, Summer Hill Farm, Waterfront B&B
Bikes:	B.I. Cycle Rentals (206) 842–6413, Bainbridge Boat Rentals (206) 842–9229, info at www.pugetsoundkayak.com
Etc.:	Chamber of Commerce (206) 842–3700, www.bicomnet.com/bichamber, Farmer's Market (Saturdays, April through October), Bainbridge Gardens, Bloedel Reserve (206) 842–7631 (reservations required), Living Memorial Center, Historical Museum

Imagine calling a biking event the "Chilly Hilly"! Makes you want to crawl back in bed. But this organized ride each February marks the opening of biking season in the Northwest, and no upstanding biker would miss it. The exhilaration of freezing on the ferry dock with 2,500 other fanatics can't be beat. Of course, savoring Bainbridge on a warmer, peaceful day has its benefits—such as enjoying the contemporary and Victorian waterfront homes and Seattle skyline views in solitude (to say nothing of riding less than six abreast).

Alone, and not packed in like a sardine, you'll delight in Bainbridge's narrow, hilly, twisted roads that wend, like an *Alice in Wonderland* maze, among towering firs, cedars, and madronas besieged by blackberry and ivy vines. Formerly a farming and logging community, much of the island now serves as a Seattle bedroom. Residents work vigorously to preserve natural resources.

Traveling to a ride via ferry bestows a luscious "nothing to do" interlude. Conversation flows, newspapers are shared, and food enjoyed. Biking from the ferry's mouth lifts any spirit, providing a unique sense of car-less freedom—even on this uphill pull. Depending on your strength and interest in exploring, this ride can be done in one or two days. Check with the Chamber of Commerce for B&Bs.

Don't miss Fay Bainbridge State Park, a driftwood-covered beach that offers a richness of splendors. Stunning Seattle vistas are topped by volcanic-peaked Mount Baker and Mount Rainier. Interpretive signs detail Puget Sound's 900-foot depths, views, and extensive sand spit formed by cliff erosion. Dig out the camera.

A 0.5-mile uphill leads to historic Kane Cemetery, an interesting spot if you're into headstones. The descent through dense forestland passes the entrance to Port Madison, site of Bainbridge's first sawmill, run by George Meigs. Nearby, say hello to the colorful, tacky Frog Rock, a humorous sort of historic marker.

The Bloedel Reserve sprawls along Bainbridge's north point. Owned and maintained since 1988 by a nonprofit foundation, this spectacular 150-acre, English country estate exquisitely weaves formal gardens into a natural setting. Diverse foliage and Northwest cultural influences are evident in mossy gardens, a bird marsh, a reflecting pool, Japanese and English gardens, and the former Bloedel home (they were a lumber family). Tour reservations are required.

On the island's west side, a string of gorgeous estates and marvelously painted Victorians glow beneath spiring firs along Manzanita Road NE. Battle Point Park makes a welcome rest spot (rest rooms). On a flat stretch of Battle Point Drive NE just after Island Center Community Hall, a stop sign marks the Bucklin Road/Vincent Road decision point; left to Bucklin Road for the shortcut with a steep hill (joins the basic route at Wyatt Way) or straight for the big loop.

Another option loops Crystal Springs, a hilly area with a spectacular, flat waterfront cruise that edges Port Orchard and Rich Passage. It's perfect for rubberneckers—don't miss it. Stare to your heart's content at starkly modern architectural gems interspersed with colorful, gingerbread Victorians, New England cottages, and Northwest shingled beach homes. Even the dogs are friendly on this idyllic point.

In Lynwood Ruby's Bistro's alluring aromas of Italian foods may get those digestive juices flowing. It's tasty fare and a perfect lunch spot. Or come back for dinner—you'll be hungry enough.

At NE 3 T Road above Blakely Harbor, read the pictorial historical marker. It describes and shows William Renton's massive sawmill (the world's largest from 1885 to 1895) and shipbuilding facility, which badly polluted this bay. Now deindustrialized and recovered, the bay is home to flocks of birds and wintering ducks. In its heyday Port Blakely boosted central island agricultural development. Norwegian and Japanese farmers transformed the economy with strawberries, vegetables, and flowers. During the World War II Japanese internment, Filipinos cared for some farms, but most lay fallow.

Take care at a complex intersection to get onto Halls Hill Road. Ascend its narrow, forested road between mossy, vine-wrapped trees and drop down a steep, clench-your-brakes hill. From Rockaway Beach Road gaze in awe at the beachfront mansions and Seattle skyline. Wind around Eagle Harbor, finishing uphill on Wyatt Way

West. Grab a well-deserved, foamy latte and tasty treat at Bainbridge Bakers. For bigger appetites try Pegasus, a charming ivy-covered 1937 brick building that served as a hardware store, or Europa Take Outs for a picnic. On a more aesthetic level, wander around the artsy shops. Don't miss the top-notch Eagle Harbor Bookstore before heading to your B&B or home.

DIRECTIONS

FOR

THE RIDE

0.0   Right from ferry onto Winslow Way West. Rest rooms. Uphill.

0.4   Left onto Ferncliff Avenue NE.

1.5   Cross High School Road.

2.4   Left curve onto Lofgren Road NE. Tree farm. Downhill.

2.6   Right curve onto Moran Road NE. Murden Cove.

2.8   Right onto Manitou Beach Drive.

3.0   Veer right at the Y-intersection. Downhill.

4.1   Left curve.

4.7   Left curve as Manitou Beach Drive becomes NE Valley Road.

4.9   Hay and Feed Store. Right onto Sunrise Drive NE. Downhill.

7.0   Straight or right for side trip to Fay Bainbridge State Park.

7.1   Left onto Lafayette Avenue. Uphill.

7.5   Kane Cemetery.

7.8   Left onto Euclid Avenue NE. Downhill.

8.4   Left onto Phelps Road NE. Port Madison Park entrance.

8.5   Right curve at Frog Rock, continuing on Phelps Road NE.

8.8   Right onto NE Hidden Cove Road. Hilly.

10.0 Cross Route 305. Use caution. See Bloedal Reserve option.

10.6 Left onto Manzanita Road NE (becomes Bergman Road NE). Uphill.

11.9 Right onto Peterson Hill Road NE.

12.0 Right onto Miller Road NE at the T-intersection.

12.5 Right onto Arrowhead Drive NE. Battle Point Park.

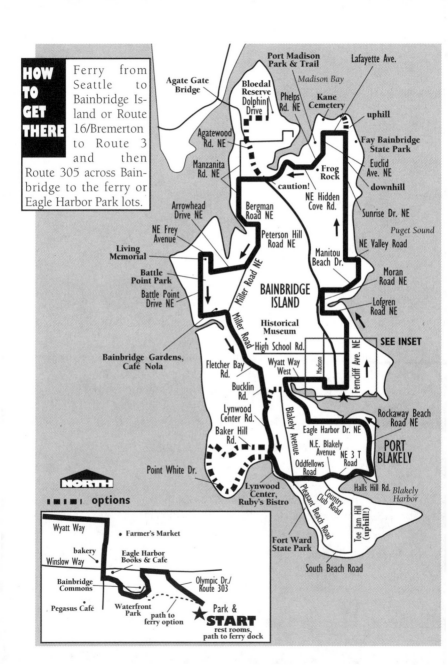

HOW TO GET THERE

Ferry from Seattle to Bainbridge Island or Route 16/Bremerton to Route 3 and then Route 305 across Bainbridge to the ferry or Eagle Harbor Park lots.

Port Madison Park & Trail
Lafayette Ave.
Agate Gate Bridge
Bloedal Reserve
Madison Bay
Phelps Rd. NE
Kane Cemetery
Dolphin Drive
uphill
Agatewood Rd. NE
Fay Bainbridge State Park
Euclid Ave. NE
downhill
Manzanita Rd. NE
Frog Rock
caution!
NE Hidden Cove Rd.
Sunrise Dr. NE
Arrowhead Drive NE
Bergman Road NE
Puget Sound
NE Frey Avenue
Peterson Hill Road NE
NE Valley Road
Living Memorial
Manitou Beach Dr.
Moran Road NE
Battle Point Park
BAINBRIDGE ISLAND
Battle Point Drive NE
Lofgren Road NE
Historical Museum
Bainbridge Gardens, Café Nola
High School Rd.
SEE INSET
Fletcher Bay Rd.
Wyatt Way West
Madison
Ferncliff Ave. NE
Bucklin Rd.
Rockaway Beach Road NE
Lynwood Center Rd.
Eagle Harbor Dr. NE
Baker Hill Rd.
N.E. Blakely Avenue
NE 3 T Road
PORT BLAKELY
Point White Dr.
Oddfellows Road
Lynwood Center, Ruby's Bistro
Halls Hill Rd.
Blakely Harbor
Country Club Road
Toe Jam Hill (uphill!)
NORTH
▪▬▪▬▪ options
Fort Ward State Park
Pleasant Beach Road
South Beach Road

Wyatt Way
Farmer's Market
bakery
Winslow Way
Eagle Harbor Books & Cafe
Bainbridge Commons
Olympic Dr./Route 303
Pegasus Café
Waterfront Park
path to ferry option
★ **START**
rest rooms, path to ferry dock

14.1 Left onto NE Frey Avenue.

14.3 Left onto Battle Point Drive NE.

16.4 Right onto Miller Road, which becomes Fletcher Bay Road near Island Center Community Hall.

18.6 Bucklin Hill/Vincent Road stop sign. See shortcut option.

18.8 Right onto Lynwood Center Road.

19.5 Lynwood Center shops. Straight at Baker Hill Road or right for Crystal Springs Loop. See option. Road becomes Pleasant Beach Road.

20.5 Left onto Oddfellows.

21.1 Right onto NE Blakely Avenue.

21.8 Right onto NE 3 T Road. Blakely Harbor.

23.0 Right onto Halls Hill Road (complex intersection). Steep hill up and down.

23.0 Left curve onto Rockaway Beach Road NE. View Point.

23.7 Left curve onto Eagle Harbor Drive NE.

26.8 Right at the T-intersection onto Eagle Harbor Drive NE.

27.1 Right onto Wyatt Way West. Uphill.

28.0 Right onto Madison Avenue. Farmer's Market.

29.0 Left onto Winslow Way West (or straight across, right on Bjune, left on Shannon to Waterfront Park and footpath to ferry).

30.0 Right onto Olympic Drive/Route 305 to the ferry.

Option to Bloedel Reserve

0.0 Right onto Route 305.

1.0 Right onto Agatewood Road NE.

1.3 Right curve onto Dolphin Drive.

1.5 Reserve. Return to Hidden Cove Road via Route 305.

3.0 Right onto Hidden Cove Road, rejoining basic route.

Shortcut Option

0.0 Left onto Bucklin Road.

0.3   Left at the T-intersection onto Hill Road, which becomes Eagle Harbor Drive NE.

0.8   Right onto Wyatt Way West. Pick up basic route directions.

Crystal Springs Loop Option

0.0   Right onto Baker Hill Road. Up and downhill.

1.9   Left at the T-intersection onto Crystal Springs Road, which becomes Point White Drive. Uphill.

5.6   Right onto Pleasant Beach Road. Downhill. Lynwood Center.

King County: Seattle
Elliott Bay Trail & Pier 91 Bike Path

Distance & Rating:	2.6 or 4.0 miles one-way; easy, flat
Surface & Traffic:	Paved path; one busy crossing
Highlights:	Myrtle Edwards Park, grain elevator, fishing dock, views Longer route: Smith Cove Park, marina
Links to:	Magnolia Loop and Discovery Park routes (Rides 18 and 19)
Eats:	Picnic, Palisades Restaurant

Connecting downtown Seattle with Magnolia, the Elliott Bay Trail is an urban delight. Linked with the Pier 91 Bike Path, it juxtaposes a breathtaking waterfront park with a busy industrial port. The Elliott Bay section passes the Pier 86 Grain Elevator, gardens, benches, a massive boulder sculpture, and a popular fishing pier. Separate cycling and jogging paths make riding a breeze.

The Pier 91 path, developed in 1987 by the Port of Seattle, remains open from 6:00 A.M. to 7:00 P.M. standard time and 6:00 A.M. to 9:00 P.M. daylight saving time. Where the path passes unmarked 20th Avenue, continue left to an upscale marina and the flashy Palisades Restaurant. Cycling is prohibited on the boardwalk, but lock up and check out the views of downtown while picnicking. Backtrack or head up 20th or 21st Avenue to link up with the Magnolia Loop.

DIRECTIONS
FOR
THE RIDE

0.0 Myrtle Edwards Park.

2.6 End of Elliott Bay Trail. Left from trail across tracks enters Pier 91 Trail. Right on 20th or 21st links up to the Discovery Park/Magnolia rides.

3.4 Right at Smith Cove Park onto Marine Drive.

4.0 End of road.

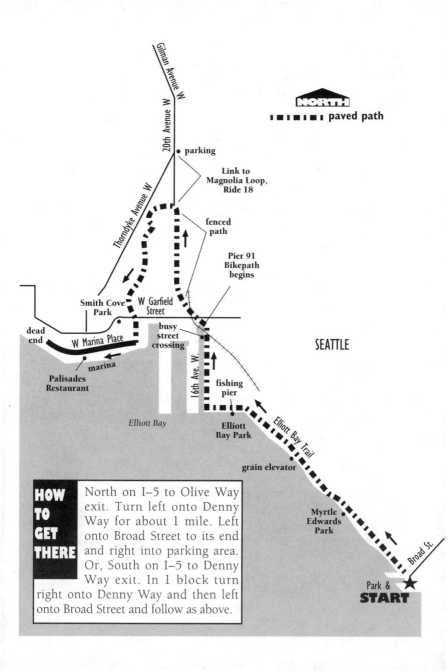

Gilman Avenue W

20th Avenue W

● parking

Link to Magnolia Loop, Ride 18

Thorndyke Avenue W

fenced path

Pier 91 Bikepath begins

Smith Cove Park

W Garfield Street

dead end

W Marina Place

busy street crossing

SEATTLE

16th Ave. W.

marina

Palisades Restaurant

fishing pier

Elliott Bay

Elliott Bay Park

Elliott Bay Trail

grain elevator

Myrtle Edwards Park

HOW TO GET THERE North on I–5 to Olive Way exit. Turn left onto Denny Way for about 1 mile. Left onto Broad Street to its end and right into parking area. Or, South on I–5 to Denny Way exit. In 1 block turn right onto Denny Way and then left onto Broad Street and follow as above.

Broad St.

Park & START

NORTH
▮▬▮▬▮▬▮ paved path

King County: Seattle
Magnolia Loop

Distance & Rating:	Approximately 8 miles; moderate, with some brief steep hills
Surface & Traffic:	Bike lanes, paved paths; moderate traffic to no cars
Highlights:	Ship Canal and Locks, Discovery Park
Links to:	Elliott Bay Trail & Pier 91 Bike Paths and Discovery Park (Rides 17 and 19)
Eats:	Upper Crust Bakery, Szmania's

Though short in mileage, this loop serves a hearty slice of Seattle. Plan a full day to savor the sights, taking the Options described. This listing begins at 20th Avenue W in order to combine the loop with the Elliott Bay/Pier 91 paths and Discovery Park (see Rides 17 and 19) for a blue-ribbon day. If cycled without additions, start anywhere you like.

Magnolia, situated on a peninsula bluff, commands stunning views of Puget Sound and the Olympics. Rising above Shilshole Bay and the Lake Washington Ship Canal on the north, Puget Sound and the Olympics on the west, and Elliott Bay and downtown Seattle on the south, Magnolia wins four stars for sweeping views. Spectacular manicured homes provide a feast for rubberneckers and a plethora of gardening ideas. Mix in huge park acreage and an upscale neighborhood shopping area for the deluxe package deal. Sample the topnotch Upper Crust Bakery and three-star Szmania's restaurant. The bakery and restaurant are closed Sundays, open for lunch other days.

Home of Herschel the seal and his insatiable salmon appetite, the Lake Washington Ship Canal and Hiram M. Chittenden Locks is well worth visiting. Lock or walk your bike—no cycling on the locks or in the gardens allowed. From the Magnolia side enter through Commodore Park and head down to the fish ladders. Here's where the controversy takes full shape: Should seals, an endangered species, be allowed to gorge on another endangered species, the salmon struggling upstream? (At the fish ladder you might see these once-plentiful salmon fight the current.) The elusive answer escapes resolution. Netting and removing seals has failed—even Herschel returned after being carted to Southern California waters. Killing seals meets with violent furor. Well, cycle on. Perhaps, once Mother Nature is disturbed, no single answer provides the fix.

Constructed in an era of altering the environment for human use, the ship canal cut a commercial link from Puget Sound to Lakes Washington and Union. The locks prevent salt water from intruding into the freshwater lakes and destroying the ecosystem. Observing the ten- to twenty-five-minute rising and lowering of pleasure and commercial crafts is like watching a nautical pageant. Tots (and adults) are mesmerized. Boaters tie and release thick ropes, lounge between efforts, wave, and entertain the viewing folk—it's superb people-watching. Across the canal the seven-acre Carl S. English Jr. Botanical Garden displays masterful horticultural design and beauty; a picnic spot worthy of the Impressionists. Peruse maps, information, and the bookstore at the Visitor Center.

Highlighting the nature component of this route, Discovery Park (Ride 19) stands out as a gold-medal urban treasure. South of the park, Magnolia Boulevard leads to breathtaking panoramas, *Sunset* magazine homes, serene Magnolia Park, and the bakery and restaurant side trip. What more could one ask?

DIRECTIONS
FOR
THE RIDE

0.0 Thorndyke Avenue W and 20th Avenue W (connects with Elliott Bay/Pier 91 Bike Path via 20th Avenue W). Parking on grassy shoulder.

0.2 Straight at Dravus. 20th Avenue becomes Gilman Avenue W. Bike lane begins.

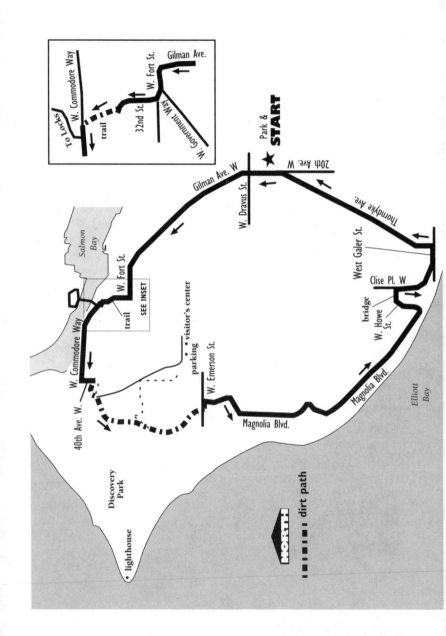

2.1 Veer right onto W Fort Street to the Hiram M. Chittenden Locks. Do not follow the Scenic Bike Route left onto W Government Way. Visit the locks and fish ladder, and cross to the gardens.

2.2 Right onto 32nd Avenue W (DEAD END sign).

2.3 Road ends. Veer right onto forested path. Cross RR bridge. Downhill.

2.6 W Commodore Way. Cross to Commodore Park and the Locks; left to Discovery Park.

3.2 Left onto 40th Avenue W. Short, steep uphill.

3.5 Enter Discovery Park. To ride through the park see Ride 19. North Parking Lot; straight onto trail ahead.

3.8 Right to Daybreak Star Indian Cultural Center. Grassy viewpoint.

3.9 Left along parking area and straight onto path.

4.5 Left at T-intersection. Option: Right to lighthouse and backtrack.

4.6 Right before yellow building.

4.7 Right at T-intersection.
Option: Left uphill to Officers' Quarters and historic marker. Backtrack.

4.8 Left to W. Emerson Street at South Parking Lot entrance.

4.9 Right onto Magnolia Boulevard.

HOW TO GET THERE

North on I–5 to Olive Way exit or South on I–5 to Denny Way exit.) In several blocks turn left onto Denny Way. Veer right as Denny Way merges into Western Avenue. Veer right onto Elliott Avenue W. Turn right onto 14th Avenue W, following signs to W Garfield Street and cross the Magnolia Bridge. Turn right onto Thorndyke Avenue W for 1 mile to the grassy area at 20th Street and park (merge point with Elliott Bay Trail & Pier 91 Bike Path).

6.6 Right onto W. Howe Street. Cross bridge and right onto Clise Place W/Magnolia Boulevard. Magnolia Park.
Option: Left onto Clise Place W, veering right at the Y-intersection onto 32nd Avenue W. Upper Crust Bakery. Left onto W McGraw Street 1 block to Szmania's restaurant. Backtrack to Magnolia Boulevard.

6.9 Magnolia Boulevard becomes W. Galer Street.

7.0 Left onto Thorndyke Avenue W.

8.0 Return to start.

King County: Seattle
Discovery Park

Distance & Rating:	5+/- miles; moderate hills
Surface & Traffic:	Paved paths, bike lanes
Highlights:	Wildlife, beaches, Daybreak Star Center, West Point Lighthouse, Fort Lawton Historic District, Visitor Center
Links to:	Elliott Bay Trail & Pier 91 Bike Path and Magnolia Loop (Rides 17 and 18)
Eats:	Picnic

In 1894, just five years after Washington gained statehood, the Seattle business community lobbied Congress to construct a fort 6 miles north of downtown, on the land that is now Discovery Park. The rapidly growing population was, they wrote, "restless, demonstrative, and oftentimes turbulent." Brigadier General Elwell Otis selected the wilderness site because it was "the place at which exhibitions of lawlessness . . . have so frequently manifested themselves."

Built at the turn of the century, the fort was named after Henry Ware Lawton, a general killed in the Philippines in 1899 as the nation's focus shifted from "domestic peace" to President Teddy Roosevelt's "big stick" international policies. Fort Lawton served as a jumping-off point for Pacific destinations. When outdated, Senator Henry M. "Scoop" Jackson sponsored the "Fort Lawton Bill," allowing the government to give surplus lands to the community for recreation. At the flagpole a pictorial details the fort's history and honors Jackson.

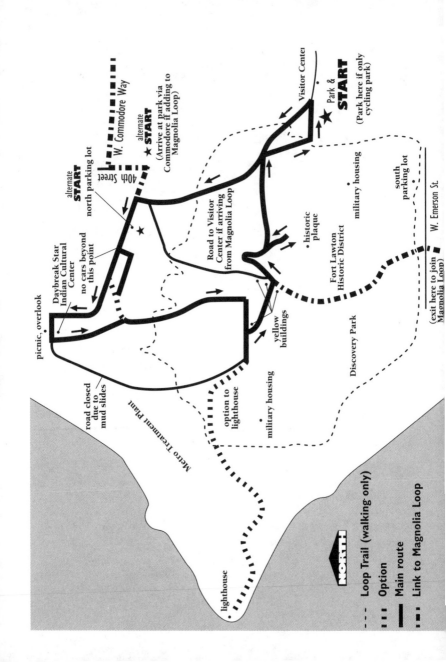

NORTH

Loop Trail (walking only)

Option

Main route

Link to Magnolia Loop

Park & **START**
(Park here if only cycling park)

Visitor Center

military housing

south parking lot

historic plaque

W. Emerson St.

(exit here to join Magnolia Loop)

Fort Lawton Historic District

Discovery Park

Road to Visitor Center if arriving from Magnolia Loop

alternate **START**
(Arrive at park via Commodore if adding to Magnolia Loop)

W. Commodore Way

40th Street

alternate **START**
alternate north parking lot

no cars beyond this point

Daybreak Star Indian Cultural Center

picnic, overlook

road closed due to mud slides

Metro Treatment Plant

yellow buildings

option to lighthouse

military housing

lighthouse

Before the military and white settlers, Native Americans fished and foraged this lush land. The Daybreak Star Indian Cultural Center depicts their lives through displays—canoes, carved statues, and artwork. Across the road a grassy plateau and overlook offer a stunning picnic spot with a nonstop view.

To cycle the paths pick up a map (35 cents) and historical booklet (75 cents) at the Visitor Center. Combining the park with the Magnolia Loop delivers you to the North Parking Lot. Head left uphill on the road to reach the Visitor Center if you want more than a quickie ride-through.

Maintained as an urban wilderness, rather than a groomed park, Discovery Park's 534 acres provide unique opportunities to observe wildlife. Fir, cedar, maples, and wetlands are inhabited by more than 230 species of birds. Mountain beaver and deer mice skitter through dense shrubs.

Free, guided nature walks, bird tours, or wildflower strolls begin at the Visitor Center on Saturdays. Environmental programs teach children about nests, forests, tide pools, and wetlands in two-hour classes, allowing parents to explore on their own. Family-oriented sessions explore ponds, frogs, and beaches. On other days walk the self-guided 0.5-mile Wolf Tree Nature Trail or the 2.8-mile Loop Trail.

HOW TO GET THERE North on I–5 to Olive Way exit. (South on I–5 to Denny Way exit.) Left onto Denny Way. Veer right as Denny Way merges into Western Avenue. Veer right onto Elliott Avenue W, which becomes 15th Avenue W. At W Emerson Place/W Nickerson Street, exit right, looping around to Emerson. At T-intersection turn right onto Gilman Ave W, which becomes W Government Way and leads to Discovery Park's Visitor Center and east parking lot.

King County: Seattle
Green Lake Loop

Distance & Rating:	3.2-mile loop; easy
Surface & Traffic:	Paved; no cars but cycle early as path gets crowded
Highlights:	Charming lake surrounded by park, swimming areas, boat rentals, play lots; next to Woodland Zoo Park
Eats:	Picnic, cafes on north end, Mona's, Honey Bear Bakery, Brie and Bordeaux
Bikes:	Gregg's Greenlake Cycle (206) 523–1819

Kids find this area a perfect place for a city play day. For adults it's people-watching at its best.

Start with a morning ride on the paved path that circles the lake. Lanes are marked for walking, jogging, cycling, and in-line skating. Consider a picnic on the broad sloping lawns, in view of waterfowl, windsurfers, dogs, and local folk. Or instead, rent a canoe or paddleboat at the lake's north end (the top kid choice) and picnic while floating. Swimming and play areas soak up any leftover energy. Explore the shops and eateries lining the north edge of the park and east of park on 55th Street. Finishing the day on the south end, at Woodland Park Zoo or Poncho Theater, assures you of an early bedtime for kiddies.

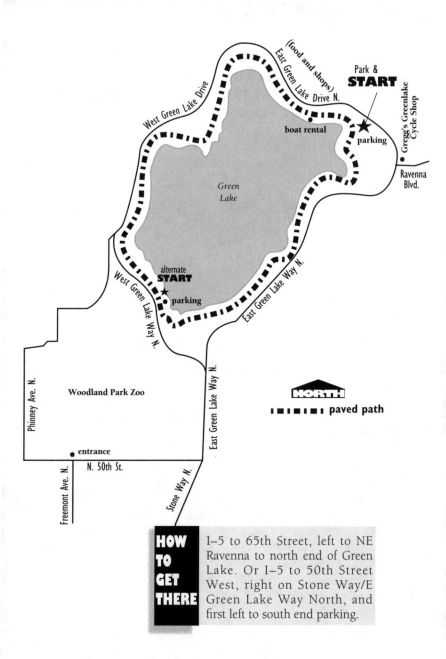

West Green Lake Drive

East Green Lake Drive N.

(food and shops)

Park &
START

Gregg's Greenlake
Cycle Shop

boat rental

parking

Ravenna
Blvd.

*Green
Lake*

alternate
START

parking

West Green Lake Way N.

East Green Lake Way N.

East Lake Way N.

East Green Lake Way N.

NORTH

Phinney Ave. N.

Woodland Park Zoo

paved path

entrance

N. 50th St.

Freemont Ave. N.

Stone Way N.

HOW TO GET THERE I–5 to 65th Street, left to NE Ravenna to north end of Green Lake. Or I–5 to 50th Street West, right on Stone Way/E Green Lake Way North, and first left to south end parking.

King County: Seattle
Seward Park Loop and Bicycle Saturdays/Sundays on Lake Washington Boulevard

Distance & Rating:	5.5 miles, Seward Park loop only, 2 miles; easy
Surface & Traffic:	Paved, packed dirt and gravel trail in Seward Park; see text
Highlights:	Lakeside mansions and park, waterfront park path, play areas, swimming
Eats:	Picnic

Seward Park is a jewel. Jutting into gorgeous Lake Washington, it forms Andrews Bay, a calm spot for swimming and paddling. Rustic brick buildings, an art studio, and a fish hatchery appear as relics from some genteel era. But you're here for the memorable lake path, a beautiful 2-mile loop. Add miles for adults and older children by continuing north on Lake Washington Boulevard, slipping by Leschi Park and Madrona Park and ending at the Seattle Tennis Club. This section of Lake Washinton Boulevard is closed to cars the second Saturdays and third Sundays of May through September. If these two days fall on the same weekend, the schedule changes to avoid a two-day closure. Check with Seattle Parks and Recreation (206) 684–7092. Where the road reopens, use the parallel path (paved and dirt).

Drivers are accustomed to cyclists here; in fact, signs state CY-CLISTS HAVE THE RIGHT-OF-WAY. A classy Seattle address, the boulevard boasts striking waterfront estates and charming homes perched on its steep hillsides. Marinas are chock-full of well-kept pleasure crafts. Pocket parks offer access to the shore, great picnic spots, and play areas.

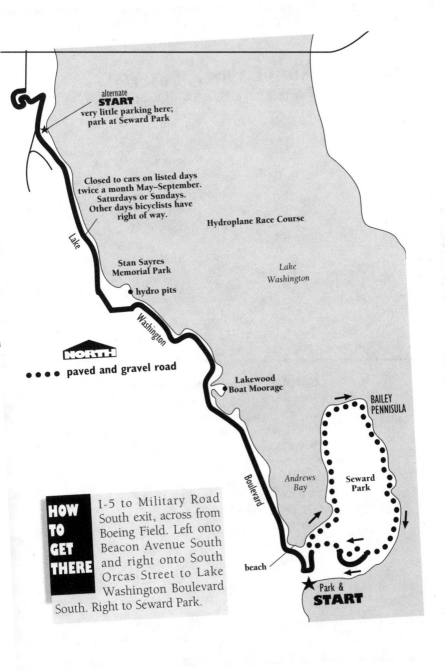

alternate
START
very little parking here;
park at Seward Park

**Closed to cars on listed days
twice a month May–September.
Saturdays or Sundays.
Other days bicyclists have
right of way.**

Hydroplane Race Course

**Stan Sayres
Memorial Park**

*Lake
Washington*

● **hydro pits**

Lake

Washington

NORTH

●●●● **paved and gravel road**

**Lakewood
Boat Moorage**

**BAILEY
PENNISULA**

*Andrews
Bay*

**Seward
Park**

Boulevard

beach

**HOW
TO
GET
THERE** I-5 to Military Road
South exit, across from
Boeing Field. Left onto
Beacon Avenue South
and right onto South
Orcas Street to Lake
Washington Boulevard
South. Right to Seward Park.

★ **Park &
START**

King County: Seattle
Burke Gilman/Sammamish River Trails

Distance & Rating:	Any amount desired (26+ miles one-way); 15 mph limit, easy, flat
Surface & Traffic:	Paved; no cars—weekends crowded with cyclists, in-line skaters, joggers; one main street crossing before and after University of Washington
Highlights:	Spectacular—that covers it! Nature, lakes, wineries, brewery
Eats:	Picnic

This 26-mile path between Gas Works and Marymoor Parks runs through shaded woods, lakeside communities, and broad river flats. Choose all or a section; there's no traffic and few street crossings beyond UW.

Don't miss Château St. Michelle Winery's "old money" castle structure and top-notch gardens, Columbia Winery's "nouveau riche" faux (pale yellow) Victorian house, or the brewery, all on NE 145th Street. From the path watch for the avant-garde Red Hook Brewery. Oddly there are no signs labeling the route or the exit at NE 145th Street, the connection point.

NE 145th Street leads to Bothell Landing's shops to the left and the wineries and brewery to the right. Its wide shoulders accommodate cyclists safely. Rest rooms can be found along the trail and at attractions described above.

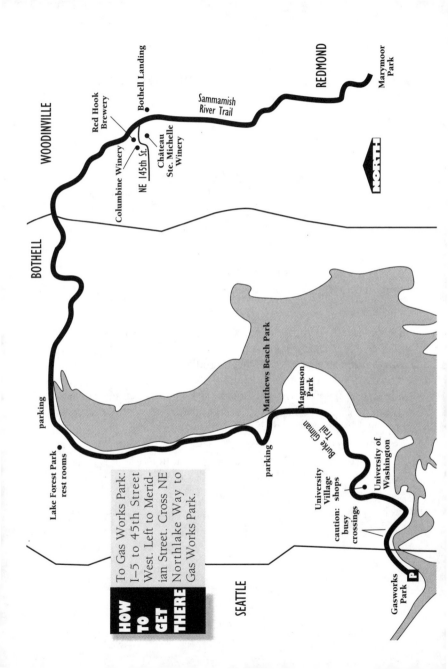

King County: Maple Valley
Soos Creek Trail

Distance & Rating:	4.4 miles each way or 4.9 from Lake Meridian parking; easy
Surface & Traffic:	Paved path; 0.5 mile on wide shoulder if starting from the lake; no cars but several road crossings.
Highlights:	Wetlands, Lake Meridian, Soos Creek Parks, forests, pastures
Links to:	Lake Youngs Loop (Ride 24)
Eats:	Picnic

If I had to choose the loveliest path of all, the Soos Creek Trail would be high on my short list. Mostly flat, it slices through verdant forests, sprawling wetlands, wildlife-filled ponds, serene pastures, and over a charming bridge. Starting at the south end puts the lakeside at your disposal for post-ride picnicking or play time. The north end also has a well-kept park and kiddie equipment. Benches and picnic tables are scattered along the route.

To connect with Lake Youngs Loop, turn right onto 208th Street SE and cycle uphill to 148th Avenue SE. Caution! There is no shoulder on this 0.7-mile link. Cross to the dirt trail.

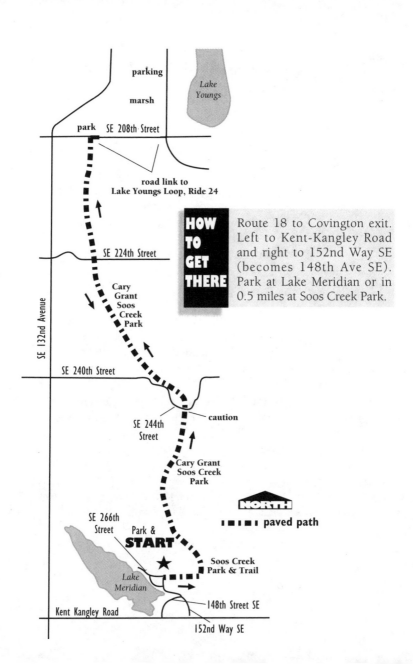

parking

marsh

Lake Youngs

park   SE 208th Street

road link to
Lake Youngs Loop, Ride 24

SE 224th Street

Cary Grant Soos Creek Park

SE 132nd Avenue

SE 240th Street

SE 244th Street

caution

Cary Grant Soos Creek Park

HOW TO GET THERE

Route 18 to Covington exit. Left to Kent-Kangley Road and right to 152nd Way SE (becomes 148th Ave SE). Park at Lake Meridian or in 0.5 miles at Soos Creek Park.

NORTH

▪▬▪▬▪ **paved path**

SE 266th Street

Park &
START

Soos Creek Park & Trail

Lake Meridian

148th Street SE

Kent Kangley Road

152nd Way SE

King County: Maple Valley
Lake Youngs Loop

Distance & Rating:	9.3 miles; easy to moderate—two steep hills
Surface & Traffic:	Compact dirt, occasional rocky spots; 0.5-mile road section with moderate traffic
Highlights:	Forested ride; mountain-biking practice
Link to:	Soos Creek Trail (Ride 23)
Eats:	Picnic

Lake Youngs is actually a Seattle water reservoir, untouchable and unviewable. The surrounding forested trail runs between two fences. Mostly, it's packed dirt—easy, wide, and delightful. Short segments are single track. Get out the treaded wheels; this is a perfect spot for novice to intermediate mountain bikers.

Circling clockwise puts the steeper grades on the downhill and keeps you in the same direction as traffic for the brief road sections. The steepest rocky downhill, along SE 224th Street, can be avoided, if desired, by riding on the road's wide shoulder; there's no double fence here. Unless you're a macho mountain biker, you might have to push your bike on two brief rocky sections along the road. During summer the route remains shaded and cool. To connect with the Soos Creek Trail (Ride 23), go downhill on 208th Street SE.

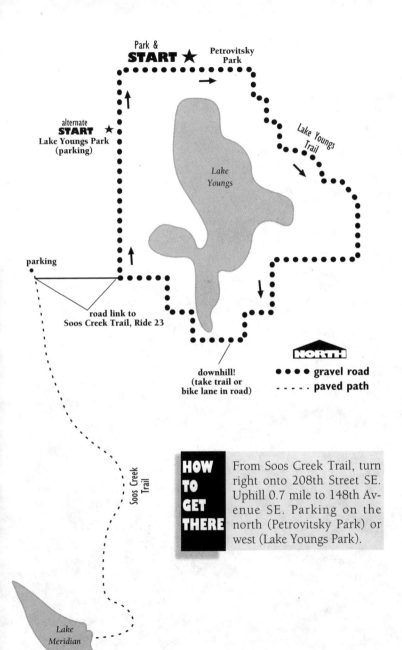

Park &
START ★ Petrovitsky
Park

Lake Youngs Trail

alternate
START ★
Lake Youngs Park
(parking)

*Lake
Youngs*

parking

road link to
Soos Creek Trail, Ride 23

downhill!
(take trail or
bike lane in road)

NORTH

● ● ● gravel road
- - - - paved path

Soos Creek Trail

HOW TO GET THERE From Soos Creek Trail, turn right onto 208th Street SE. Uphill 0.7 mile to 148th Avenue SE. Parking on the north (Petrovitsky Park) or west (Lake Youngs Park).

*Lake
Meridian*

King County: Bellevue
Phantom Lake Loop and Lake Hills Greenbelt

Distance & Rating:	Each section 2.5 miles; mostly flat
Surface & Traffic:	Bike lanes, paved paths, gravel trails (need mountain bike); no cars
Highlights:	Phantom Lake, Larsen Lake, Community Demonstration Garden, Blueberry Farm
Bikes:	Bike Map (425) 452–2894

Bellevue teems with bike lanes and paths; nature preserved by city officials' foresight. One safe cycling area, the Lake Hills Greenbelt, is part of a future network. Its Phantom Lake Loop path, somewhat of a misnomer, runs on the non-lake side of the roads. You can't see the lake, but the path is paved, wooded, and delightful.

An 1895 U.S. Geological Survey shows a footpath skirting Phantom Lake, probably a Snoqualmie tribe trail used to transport canoes from Lake Washington to Lake Sammamish. On the Pacific Flyway, the lake hosts twenty types of waterfowl; migrating ducks, Canada geese, merganza, teal, Northern shovelers, and great blue herons. Hidden in the lily pads, reeds, and marshes are yellow perch, black crappie, river otters, salamanders, and frogs. Observe from the pier.

In the 151-acre Greenbelt, gravel paths wend through farms, ponds, marshes, and woods to Larsen Lake. Farmers grow berries, a tradition begun by Japanese immigrants. Keep your eyes peeled for red-tailed hawks, muskrats, coyotes, and hummingbirds.

On Saturdays join a nature walk or talk at the Demonstration Gardens, where everything from common peas to obscure oriental vegetables grows in terraced plots. Purchase summer crops at the

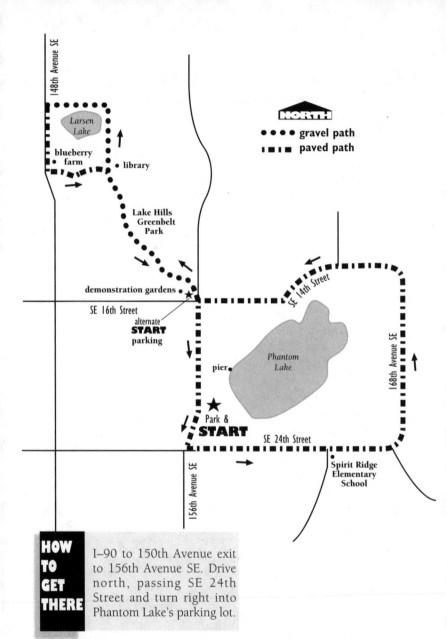

148th Avenue SE

NORTH

● ● ● gravel path
▪ ▪ ▪ paved path

Larsen Lake

blueberry farm

library

Lake Hills Greenbelt Park

demonstration gardens

SE 16th Street

alternate START parking

SE 14th Street

168th Avenue SE

Phantom Lake

pier

★ **Park & START**

SE 24th Street

156th Avenue SE

Spirit Ridge Elementary School

HOW TO GET THERE

I–90 to 150th Avenue exit to 156th Avenue SE. Drive north, passing SE 24th Street and turn right into Phantom Lake's parking lot.

gardens or the old blueberry farmhouse. In 2000 a pedestrian/bike bridge across 148th Street will connect with the now short trail, soon to be expanded.

To Phantom Lake Path

0.0 Left from Lake Hills Greenbelt parking area. Rest rooms.

0.1 Left across SE 24th Street onto path. Downhill. Bath House.

0.6 Spirit Ridge Elementary School.

1.0 Curve left next to 168th Avenue SE and left next to SE 14th Street.

1.4 Lake Hills Community Park.

1.6 Left curve along SE 16th Street.

2.2 Left onto path next to 156th Avenue SE.

2.5 Lake Hills Greenbelt parking and Phantom Lake.

To Greenbelt

0.0 Northeast corner of SE 156th Avenue and SE 16th Street.

0.9 Pass Lake Hills Library on right over bridge.

1.1 Larsen Lake. Not open to the public.

1.3 Left on sidewalk edging 148th Avenue SE.

1.5 Left after blueberry farmhouse onto SE 8th Street

1.6 Left onto path toward Lake Hills Library.

2.5 Return to start.

King County: Pacific/Tukwila
Interurban & Christensen–Green River Trail

Distance & Rating:	Loop—20.5 miles, complete trail—35 miles; do any distance; easy
Surface & Traffic:	Paved; several street crossings
Highlights:	Safety, Green River, parks, rest rooms
Eats:	Picnic, fast-food eateries

Safe, paved, flat, riding along a river, parks, Mount Rainier views, and beauty. What more could one ask?

Well, better shielding of industry's backyard on the 14-mile Interurban Trail (IU). Though agricultural remnants remain, most of this rich glacial valley has succumbed to industry: lumber, railroads, manufacturing, offices, and housing. Wetlands, drained and filled with concrete, bare urban sprawl's negative effects. On the bright side, new wetland plantings of willow, cattail, wild rose, and snowberry screen commercial enterprises and provide a wildlife habitat. Environmental awareness is taking hold; the new racetrack and proliferating developments go for the green, in plantings, paths, and parks, and money.

The 14-mile Christensen–Green River Trail (GRT) exhibits urbanization at its best. Meandering through serene riverside parks, it is sheer delight. Brisco Meander and Anderson Parks make splendid picnic spots. Don't miss the whimsical "Slipstream" bicycle art.

Pedaling both trails adds up to 35 miles; skipping the IU below the GRT connection makes a 20.5-mile loop. Limited segments of the GRT run on small local roads. On the IU, at several major street crossings, head for the stoplights. The GRT, which once ended at I–405, now crosses beneath it, following the Green River's winding course. Currently, the GRT ends at East Marginal Way, which leads to Seattle. Eventually it will continue along the Duwamish Waterway to Alki Beach in West Seattle and the IU will link directly to the GRT.

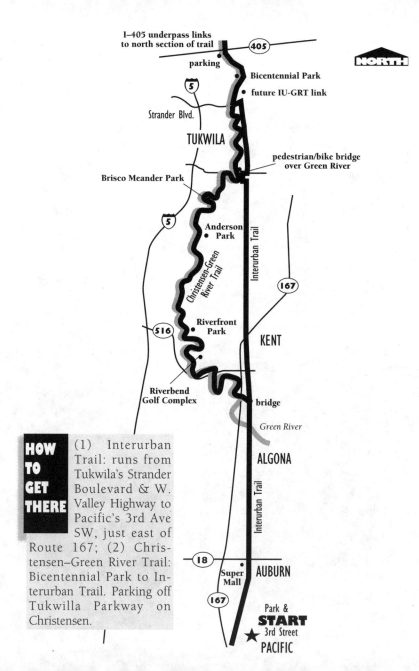

I–405 underpass links
to north section of trail

405

parking

5

Bicentennial Park

future IU-GRT link

Strander Blvd.

TUKWILA

**pedestrian/bike bridge
over Green River**

Brisco Meander Park

5

**Anderson
Park**

Christensen-Green
River Trail

Interurban Trail

167

**Riverfront
Park**

516

KENT

**Riverbend
Golf Complex**

bridge

Green River

ALGONA

HOW TO GET THERE (1) Interurban Trail: runs from Tukwila's Strander Boulevard & W. Valley Highway to Pacific's 3rd Ave SW, just east of Route 167; (2) Christensen–Green River Trail: Bicentennial Park to Interurban Trail. Parking off Tukwilla Parkway on Christensen.

Interurban Trail

18

**Super
Mall**

AUBURN

167

Park &
START
3rd Street
★
PACIFIC

NORTH

King County: Kent
Cedar River Trail—Lake Wilderness to Landsburg Park

Distance & Rating:	13.2 (lake) or 16 (trailhead) miles; easy on all-terrain bike
Surface & Traffic:	Compact dirt and pea gravel; no cars
Highlights:	South King County Arboretum, two parks, Cedar River
Eats:	picnic
Etc.:	Isolated area—not recommended for women alone.

Whether starting at the Kent-Kangley Road trailhead or Lake Wilderness Center, take in Lake Wilderness Park. Its stunning shore, though no longer in the wilderness, sports broad lawns, fishing piers, sandy swimming spots, marshes, wooden walking bridges, and playlots.

The trail, built of compacted dirt and pea gravel on an old railroad bed, is easily rideable on an all-terrain bicycle. Slicing through a quiet, forested valley, it skims along a raised base. Wildflowers bloom prolifically in the sunny forest cut, high above the floodplains and scattered rooftops. Somehow, back in 1902, the railroad architects knew better than to build in a floodplain, unlike the builders of the riverside homes clustered below. The ribbony river, rushing over a rocky bed, runs a tortuous path. Repeatedly, it bends, divides, and wends beneath train trestles. Evidence of its rampages appears as fallen trees and mud slides.

High above the sparkling water, around 1908, the railroad installed sturdy steel bridges shipped from Pennsylvania steelyards. The valley then resounded with the clickety-clack of Black Diamond coal trains hauling their loads to Seattle or back East. With mining's

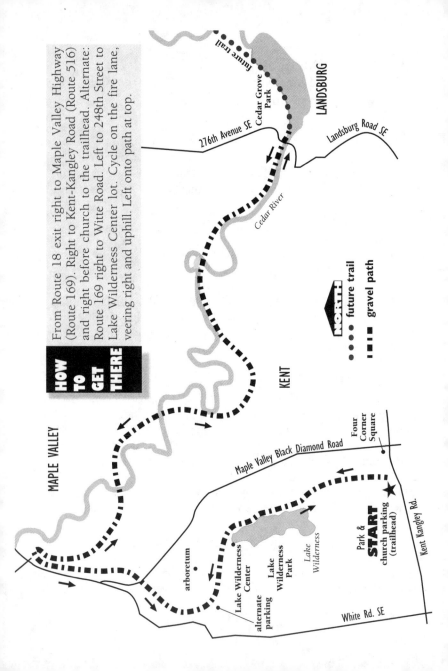

HOW TO GET THERE

From Route 18 exit right to Maple Valley Highway (Route 169). Right to Kent-Kangley Road (Route 516) and right before church to the trailhead. Alternate: Route 169 right to Witte Road. Left to 248th Street to Lake Wilderness Center lot. Cycle on the fire lane, veering right and uphill. Left onto path at top.

NORTH

●●● future trail
■■■ gravel path

MAPLE VALLEY

KENT

LANDSBURG

276th Avenue SE

Cedar Grove Park

future trail

Landsburg Road SE

Cedar River

Maple Valley Black Diamond Road

Four Corner Square

Kent Kangley Rd.

Park & church parking (trailhead)

★ START

Lake Wilderness Center

Lake Wilderness Park

Lake Wilderness

arboretum

alternate parking

White Rd. SE

demise the railroad fell into disuse, making it available for recreation. Negotiations are under way to convert additional tracks to trails. Continuing from Landsburg Park, the railroad bed traverses the City of Seattle Watershed. The completed path to Rattlesnake Lake will join the Iron Horse State Park and Snoqualmie Trails. To complete the original run, it will also be paved south to Black Diamond.

On the return cut left back uphill. Forget the trail straight ahead. It's great for 1.5 miles to a bridge but turns to chunky gravel and runs unpleasantly along noisy Maple Valley Highway. Back at the Arboretum, however, narrow walking and biking trails loop through acres of dense trees and ferns, almost untouched by sun. Lake Wilderness Park has a stunning lakefront where you can picnic, fish, take out a rowboat, or just sit.

DIRECTIONS
FOR
THE RIDE

0.0 Trailhead, Lake Wilderness Trail section.

1.1 Lake Forest Estates.

1.9 Arboretum. Trailhead map. Bicycling okay on loop trail.

3.4 Gravel downhill. Right onto Cedar River Trail at junction.

8.0 Trail ends. Parking lot next to river. Cross road to Landsburg Park.

16.0 Backtrack to start.

Distance & Rating:	29.2 miles; moderate effort, long flat stretches and a few steep hills
Surface & Traffic:	Paved; light; avoid King County Fair in August
Highlights:	Enumclaw plateaus, Flaming Geyser Recreation Park, Black Diamond
Eats:	Black Diamond Bakery
Bikes:	Enumclaw Cyclery (253) 825–4461

Enumclaw, a Muckleshoot Indian word for "home of evil spirits," hardly describes this route. Situated in the shadow of Mount Rainier, this valley ride seems more a gateway to heaven.

According to archaeologists, nomadic Native Americans roamed the Green River Valley for 6,000 years, partaking of its abundant plants, animals, and water. White homesteaders arrived in the 1850s. Forced to Fort Steilacoom during the subsequent Indian wars, they returned to reclaim their farms and platted the town in 1885.

Danish immigrants formed a cooperative cannery and milk condensery. Farming, coal mining, and timber jobs attracted other settlers. Crops grew prolifically in the rich, mud-flow soil. Grassy fields nourished dairy cows. Thoroughbred horses thrived alongside timbering enterprises. Spring-flowering hawthorns, dogwood, crab apple, and cherry trees that could make a "young man's fancy turn to love" contrast with flaming maples that lure autumn fans. No matter the season, for cycling, these pastoral plateaus can't be beat.

Start at Martin Johnson Park, located in a quiet residential area about 0.5 mile from rural farms and backcountry roads. Rising abruptly from these open fields are the Cascade Foothills. You can imagine a vast glacier pushing tons of dirt down valley. Forest patches, scattered reminders of lush bygone eras, stand isolated like ships at sea. Emus dash about enclosures. Pungent manure odors emanate from prosperous farms. Names on entry signs reflect the area's Danish heritage: Krainik, Sunoversnik, and Zurcher. Jim and Cindy Shuobersnick's 1990 Dairy Farm of the Year could get an award just for location (though their home and garden are picture perfect, too). It seems as if you could touch Mount Rainier behind it.

Leaving the plateau, glide down forested SE 368th Way and 212th Avenue SE to the Green River. Cross the concrete Whitney Bridge, a slick new affair that replaced the charming green metal bridge, now retired peacefully amid the tall, waving grass. A sprawling farm with picturesque barns, silos, and horse pastures lies kitty-corner from a Christmas tree farm. Along the road blackberry vines encroach like marching ants.

Don't skip a visit to stunning Flaming Geyser Recreation Park. Its bridge, once a twin to the Whitney green metal one, has been replaced by a unique, futuristic concrete and aluminum structure that rises in peaks. At the road's end a short walk leads to a cascading creek, the former flame geyser, and the bubbling geyser that emits sulfur and turns the soil gray. Other trails edge the Green River.

You'll need your stamina to climb 218th Avenue SE. Stock up on calories and water; it's 0.9 mile. Panting, sweating, and creeping at a snail's pace, especially on a hot day, this is a tough incline. Remember the little engine: "I think I can, I think I can."

After the crest head onto Auburn Black Diamond Road's wide shoulder. Sprawling development on Horseshoe Lake and massive clear-cuts afford resplendent Mount Rainier and Cascade views. Coast downhill after the Black Diamond sign to Morganville, a late-nineteenth-century logging and coal-mining town. European immigrant workers purchased homes here but had to rent the lots from the company. During the 1921 nationwide coal strike, management forced workers to move their homes. Those who couldn't afford it (pay was 20 cents an hour) just left. Thus, many of these humble cottages date from that era. Even after the settlement, life would never be the same. Changing fuel demands and a fatal mine accident precipitated an economic shift to logging. If you have time, cruise the side streets.

After the King County Library, Morgan Street heads to Black Diamond, a historic spot tucked below the foothills. In 1855 a blemish fell upon this village. Starting here and spreading throughout Puget Sound, Chinese immigrants were terrorized by "American" (European immigrant) miners. After six months President Grover Cleveland declared martial law, ending the racist attacks.

Visit the Depot Museum, vintage caboose, original jail, and Baker Street Books (connected to an antiques shop) in a hundred-year-old tavern. It offers a fantastic array of books and you can sink into massive armchairs. In another block visit the Black Diamond Bakery and Restaurant (closed Mondays). Geared more to Cascade Loop car travelers than to the granola or sports-drink crowd, the bakery's stocked with fried donuts, fritters, and cookies. Warning! Even purists may be tempted. The cheery restaurant serves salads and sandwiches on fresh-baked bread.

Backtracking to Baker Street, turn right and uphill at the corner antiques shop that's crammed with quilts, dishes, and unique jewelry. At the T-intersection and a tire store, turn right onto heavily traveled Route 169. Quickly, make the first left onto Lawson (becomes Green River Gorge Road). An eyesore gravel pit eats at the hillside ahead, visible until hidden by a wood fence. Well, we do need the stuff.

A gradual descent to the Green River cuts through woods and clear cuts. River updrafts create a chilling breeze. At the new one-lane bridge, take in this lovely, deep ravine before the well-graded, short climb. It's pretty isolated out here. You may not want to cycle alone. Fireweed carpets open spaces, competing with seedlings for sun. A left curve onto SE 352nd Street lands you at a T-intersection and electrical station. Head south on Veazie Cumberland Road to tiny Cumberland, home of the Eager Beaver Tavern and a fire station.

A shaded Nolte State Park, secluded Deep Lake's grassy patches and massive maple trees invite picnicking (rest rooms, too). A family-owned retreat, the 117 acres were donated to the state in 1972 at Miss Minnie Nolte's death. A hiking trail circles the 100-foot-deep lake. Area miners tell of running twenty-four-hour pumps to drain their shafts of water that seeped in from the lake's depth. Trout, catfish, perch, and bluegill make it a popular fishing hole.

After the park return to the broad, flat valley, turning right onto SE 392nd Street. Passing Huizenger and Sea-Bee Dairies, climb briefly and head left onto 278th Way SE to 416th Street SE. The terrain gives a sense of the riches available to nineteenth-century immigrants. Watch for the Skaker Dairy and left turn onto 252nd Way SE, backtracking the early segment to Martin Johnson Park.

DIRECTIONS
FOR
THE RIDE

0.0 Begin at Martin Johnson Park, heading north on Harding Street.

0.2 Left onto McHugh Avenue SE at the T-intersection.

0.6 Left curve onto SE 433rd Street.

1.1 Right turn onto 248th Avenue SE, which becomes 252nd Way SE.

1.3 Cross SE 424th Street, staying on 252nd Way SE.

1.8 Left onto SE 416th Street.

2.3 Cross 244th Avenue SE. Blinking red light and stop sign.

2.5 Evergreen Cemetery. Dairy farms.

2.7 Right onto 236th Avenue SE. Darigold dairy farm.

3.3 Emu/ostrich farm on left. Krainik Dairy.

3.7 Cross SE 400th Street.

4.2 Zurcher Dairy Farm.

4.5 Left onto SE 384th Street, which curves right into 236th Avenue SE. Hills.

5.6 Picturesque old barn.

6.2 Sunoversnik Dairy. Downhill, curving left onto SE 368th Street.

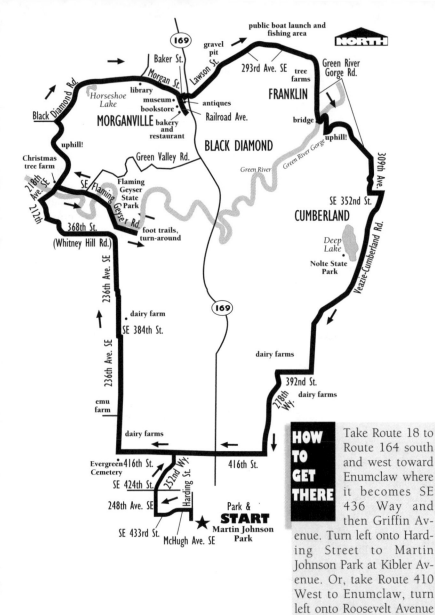

NORTH

169

Baker St.

gravel pit

public boat launch and fishing area

Lawson St.

293rd Ave. SE

Green River Gorge Rd.

tree farms

Morgan St.

Black Diamond Rd.

Horseshoe Lake

library

museum

Black Diamond

FRANKLIN

bookstore

antiques

MORGANVILLE

bakery and restaurant

Railroad Ave.

bridge

BLACK DIAMOND

Green River Gorge Rd.

uphill!

Christmas tree farm

Green Valley Rd.

Green River

309th Ave.

218th Ave. SE

212th

SE Flaming Geyser Rd.

Flaming Geyser State Park

uphill!

SE 352nd St.

368th St.

(Whitney Hill Rd.)

foot trails, turn-around

CUMBERLAND

Deep Lake

Nolte State Park

236th Ave. SE

Veazie-Cumberland Rd.

dairy farm

SE 384th St.

236th Ave. SE

169

emu farm

dairy farms

392nd St.

dairy farms

278th Wy.

dairy farms

Evergreen Cemetery

416th St.

416th St.

SE 424th St.

252nd Wy.

Harding St.

248th Ave. SE

Park & **START**

SE 433rd St.

McHugh Ave. SE

Martin Johnson Park

HOW TO GET THERE Take Route 18 to Route 164 south and west toward Enumclaw where it becomes SE 436 Way and then Griffin Avenue. Turn left onto Harding Street to Martin Johnson Park at Kibler Avenue. Or, take Route 410 West to Enumclaw, turn left onto Roosevelt Avenue E and right onto Harding Street to park.

6.8 Right onto 212th Way SE at the stop sign. Becomes 218th Avenue SE at right curve. No sign.

7.2 Cross SE 358th. Horse pasture and massive farm on right.

7.3 Cross the Green River. Whitney Bridge Park. Christmas tree farm. (Christmas tree farm is on the corner at the right turn to park. Pass it also on way out.)

7.4 Right onto SE Green Valley Road. Great shoulder.

8.0 Right onto SE Flaming Geyser Road.

8.2 Bridge over Green River. Flaming Geyser Recreation Park.

8.4 Veer right.

9.2 End of road turn-around. Trails begin. Backtrack over bridge.

10.5 Left onto SE Green Valley Road.

11.0 Right onto 218th Ave SE. Christmas tree farm. Climb long hill.

11.9 Crest of hill!

12.3 Right onto Auburn Black Diamond Road. Excellent shoulder.

13.0 Horseshoe Lake and development.

13.6 Pass Lake Sawyer Road SE. Black Diamond sign. Downhill.

14.1 Right onto Morgan Street after King County Library. Cemetery.

14.6 Morgan Street becomes Railroad Avenue. Historic Black Diamond—Depot Museum, Baker Street Books, antiques shops, Black Diamond Bakery, just south of Baker Street.

14.7 Left onto Baker Street. Uphill. Fire station.

14.9 Right onto unmarked Route 169 at the T-intersection. Quick left onto Lawson. City Hall.

15.5 Gravel pit. Clear-cuts. Long downhill.

16.7 Public fishing sign.

17.6 Curve right as road becomes 293rd Avenue SE.

18.6 Road becomes Green River Gorge Road. Downhill.

18.8 Green River Bridge—single lane. Gorge. Begin climb.

19.1 Sharp left, staying on SE Green River Gorge Road (briefly signed 293rd Avenue SE). Enumclaw Franklin Road SE on right.

20.1 Road becomes 309th Avenue SE.

20.8 Left curve onto SE 352nd Street.

21.1 Right onto Veazie Cumberland Road's shoulder at the T-intersection. Cumberland—Eager Beaver Tavern, fire station.

22.5 Nolte State Park (rest rooms).

23.9 Right onto SE 392nd Street. Dairies. Uphill.

24.1 Left onto 278th Way SE.

25.8 Stop sign; right onto SE 416th Street.

26.7 Cross 264th Ave SE/Route 169. Skaker Dairy.

27.4 Left onto 252nd Way SE.

27.9 Cross SE 424th Street. Road becomes 248th Avenue SE.

28.4 Veer left onto SE 433rd Street. Becomes McHugh Avenue.

29.0 Right onto Harding Street.

29.2 Return to Martin Johnson Park.

King County
Vashon Island Loop

Distance & Rating:	32 miles, 9.7- or 14.7-mile options; moderate to difficult
Surface & Traffic:	Paved; moderate on main road, light on back roads
Highlights:	Rural roads; waterfront, spectacular views, Blue Heron Art Center, Vashon Center, Seattle's Best Coffee, ferry ride; local industries, bed and breakfasts
Eats:	Seattle's Best Coffee, Dog Day Cafe and Juice Bar, Turtle Island Cafe, Maury Island Farms, Mary Martha's
Sleeps:	Vashon-Maury Island Chamber of Commerce, 206–463–6217 or www.vashonchamber.com; Castle Hill lodging reservations, www.vashonisland.com, (206) 463–5491 or (206) 463–3556; Angels of the Sea B&B, Artist's Studio Loft B&B, Harbor Inn, Peabody's B&B, Emerald Isle Guest House, Tjomsland House B&B, American Youth Hostel/B&B Ranch, Back Bay Inn
Etc.:	Bike Shop (206) 463–6225; kayaks (206) 463-9257; Strawberry Festival (July)

Home to artists, counterculture types, and weekenders, Vashon Island retains a rustic ambience despite its proximity to mainland cities. Thriving businesses, such as K-2 Skis, Wax Orchards (preserves, syrups, and cider), Maury Island Farms (berries and preserves), Seattle's Best Coffee (SBC), Andrew Will Winery, and a tofu company, make the island more self-contained than other bedroom islands.

Scenic roads, flanked by prolific pastel sweet peas, succulent blackberries, rolling pastures, verdant forests, and brilliant orange maples in autumn, can be explored year-round. Vashon Island requires an entire day—to travel by ferry, to ride, and to savor. Two days provide leisurely cycling: Stash jeans, a T-shirt, a nightshirt, and a toothbrush in your panniers. Relaxed is the name of the game here. Rushing is déclassé. Waiting, as in "for the ferry," is a way of life. Dress is rustic Northwest; basic REI. Stay near Vashon Center to walk or cycle to dinner or at a B&B with a restaurant. A favorite with bicyclists is the Ranch Hostel and B&B, complete with teepees, Old West buildings, and a covered wagon.

Vashon street names change as often as the weather. Watch carefully for turns. Also, beware here of Murphy's First Law of Bicycling: No matter which way you ride, it's uphill against the wind. Take heed; the wind hits right off as you emerge from the oldest (brass railings and soft armchairs) and smallest Washington ferry at Tahlequah and climb a steep hill. Gear down and forget macho; you're not warmed up yet. Walking part way is not a sin. Local drivers, accustomed to panting bicyclists, provide a wide berth.

Re-oxygenate on Vashon Highway SW, a forested road, often shrouded in morning fog. Rest at Inspiration Point above Quartermaster Harbor. Vashon, "discovered" in 1792 by Captain George Vancouver, had no homesteaders (except Native Americans) until 1877. "Old" in the Northwest is green behind the ears by Eastern standards.

Soar down a forested mile to placid Quartermaster Harbor where blue herons and other waterfowl feed. Leaving the shore, head uphill to Burton, founded with a turn-of-the-century private college, which burned in 1910. The Harbor Mercantile's 1908 roots are evidenced in timeworn shelves and creaky wood floors. Burton's Back Bay Inn and Restaurant is an island favorite for gourmet fare. The Silverwood Gallery showcases fine and functional contemporary art.

SW Burton Drive circles a bucolic area of shingled cottages, frame and porched farm homes, and artistically painted Victorians that surround Burton Acres Park and Lodge. The park's tranquil shoreline boat access brims at the seams with sweet blackberries. Overhead, mammoth, plate-sized leafed maples and shiny red-trunked madronas block the sun. Returning to Vashon Highway, skirt a marina tucked in the protected cove that connects to the Judd Creek estuary.

The T-intersection with Dockton Road SW separates the wheat from the chaff. The Maury Island option (see below) is not for the young at heart but weak of knees. Rather, it is for strong bicyclists accustomed to fairly brutal hills. Fair warning.

For those sane folks skipping the option, you might linger at Tramp Harbor Fishing Pier (rest room) to see blue herons, contemplative fishermen, and picturesque views. At the harbor's end ducks galore feed frenziedly amid rotting pilings that stand like soldiers at attention. Climb Chautauqua Beach Drive SW toward Ellisport's striking, high-bank homes and Tramp Harbor Inn. Empower those thighs to propel you up steep 204th Street to a high plateau traverse leading to Downtown Vashon. This thriving marketplace is jam-packed with shops. Browse in Books by the Way on SW Bank Road, adorned with plush carpet and comfy wingback chairs. Check out Vashon artists' arts and crafts at the Heron's Nest. Refresh at Dog Day Cafe and Juice Bar with a healthy, yummy lunch or fresh-squeezed juice (breakfast and lunch only). For a sit-down meal, sample Turtle Island Cafe's salivating good stuff (lunch weekdays, dinner daily). Rich herby aromas emanate from Mary Martha's, purveyor of melt-in-the-mouth delicacies, and Bob's Bakery, stocked with hearty whole-grain breads. Save room in your panniers.

An optional 4-mile flat round-trip to Valley Center heads south. Wander into Seattle's Best Coffee Rotisserie; the rich aromas would have brought Mrs. Olsen to ecstasy. Visit the Blue Heron Arts Center, a showplace for local artists.

Ahead, Minglement Marketplace sells in-season organic produce, natural foods, and gifts. Nearby are the Maury Island Farm store, famous for fruity jams, and Sound Foods, once an artsy hippie haven that now serves middle-of-the-road hearty food and baked goods.

Back in Downtown Vashon, locals hold Saturday Country Market at Ober Park. Special festivals include the Harvest Fair, Barnworks Watercolor Show, Potter's Tour, Discovery Days, Strawberry Festival, and Burton Pioneer Days. Stretch out like a marmot on the grassy knoll and enjoy some treats.

North on Vashon Highway watch for Vashon Realty at SW Cedarhurst Road, your cue to a sharp backward left. (Staying on Vashon Highway leads you to the Heights Ferry Dock to Seattle.) Drop down steep Cedarhurst Road and wend up and down around plunging, forested ravines. Open fields on Westside Highway SW, a name that fails to depict its rural character, reveal stunning views.

Passing 121st Avenue SW, climb Westside Highway's well-graded mile through farmland. Cresting (hallelujah!), sail down to the Cemetery Road/Westside Highway T-intersection, turn right, and (you guessed it) cycle uphill to SW 220th Street. Jog right and left to flat Wax Orchard Road and Wax Orchard's sprawling acres. Horses visit over barbed-wire fences, nuzzling for a treat.

After merging with Vashon Highway, there's one last (honest) rise. Your marathoner thighs get payback coasting down to the Tahlequah Ferry Dock on Commencement Bay. Above, Mount Rainier dominates like a silent guardian. Fishermen, ships, and football-field–sized barges sail by. Stately blue herons, squawking seagulls, and flitting shorebirds zero in on abandoned pilings. Here's your chance to do as the islanders do: Relax, read, and wait for the ferry.

Option to Maury Island (9.7 or 14.7 miles)

For this hearty option turn right at the T-intersection to Dockton Road SW. Cycle past the KIRO radio transmitter and Pete's Farmstand (open in autumn to sell crunchy apples, nuts, and pears). A golf course seems populated mostly by feeding birds. On hilly acreage holly grows and woolly sheep graze.

For the 9.7 mile loop, head left up SW 248th (steep!), joining the longer loop at 75th Avenue SW. Rolling wooded terrain opens to dazzling Puget Sound and Mount Rainier views. Here rests the original Swallow's Nest, funky cottage lodgings that seem relics of the 1960s. The site is an ornithologist's delight.

Point Robinson Road descends steeply to it's namesake park, the Coast Guard Station, and the diminutive white 1888 lighthouse perched on the point, like a toy. Flocks of birds, chirping like a cathedral choir, nestle in wooded cliffs that border the grassy flats and driftwood-scattered beach. Rest up for the uphill return and SW Luana Beach Road, a secluded, serpentine lane that drops and ascends through luxuriant vine- and fern-covered ravines that are bereft of sunlight, and rises to a sunny plateau and SW Point Robinson Road. Return on Dockton Road SW, joining the basic route.

Option to Dockton (14.7 miles)

Soar down to sleepy Dockton, home of a defunct shipbuilding industry. A turn-of-the-century village, it is replete with false-fronted shops and gingerbread Victorians. Unpretentious fishing and tugboats belong to the town's working population. Visitors may stay at the Angels of the Sea B&B, where the owner serenades breakfast guests with her harp. Returning to Dockton Road SW, climb past Dockton Park and turn right up steep SW 260th Street, creeping slower than a government check. Cutting through a housing development, glide downhill on 75th Avenue SW to join the shorter option at SW 248th Street.

DIRECTIONS
FOR
THE RIDE

0.0 Ferry dock. Right up steep W Tahlequah Road.

0.2 Switchback left onto 131st Avenue SW.

1.0 Veer right onto Vashon Highway SW at the Y-intersection.

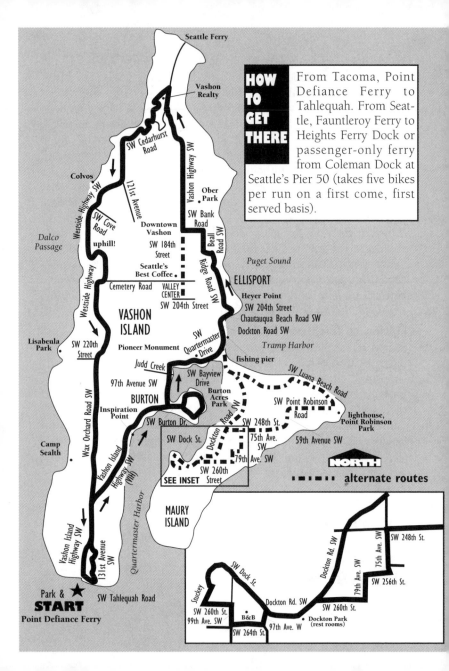

2.2 Veer right, passing Wax Orchard Road SW.

2.5 Inspiration Point. Mile downhill.

5.0 Left curve uphill to Burton and right onto SW Burton Drive.

5.6 Right onto 97th Avenue SW. Burton Acres Park and Lodge.

6.4 Marine frontage. Road becomes SW Bay View Drive.

6.8 Left curve onto 97th Avenue SW. Right onto SW Burton Drive.

7.5 Right onto Vashon Highway. Silverwood Gallery, Back Bay Inn, Swallow's Nest Cottages. Marina.

8.3 Judd Creek. Quick right onto SW Quartermaster Drive.

9.3 Straight at Pioneer Monument.

9.8 Left onto Dockton Road SW at the T-intersection. Or see option to Maury Island, below.

10.0 Tramp Harbor Fishing Pier. Rest room.

10.6 Veer right up Chautauqua Beach Road SW. Ellisport. Tramp Harbor Inn.

11.0 Left up steep SW 204th Street or right to visit Heyer Point.

11.4 Right curve onto Ridge Road SW.

14.2 Left curve onto SW 184th Street.

14.4 Right onto Beall Road SW. Van Gelders' B&B.

14.9 Left curve onto SW Bank Road. Downtown Vashon.

15.2 Right to Vashon Highway SW. Mary Martha's cafe, Bob's Bakery. See option to Valley Center.

15.4 Ober Park. Public Library. Rest rooms. Country Market. Old Tjomsland House B&B.

18.2 Left switchback onto SW Cedarhurst Road at Vashon Realty. Downhill. (Straight to Heights Ferry Dock to Seattle.)

19.0 Pass Burma Road SW. Saltwater estuary.

20.4 Left curve onto Westside Highway SW. Colvos.

22.4 Veer right past 121st Avenue SW at the Y-intersection.

23.2 Pass SW Cove Road. Steep uphill. (AYH Ranch Hostel to left.)

23.7 Crest hill. Pass Thorsen Road SW.

25.4 Right onto SW Cemetery Road/Westside Highway SW.

27.0 Right onto SW 220th Street. Lisabeula Park ahead.

27.1 Left onto Wax Orchard Road SW. Wax Orchards.

29.0 Camp Sealth.

29.4 Veer right onto Vashon Highway SW.

32.0 Downhill to Tahlequah Ferry Dock.

Option to Valley Center (4 miles)

0.0 Left onto Vashon Highway SW. Chamber of Commerce.

1.0 Seattle's Best Coffee Rotisserie. Blue Heron Arts Center. Antiques shops. Coral Bay Trading café.

2.0 SW 204th Street. Maury Island Store. Sound Foods. Bicycle in a Tree.

4.0 Backtrack to Vashon Center.

Option to Maury Island/Point Robinson (9.7 or 14.7 miles)

0.0 Right onto Dockton Road SW at the T-intersection.

0.6 KIRO transmitter. Left and right curves. Pass SW Point Robinson Road and Melita Creek Heron Rookery.

2.2 Right curve onto Dockton Road SW passing 75th Avenue.

2.7 Golf course. Holly orchard and sheep farm.

2.9 Left onto SW 248th Street. Or straight for 14.7-mile option (see below).

3.2 Cross 75th Avenue SW, joining the 14.7-mile option.

4.2 Left curve onto 59th Avenue SW. Swallow's Nest Guest Cottages. Views!

4.8 Right onto SW Point Robinson Road toward Point Robinson.

5.8 Right following Point Robinson Road downhill to park.

6.1 Coast Guard Station. Lighthouse. Backtrack uphill.

6.4 Straight onto SW Luana Beach Road. Hilly!

8.0 Crest long uphill.

8.6 Right onto SW Point Robinson Road.

9.2 Veer right onto Dockton Road SW. KIRO tower.

9.7 Pass SW Quartermaster Road, rejoining the basic ride.

Option to Maury Island/Dockton (additional 5 miles)

0.0   Pass SW 248th Street. Downhill.

2.0   Dockton Park. Rest rooms.

2.6   Veer right onto SW Dock Street, not left to 99th Avenue SW.

2.8   Right onto Stuckey Avenue SW. Left onto SW 260th Street.

2.9   Right onto 99th Avenue SW.

3.0   Left onto SW 264th Street. Angels of the Sea B&B.

3.1   Left onto 97th Avenue SW and quick right onto Dock Street.

3.5   Dock Street becomes Dockton Road SW. Dockton Park.

3.7   Right onto steep SW 260th Street.

4.4   Left curve onto 79th Avenue SW.

4.5   Right onto SW 256th Street. Uphill.

4.6   Left onto 75th Avenue SW. Downhill.

5.0   Right onto SW 248th Street. Tennis courts. Join the 9.7-mile option.

Pierce County: Gig Harbor
City Park/Ollala Loop

Distance & Rating:	25 miles; moderate to vigorous, steep hills
Surface & Traffic:	Paved; light to moderate
Highlights:	Rural farms, Burley Lagoon, Ollala Lagoon, Gig Harbor
Eats:	Picnic, Al's Market. See Ride 31.
Sleeps:	See Ride 31.
Bikes:	Old Town Cycles (253) 858–8040

"Car Talk," Boston Public Radio's car repair and therapy program, once teased an Ollala caller who cheerfully bore the brunt of Click and Clack's "Ooo-la-la" jokes. Actually, it's pronounced Oh-la-la and is a sublime rural area—home to Magical Strings, Pam and Phil Boulding's popular Celtic harp and hammered dulcimer group.

Ollala comes midpoint in this ride of roller-coaster hills. They loom threateningly but flatten considerably as you reach them. City folks trek out to this rural land to board horses or ride them. Locals use them for transportation; several small markets have hitching posts. Take along plenty of water and perhaps thick-crusted, brick-oven–baked bread or rolls from Harbor Bread Co.

Nibbling at the dense forests that at one time blanketed these parts are housing plats. Burley Lagoon remains relatively untouched, its marshy, wetland tideflats replete with wildlife. Check for waterfowl as you edge it on flat terrain that ends at Pine Road SW. There, a toilsome climb to Madrona Road begins. Madrona climbs again, albeit slowly. The good news is that cars here are rare.

The Burley Glenwood Elementary School's playing field provides a grassy rest spot if you need it. After gliding downhill, flat (really)

Bethel Burley Road SE seems a piece of cake. Stop at a dark red cottage whose yard is besieged by clever stationary and whirlygig sculptures—colorful and lively like in a kindergarten. Across the road Jadamac Arabians are raised, and a sign states JOHN DEERE X-ING.

Rolling terrain resumes near Mullenix Ridge Elementary School. Power lines—our energy umbilical cords—stretch overhead, as if heralding our industrial dependence. Along rolling Ollala Valley Road, plump sheep graze languorously, growing wool. Timeworn and fading gray and red barns, artifacts of a disappearing family-farm era, dot the valley floor—evidence of the struggle to wrest an independent existence from the land. Prolific blackberry vines and wildflowers overflow roadside ditches. Plopped in an open pasture, the blue, wooden Virgil Stacey Memorial Complex (home to South Kitsap Little League), is reminiscent of Field of Dreams. Above, Mount Rainier looms regally like a massive watchtower.

Nestled under massive firs the postage stamp–size Ollala Triangle Park's striking totem pole reflects the Northwest Coast Indian paintings that adorn the Ollala Elementary School. The barn-like Community Center contrasts sharply with the crisp white Ollala Bible Church and a picturesque storybook farm of gray, red-roofed buildings. A downhill glide edges Ollala Bay, nature's four-star restaurant for hungry waterfowl.

Humans can feast at Al's Market. Al has retired, but son John carries forth tradition well, chatting with bicyclists. His unimposing, immaculate store (with rest rooms) offers top-grade fresh and smoked meats and poultry. Succulent smoked beef melts in your mouth. Haul home smoked bacon to sizzle up in the morning. Picnic at Al's outdoor tables, overlooking serene Colvos Passage beneath Mount Rainier—what a backdrop! A charming wood-railed bridge crosses the lagoon inlet, making for a terrific photo op.

Enough rest. It's time to creep up Crescent Valley Road's punishing incline. Sun-dappled woods and wildflowers lure you on. Catch your breath on the flat but bumpy road that slices like a knife through thick forests and verdant farmland.

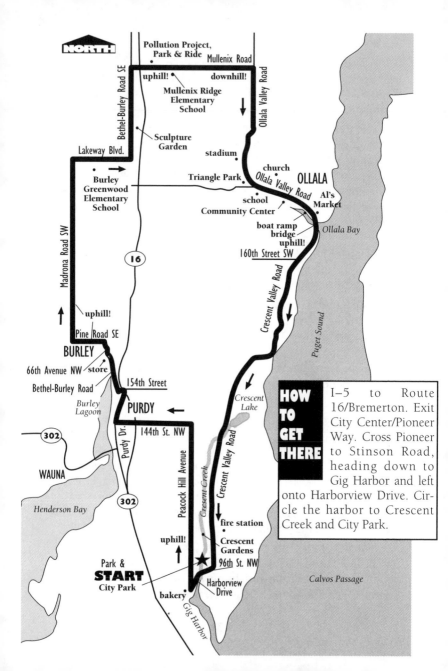

NORTH

Pollution Project, Park & Ride
Mullenix Road

uphill!   downhill!

Bethel-Burley Road SE

Mullenix Ridge Elementary School

Ollala Valley Road

Sculpture Garden

Lakeway Blvd.

stadium

church

Triangle Park   Ollala Valley Road   OLLALA

Burley Greenwood Elementary School

Al's Market

school

Community Center

boat ramp
bridge
uphill!

Ollala Bay

Madrona Road SW

16

160th Street SW

Crescent Valley Road

Puget Sound

uphill!

Pine Road SE

BURLEY

66th Avenue NW   store

Bethel-Burley Road

154th Street

Burley Lagoon

PURDY

302

144th St. NW

Crescent Lake

Purdy Dr.

302

WAUNA

Henderson Bay

Peacock Hill Avenue

Crescent Creek

Crescent Valley Road

fire station

uphill!

Crescent Gardens
96th St. NW

Park &
START
City Park

bakery   Harborview Drive

Gig Harbor

Calvos Passage

HOW TO GET THERE

I–5 to Route 16/Bremerton. Exit City Center/Pioneer Way. Cross Pioneer to Stinson Road, heading down to Gig Harbor and left onto Harborview Drive. Circle the harbor to Crescent Creek and City Park.

Nearing Gig Harbor you'll see the houses are older and more like cottages. Farms feed cows and horses; earthy manure smells permeate the air. On several acres Crescent Valley Gardens specialize in rhododendrons and azaleas. It's well worth a stop before you head back to the City Park and perhaps Le Bistro for a post-ride latte.

DIRECTIONS
FOR
THE RIDE

0.0 Right from City Park, crossing Crescent Creek.

0.2 Left onto unmarked Harborview Drive NW. Do not go straight up hill.

0.6 Right up Peacock Hill Avenue NW. (½ block farther on Harborview Drive NW visit the Harbor Bread Co.)

1.1 Crest. Future Cultural Center for the Performing Arts.

3.8 Left onto 144th Street NW.

5.3 Park and Ride. Right onto Purdy Drive/Route 302's shoulder.

5.8 Left onto 154th Street just before FREEWAY ENTRANCE sign. Immediate right onto 66th Avenue NW. Burley Lagoon on left.

6.1 Kitsap County. 66th Avenue becomes Bethel Burley Road SE. Store.

6.5 Curve left.

7.1 Left onto Pine Road SE. Uphill 0.8 miles.

8.1 Right onto Madrona Road SW.

9.5 Right onto Lakeway Boulevard.

9.8 Burley Glenwood Elementary. Downhill.

10.6 Left onto Bethel Burley Road SE at the T-intersection.

11.5 Sculpture garden and whirlygigs.

12.5 Right onto Mullenix Road and under Route 16.

12.8 Park and Ride, Pollution Project. Uphill.

13.6 Mullenix Ridge Elementary School. Downhill.

15.0 Right onto Ollala Valley Road. Flatter section.

16.4 Virgil Stacey Memorial Complex (Kitsap Little League).

17.4 Ollala Food Center, Triangle Park, school.

17.9	Community Center and Ollala Bible Church.
19.0	Ollala Boat Ramp, Al's Market. Road becomes Crescent Valley Avenue NW.
19.1	Cross bridge. 1.5-mile climb.
22.1	Pass 144th Street NW; Crescent Lake on left. Crescent Creek.
24.2	Crescent Valley Gardens. Fire Station.
24.8	Right onto 96th Street NW.
25.0	Return to City Park.

Pierce County: Gig Harbor
Three-Loop Option

Distance & Rating:	16.9 miles for basic loop, optional 6-mile Cromwell Loop and/or 7.9-mile Bridge Loop; moderate and steep hills
Surface & Traffic:	Paved; little to moderate
Highlights:	Gig Harbor, Saturday Farmer's Market, rural roads, waterfront, Kopachuck State Park, views
Eats:	Tides Tavern, Le Bistro, J.T.'s Original Louisiana BBQ, Spiro's Pizza, Green Turtle, Marco's, Harbor Breads, Suzanne's Bakery & Deli
Sleeps:	The Pillars B&B, The Maritime Inn, Mary's B&B, Water's Edge B&B, The Inn at Gig Harbor
Etc.:	Chamber of Commerce, (253) 851–6865, www.gigharbor.com

Puget Sound, Mount Rainier, and Olympic Mountain views. Dense forests, sprawling farmland, scenic cycling. Experience it all by using the basic route or designing your own from the options. Make it short and sweet or a thigh challenger. Build up cycling skills and muscles or squeeze in a quickie before twenty other tasks.

Idyllic Gig Harbor is frequented by seasoned fishermen, the pleasure-craft crowd, and scenery-hungry tourists. Restaurants and shops abound. Downtown accommodations are cropping up, such as the new Maritime Inn, Mary's B&B, and bed-and-breakfast standbys.

The peninsula's early twentieth-century fishing and farming communities depended on broad, frigid Puget Sound as their supply and commerce lifeline. Reminiscent of Norwegian fjords, the peninsula, called "Little Norway," drew settlers from that country. Lacking road and steamer linkages, early residents bucked shifting tides, rowing to Tacoma markets. These were sturdy Scandinavian stock, whose hardy descendants populate Gig Harbor.

Starting at sea level, you have only one way to go—up. So, without further ado, head up Pioneer Way at The Harbor Inn Restaurant, rebuilt after a brakeless truck careened down Pioneer Way, plowing into it. The hill looks daunting and is, but haste makes waste. Go one pedal at a time.

After cresting and passing residential and commercial enterprises, skirt Wollochet Bay's tip. Pass the timeworn Artondale Grange, a relic from rural days. The native word *wollochet* has two possible meanings: "Cut throat" refers to a story about a young brave who, unable to marry his lady of choice, cut his throat. Less romantic is the other possible meaning of the word, "squirting clams."

At 40th Street NW the basic route turns right (Cromwell option heads straight). Cutting through stately firs, descend onto 92nd Avenue NW to the triangle intersection, where the Cromwell option joins in. Enter Arletta, a late-nineteenth-century settlement, named for a Mrs. Powell's daughter Arla and her friend Lecetta. Near Horsehead Bay, Arletta was home to loggers, fishermen, trappers, and berry and holly growers. The rich green, crimson-berried holly gained fame through White House purchases each Christmas.

From Arletta's business section (the Arletta Store), rolling terrain holds pastures where frisky horses graze. Gliding down, don't miss the sharp, angled left to steep, wooded Artondale Drive NW. Creeping up is like being pulled back by an undertow. At the top enjoy the stupendous views. The site, once a camp, now sprouts high-end real estate.

Below, visit Kopachuck (meaning "near water") State Park, a hundred-acre, 5,600-foot waterfront gem. Bring out the snacks as you beachcomb its rocky shores. Miniature scrambling crabs dash from overturned rocks. Marine birds dunk for food. Abundant deer, rabbits, and even bears (you probably won't see one) make this home.

Rosedale, named for its abundant, pink-red wild roses, was settled in 1882 before roads existed. Land sold for $60–$100 per acre to hardy residents who depended on boats for weekly mail delivery, travel, and commercial sales of fruit, oysters, timber, and Christmas trees. Timber sales evolved to electric and telephone pole construction (but not for Gig Harbor, which had neither service until 1920!).

Across Henderson Bay is Raft Island (a wood sign is obscured from this direction). Between low water, pleasure craft stagnate like beached whales while abundant waterfowl peck the muddy bottom.

A bridge crosses to Ray Nash Drive NW (the shortcut joins here). Waterfront homes crowd the bay's shore to its end. A right shortcuts to downtown Gig Harbor but climbs a long hill. A left follows the basic route to 86th Avenue NW, edged by Rosedale Playfield, Templeton's Grocery, and the Rosedale Community Center. Lay Inlet, named for the original settler, Benjamin Lay, lies serenely to the left. After trickling Nelyaly Creek, a gargantuan, white farmhouse and red barn loom, like a mirage in the desert.

From rural 86th Avenue NW wend uphill through a dense, coniferous, luxuriantly ferned forest on Sehmel Drive NW, named for the early settler who grew Christmas trees. Finding no market in the Northwest, Sehmel trucked them to California for a hefty profit.

Coast to the hill's base where a sprawling country home dominates the slope. Along 70th unkempt pastures and timeworn homes whither, like Salvation Army castoffs, between encroaching city slickers. Snow-topped Olympic Mountain pinnacles float above Henderson Bay, before the downhill past hay fields and dense forests.

Across Route 16 a welcome flat stretch passes the Eagles Lodge and Hy-iu-hee-hee Tavern. Take care to veer left at the Y-intersection past a Mexican restaurant. Cruise past vintage frame homes down to the harbor. Visit the Harbor Bread Company, where they bake crusty, firm French country breads, tasty rolls, and yummy cookies. Le Bistro Coffee House, at the tip of the harbor, steams yummy lattes and whips up fine soups. Louisiana BBQ serves real deal ribs, chicken, and catfish.

Downtown, frame and brick fishermen's homes line the streets. Don't forget Mostly Books, where volumes bulge from shelves, stuffed in like sacked potatoes. Plop down and peruse. The store is like a honey dish for flies; *ring!* goes the cash register.

To stave off the hungers, try the venerable Tides Tavern. Known as "The Tides," it caters to a beer and pizza crowd. Sturdy wood tables sit on creaky wood floors. Nothing fancy here, just tasty dripping sandwiches and cheesy whole-wheat crust pizzas. Try the outdoor deck that hangs over the boat-crammed dock. (Note that Tides Tavern is a bar and won't admit persons under twenty-one.) And off you go to complete the chores.

Optional Cromwell Loop

For a thigh-burner remain on Wollochet Drive. Experienced riders find this hilly, rural farmland and shoreline venture challenging and visually rewarding. Red-barned farms bask on golden plateaus harboring riding horses. Warning! Unchained dogs charge like crazed militia. Stop and walk.

As you crest the hill, street names change frequently; just keep going. Drop to Carr Inlet and skirt placid Hale Passage—great photo ops. Fox Island, connected to Gig Harbor by a bridge, slumbers across the way. Behind, Mount Rainier and the Cascade Mountains form a dazzling vista. Ahead are serene Carr Inlet and the jagged Olympic Mountains.

East Cromwell was settled in 1883 by Wisconsiner John Cromwell, a real estate agent and Cromwell's first postmaster. Homesteaders farmed fruit, berries, and produce and raised dairy cows, selling from the steamer landing at Sunny Bay Dock. As roads were constructed, East Cromwell had an influx of vacationers and permanent residents.

A steep climb inland leads to the Cromwell Cemetery and a great downhill. Another rise then soars down toward the Fox Island Bridge Y-intersection at Warren, where Mr. and Mrs. Charles Warren (Mrs. was a mail-order bride in 1911) operated Warren's Dock and a store. Veer right uphill to the triangle intersection, joining the basic route.

Optional Bridge Loop

From Jerisich Park follow Harborview Drive, curving right onto Soundview Drive NW, a 0.8-mile uphill with unremitting traffic but a bike lane. A glance to the left reveals Puget Sound and snow-topped Mount Rainier, so unreal it could be a movie backdrop. Escape left to quiet 64th Street Court NW (becomes Reid Drive NW at curve). Rolling hills and wooded curves preserve the rural flavor, but development is pushing the suburban edge.

Crossing beneath the Tacoma Narrows Bridge (successor to the original that gained fame in Hollywood movies as the collapsing "Galloping Gertie"), cars drone like hived bees on the overhead metal. Huff and puff up Stone Drive NW to Tacoma Narrows Airport. Along East Bay Drive NW hills roll beneath sun-speckled leafy canopies. Below, Wollochet Bay is a muddy wetland at low tide and a glorious calm inlet at high. Its shoreline served as an Indian reservation until 1913.

Take Artondale Drive (shortcut) or 40th Street NW (joining the basic route at the triangle corner). The shorter route briefly joins the basic route on Kopachuck Drive NW, but turns right onto Rosedale, creeping up 0.8 mile to Rosedale Gardens (stupendous in rhodie season) and Gig Harbor High School. Float down to Jerisich Park.

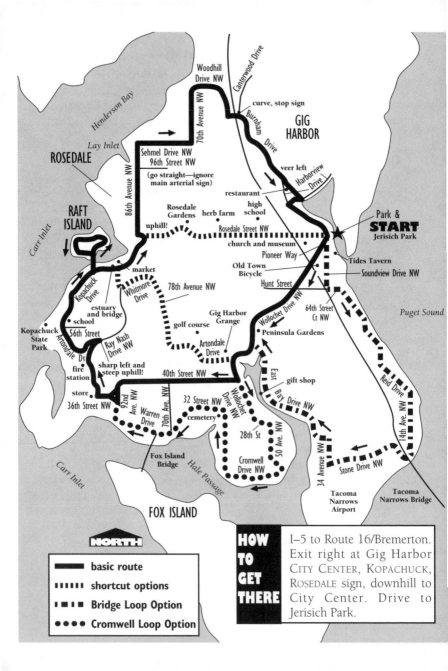

DIRECTIONS
FOR
THE RIDE

0.0 Left from Jerisich Park onto Harborview Drive NW.

0.1 Right up Pioneer Way. Harbor Inn Restaurant (*straight* for Bridge option).

0.6 Crest at Grandview Street.

0.7 Pass Kimball Drive on left (Old Town Bicycle; Saturday farmer's market on Kimball). Cross Route 16.

1.2 Cross Hunt Street NW. Pioneer Way becomes Wollochet Drive NW.

2.1 Peninsula Gardens.

2.8 Pass East Bay Drive NW and Artondale Drive NW.

3.2 Veer right onto 40th Street NW (straight for Cromwell option).

3.4 Pass Artondale Elementary School and 70th Avenue NW.

5.1 Left curve. 40th Street NW becomes 92nd Avenue NW.

5.4 Right onto 36th Street NW at the triangle intersection. Cromwell option joins.

5.6 Right onto Ray Nash Drive NW. Arletta Store.

6.2 Arletta Fire Station.

6.6 Left angle back onto steep Artondale Drive NW.

7.5 56th Street NW. Kopachuck State Park.

8.0 Voyager Elementary School; Artondale Drive NW becomes Kopachuck Drive NW.

8.6 Optional 1.5-mile loop: Left onto Raft Island Road NW, across bridge. Follow Island path. Backtrack to Kopachuck Drive.

9.0 Cross estuary bridge. Ray Nash Drive NW. Island View Market.

9.7 Left onto Rosedale Street NW at the T-intersection (right for shortcut option).

9.8 Right curve onto 86th Avenue NW at the Rosedale Playfield.

9.9 Templeton's Grocery. Rosedale Community Center. Lay Inlet.

10.4 Cross Nelyaly Creek and 92nd Street NW. Mansion on right.

10.8 Straight on 86th Avenue NW at stop sign. Do not veer right onto MAIN ARTERIAL.

11.3 Right curve onto Sehmel Drive NW. Rolling hills.

12.3 Left onto 70th Avenue NW at base of hill. Huge hillside house.

13.2 Right curve onto Woodhill Drive NW. Horse pastures.

13.9 Right onto unmarked Burnham Drive NW at the T-intersection.

14.2 Left across Route 16 on overpass to Burnham Drive NW's shoulder.

15.6 Gig Harbor city limits. Eagles Lodge, Hy-iu-hee-hee Tavern.

15.7 Veer left, remaining on Burnham Drive NW at the Y-intersection. Puerto Vallarta Restaurant.

16.0 Right onto Harborview Drive NW at the T-intersection.

16.1 Left at the stop sign, toward Tacoma. Le Bistro Coffee House.

16.3 Left onto Harborview Drive NW. Murphy's Landing.

16.5 Veer left, following Harborview Drive NW past Stinson Avenue. Wild Birds, Etc.

16.9 Return to Jerisich Park. Maritime Inn. Mostly Books.

Optional Cromwell Loop—hilly but beautiful

0.0 Straight past 40th Street NW. Stay on Wollochet Drive NW.

0.4 Left curve onto 28th Street NW.

0.7 Right curve as 28th Street NW becomes 50th Avenue NW.

1.1 Crest and curve left to Cromwell Drive NW. Downhill.

2.2 East Cromwell. Steep climb.

3.2 Crest hill. Cemetery. Left curve onto 32nd Street NW.

4.1 Straight across 70th Avenue; 32nd Street NW becomes Warren Drive NW.

5.0 Fox Island Bridge. Veer right up Warren Drive NW.

5.8 Right curve onto 92nd Avenue NW.

6.0 Join the basic route by turning left onto 36th Street at the triangle intersection.

Optional Bridge Loop

0.0   Continue on Harborview Drive. Tides Tavern.

0.1   Right onto Soundview Drive NW. Long uphill. Bike lane.

0.9   The Pillars B&B.

1.0   Left onto unmarked 64th Street Court NW. Hunt Street NW on the right. Caution crossing left.

1.2   Right curve onto Reid Drive NW. Bike lane.

2.8   Reid Drive NW becomes 14th Avenue NW.

4.1   At T-intersection veer left and under the Narrows Bridge.

4.4   Elana's Restaurant. Veer left past shops, uphill onto Stone Drive NW.

5.1   Crest at Tacoma Narrows Airport.

5.6   Right onto 34th Avenue NW at WOLLOCHET sign. Chevron Station. Rest rooms.

6.2   34th Avenue NW becomes East Bay Drive NW.

7.3   Gift Shop. Pass Murphy Road.

7.9   Left onto Wollochet Drive NW. Join basic route or turn right onto Artondale Drive NW for shortcut.

Shortcut

0.0   Right onto Artondale Drive NW. Gig Harbor Grange.

0.5   Gig Harbor Golf Club.

1.7   Artondale Drive NW curves right, becoming 78th Avenue NW, and left onto Whitmore Drive NW.

2.8   Right onto unmarked Ray Nash Drive NW at the T-intersection.

3.0   Right onto Ray Nash Drive NW at the T-intersection. Market. Kopachuck Drive NW on the left.

3.7   Right onto Rosedale Street NW. Uphill.

4.3   Rosedale Gardens and Nursery. Crest hill.

5.7   Cross Schoolhouse Avenue. Gig Harbor High School.

6.0   Cross Skansie Street/46th Avenue NW. Go under Route 16.

6.6   St. Nicholas Church. Historic Museum.

6.8   Harborview Drive at Jerisich Park.

Pierce County:
Key Peninsula
Home/Longbranch Loop

Distance & Rating:	16 miles; moderate, gentle rolling hills
Surface & Traffic:	Paved; few cars, but they drive fast
Highlights:	Penrose Point State Park, Lakebay, Longbranch, miles of undeveloped forests
Eats:	Homeport Restaurant, Longbranch Mercantile (grocery), Longbranch Chowder House
Sleeps:	Regional tourism information, www.gigharbor.com; The Olde Glencove Hotel, (253) 884–2835; Aloha Beachside B&B (888) ALOHA–BB

If you wanted to drop out of society's rat race, foregoing materialistic individualism, you might seek a place of quiet beauty and solitude. But it's too late for this spot. Back in 1896 The Mutual Home Association Cooperative, paying $65 for twenty-six acres, settled it as a utopian community geared to improve social and moral conditions. At one point the community's land grew to 217 acres. Gazing over Home's cleared idyllic setting to Von Geldern Cove (also called Joe's Bay) and the backdrop of Mount Rainier, it's clear why this site was chosen.

Precepts of tolerance and freedom of activity appealed to the founders; however, they soon learned it didn't put food on the table. Early members survived by cutting cordwood, teaching school, digging clams, farming, and building houses. Publishing a newspaper hot with topics such as free love, women's rights, anarchy, vegetarianism, a universal language (Esperanto), and religion brought Home fame and hatred. Quelling vigilante attacks, surviving imprisonment of the paper's editor, and fighting the post office closure, residents of Home lived a cooperative life. They opened a store, raised poultry, logged, and cultivated fruit. As the colony grew, the Western individualistic spirit prevailed, causing rife and disbandment of the utopian cooperative in 1919. Land reverted to the residents, many of whose descendants occupy it today.

Folks out here like their dogs. This route captures first prize for unleashed territorial dogs on its first few miles. Stop your bike and walk past them (see notes on dogs in the Introduction). On the positive side, long stretches of the route lie in undeveloped rural terrain. Roads meander through native forests, and cars are rarely in sight. Burning wood odors permeate the air. It's not ecological, but it still holds some romanticism; and for these modern-day pioneers, these fires provide heat. Residents haven't discovered that our forests are disappearing and our air is polluted. Well, enjoy these wooded roads while they last.

Begin this loop by crossing McEvan Road to D Street. Turn left in 1 block onto 10th Street, preparing for a burn-your-eyes-out Rainier view (provided the gray has lifted). Riding downhill toward the cove, curve right to A Street along the water. Turn left onto Key Peninsula Highway, crossing the wooden bridge over a marshy inlet. From the highway turn left at the first intersection onto Hoff Road, riding past open fields.

Hoff Road becomes Lorenz Road, which flanks Mayo Cove, a haven for wildlife (jumping fish and several varieties of ducks). Lakebay Marina, in a cove reminiscent of a Northwest pioneer movie set, nestles in a misty fog. Fishing boats and manicured homes speak of quieter lost times. Lakebay, settled by farmer and teacher William and Sarah Creviston in 1871, expanded in 1877 when businessman Carl Lorenz dammed a creek and built a sawmill. Unable to transport logs, Lorenz purchased a steamer fleet to serve the Sound. The town thrived, as his boats encouraged tourism, a brickyard, a farmers cooperative, a dairy farm, and the Cooper Hotel, which burned in 1922.

Lorenz Road rises to Penrose Point State Park. Open only on weekends, it is worth the mile ride to see its superb shoreline. Delano Bay, on the left, was the site of the Delano Beach Resort, built in 1889, complete with a dance hall, tennis courts, gardens, and cabins. Currently, the site is used for a camp. Look left for an awesome Rainier view. Camp Woodworth sits at the bay's end. Nearby farms dispense more protective dogs. Be forewarned and ready to walk.

Follow Lorenz Road/24th Street through a more populated area of single-family homes. The terrain flattens as a series of turns blend, wending back to Route 302, where a road sign points left to Longbranch and right to Gig Harbor/Tacoma. Ahead, a vintage stone and metal-roofed hall, the Longbranch Improvement Club, provides a gathering spot for community events and dances. A bit farther, wander about the Longbranch Cemetery and Community Church. Early settlers, bearing German names, are buried here behind ornate iron fences.

Longbranch and Filucy Bay views belong on postcards. A sleepy town now, Longbranch prospered as a resort during the first half of this century due to its scenery, activities, and Tacoma/Olympia ferries. But with the advent of major highways in the 1950s, people traveled to more distant vacation spots. Remnants of the thriving bay remain in the Longbranch Mercantile. At present the Longbranch Chowder House, across from the marina, is undergoing a major renovation. Gone are the historic family photos and laid-back atmosphere of the former owners. Opening sometime in late 1999 or 2000 with a top-notch kitchen, it aims to become a Longbranch hot-spot. In summer, eat outside or brown-bag it along the bay. Port-a-potties are at the marina.

After Longbranch, the rich manure aroma of cattle pastures greets you. A green, Victorian-style farmhouse and red barns preside at the first hilltop. Heading down, you cut right across the peninsula's tip, crossing a small bridge over Taylor Bay's head.

Heading back on the peninsula's other side, 76th Street becomes Whiteman Road in another long wooded stretch. Scattered clearings dotted with pre-fab homes interrupt otherwise unsettled forests. Halfway down the hill after Rouse Road, be wary of dogs; give them wide berth. As the road flattens, curve right at the Y-intersection to Lakebay Road and Route 302, and return to Home.

0.0 From the Chapel cross McEvan Road to D Street.

0.1 Left onto 10th Street.

0.3 Right curve onto A Street along the water.

0.5 Left onto Key Peninsula Highway, crossing the bridge.

0.8 Left onto Hoff Road at the first intersection.

1.5 Right curve as Hoff becomes Lorenz Road along Mayo Cove.

2.0 Lakebay Marina. Follow Lorenz Road's curves.

2.5 Penrose Point State Park.

3.4 Delano Bay.

4.0 Right curve onto 142nd Avenue KPS. Camp Woodworth.

4.3 Right curve onto Meridian Road/24th Street.

4.8 Left onto 158th Avenue KPS at the T-intersection.

5.1 Veer right onto Reeves Road at the Y-intersection.

5.4 Right curve. Reeves Road becomes 40th Street.

5.5 Left onto Key Peninsula Highway/Route 302 at the T-intersection to Longbranch.

7.0 Longbranch Improvement Club.

7.4 Longbranch Cemetery and Community Church.

8.0 Longbranch and Filucy Bay. Mercantile and Chowder House.

10.0 Dead-end sign. Right onto 76th Street. Cross Taylor Bay.

12.0 Right curve as 76th Street becomes Whiteman Road.

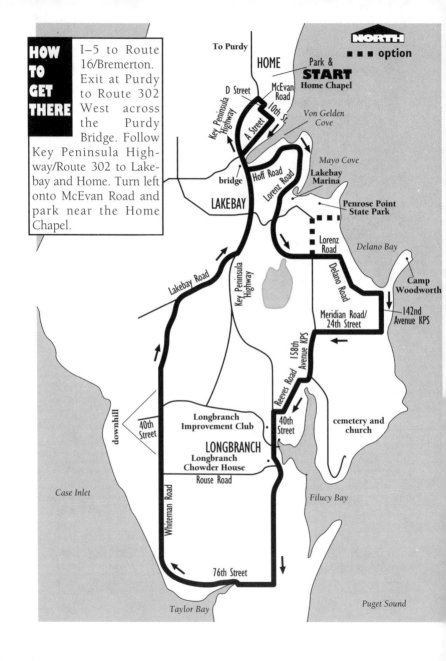

NORTH
■ ■ ■ option

HOW TO GET THERE I–5 to Route 16/Bremerton. Exit at Purdy to Route 302 West across the Purdy Bridge. Follow Key Peninsula Highway/Route 302 to Lakebay and Home. Turn left onto McEvan Road and park near the Home Chapel.

To Purdy

HOME

Park & START Home Chapel

McEvan Road

D Street

10th St

A Street

Key Peninsula Highway

Von Gelden Cove

Mayo Cove

bridge

Hoff Road

Lorenz Road

Lakebay Marina

LAKEBAY

Penrose Point State Park

Lorenz Road

Delano Bay

Lakebay Road

Key Peninsula Highway

Delano Road

Camp Woodworth

142nd Avenue KPS

Meridian Road/ 24th Street

158th Avenue KPS

Reeves Road

downhill

40th Street

Longbranch Improvement Club

40th Street

cemetery and church

LONGBRANCH

Longbranch Chowder House

Rouse Road

Case Inlet

Whiteman Road

Filucy Bay

76th Street

Taylor Bay

Puget Sound

13.4 Pass Rouse Road.

14.9 Right curve at the Y-intersection onto Lakebay Road.

15.0 Left at the T-intersection onto Key Peninsula Highway/Route 302.

15.5 Cross the bridge to Home.

15.8 Right onto McEvan Road.

16.0 Return to the Home Chapel parking lot.

Pierce County: Tacoma
Point Defiance Loop

Distance & Rating:	5 miles; easy to moderate hills
Surface & Traffic:	Paved; light traffic except on Sunday afternoons, no cars on Saturday mornings
Highlights:	Rose and floral gardens, Japanese Pagoda and Garden, zoo, boathouse/restaurant/gift shop, Owen Beach, Five Mile Drive, viewpoints, Mountaineer Tree, Fort Nisqually, Camp Six, Native Gardens
Eats:	Anthony's Restaurant, Taste of Tacoma (August), Antique Sandwich Company
Sleeps:	B&B Reservations: (800) 406–4088, www.tacoma-inns.org, Commencement Bay B&B, Chinaberry Hill B&B, Plum Duff House, Blue Willow Cottage
Note:	The park is heavily forested; women may not want to ride alone. Bikes are prohibited from the dirt trails.

Locals treasure this 700-acre, old-growth park. They ride it so often, they should get special credits—like frequent-flyer miles. Cycling it with "skeptical of Tacoma" visitors, without offering prior explanations, always blows them away. "What's with Tacoma's bad rep?" they'll exclaim.

It was in 1888 that Tacomans persuaded Congress to release this prime, untouched site for a park. Allen Mason, a real estate developer, fought hard for the cause, hoping a streetcar would cross his property and increase his wealth. Apparently, it did. His successful appeal led to a Depression-era project that resulted in the park's roads, paths, and buildings. At that time, before cars took over, visitors arrived via rail at the Pagoda railroad station. Returning to this outmoded transportation would greatly reduce the park's weekend traffic congestion.

Sloping, sprawling lawns, gardens, and island ponds constitute the park's stunning formal entry. Just beyond, the charming brick and red-tile roofed Japanese Pagoda (old railroad station) edges a bluff, as if monitoring Puget Sound and Vashon Island. In the adjacent sculpted gardens, serene paths and intimate seating beckon. Ferries, fishing boats, and commercial vessels cruise Commencement Bay below.

Cycling the park and visiting its attractions make a full day for kids or casual grown-up riders. The route is also perfect for looping several times for an aerobic, nontraffic sprint. The sunlight-speckled road feels smooth as silk as you glide its winding route beneath Douglas fir and red cedar arches that humble even jaded spirits. Here is the Northwest as it was before logging; dense forests inhabited by diverse animals such as the deer and fox you may see. Misty, damp autumns and winter fogs enhance the mysterious mood. On sunnier days breathtaking views of Dalco Passage, Vashon Island, Gig Harbor, and the Tacoma Narrows Bridge expose Puget Sound's vast meanderings. For a grander tour add the park route to the Historic Tacoma ride (Ride 35).

After the Japanese Gardens the road splits. Follow the left section past Point Defiance Zoo. Downhill to the right is the waterfront path to Owen Beach, the boathouse, the gift shop, and Anthony's Restaurant, which you might visit later for good food and great views. Vigorous cyclists can roll down and along the path but must climb the steep hill from Owen Beach.

Cutting through a small parking area that is flanked by picnic sites and the zoo's fence, look for the massive, furry, Alaskan oomingmacks grazing local zoo tundra. Continue straight through the gray stone gates, entering Point Defiance's natural forests. Wander the Big Tree Trail and the Rhododendron Gardens, resplendent in their natural shaded habitat.

Follow the Fort Nisqually and Five Mile Drive signs left as the road splits. Downhill to the right is Owen Beach, named after former Superintendent of Parks Floyd Owen, who retired after a forty-seven-year career. On the main route begin a long, moderate uphill dubbed "The Monster" by joggers. Dense old growth, thick as a rain forest, surrounds the road, except for portions blown down in the 1990 "hundred-year" storm. Massive, flat root balls of toppled trees remain as a reminder of the storm's destruction and nature's control.

Cresting, arrive at a stop sign. Straight ahead, past the white barrier gate, is the section that bars cars on Saturday mornings. On other days stick to the bike lane on the road's right. Various pull-outs offer views and photo ops of Dalco Passage and Vashon Island. On car-free mornings it's a favorite contemplative spot; other times boom boxes assault your ears.

A 400-year-old Douglas fir, called the Mountaineer Tree, indicates the massive size of trees in a first-growth forest. It is about the same size across as a bike is long. Amazing.

Farther along, the road emerges to a Tacoma Narrows Bridge viewpoint and picnic area. A historical marker commemorates Captain Charles Wilkes, who "discovered" this point on the United States Exploring Expedition of 1838–42.

When the road splits, veer right uphill toward Never-Never Land, a fairy tale play park for exuberant or whining kids. Adjacent to it, Fort Nisqually, ensconced in a timbered, sentry-towered square, depicts the Hudson Bay Company's trading heritage. Originally on the Nisqually Delta at Sequalitchew Creek, it served as a trader's rest stop and land-to-sea transfer point. Goods were transported by wagon from the Columbia River's Fort Vancouver and by boat to the Fraser River's Fort Langley in Canada. The fort was reconstructed here during the Depression-era park project.

Leaving the fort, soar downhill through a dark forest bereft of sunlight to the Camp Six Logging Museum. It and a 1929 steam train offer glimpses into our industrial past. At Christmastime the train gives "Santa Rides" to munchkins. Nearby, pass the Mildred Street exit and veer right up to the zoo parking lots.

Lock up to visit the Pacific Rim–focused Point Defiance Zoo. Totally redesigned in the mid-1980s, its rolling hills and natural exhibits are unique. Polar bears, seals, and walruses frolic in underwater viewing pools. A hands-on farm delights children. The 1989 tropical fish building is a must—definitely not the old-style wall display. Picnic on expansive lawns where you can view Mount Rainier and even Mount Baker on a clear day.

From the zoo parking lot road, veer right to complete the park loop. Near the ride's end pass the Native Garden, a natural setting complete with totem pole. Veer left to ride's end at the park entrance. To feed your hunger ride 1 block up Pearl Street to the Antique Sandwich Company, a longtime local favorite for healthy, good food. Kids are welcome—toys abound.

DIRECTIONS
FOR
THE RIDE

0.0 Begin at the park entrance. Floral Gardens.

0.1 Japanese Gardens.

0.2 Veer left toward zoo. Anthony's Restaurant and waterfront path downhill to right.

0.6 Continue straight at zoo and aquarium intersection.

0.9 Veer left to Five Mile Drive; uphill. Optional descent to Owen Beach on the right.

1.3 Straight past white metal gate. Starting here no cars are allowed on Saturday mornings.

1.9 Dalco Passage and Vashon Island viewpoint.

2.2 400-year-old Douglas fir—the Mountaineer Tree.

2.4 Gig Harbor viewpoint.

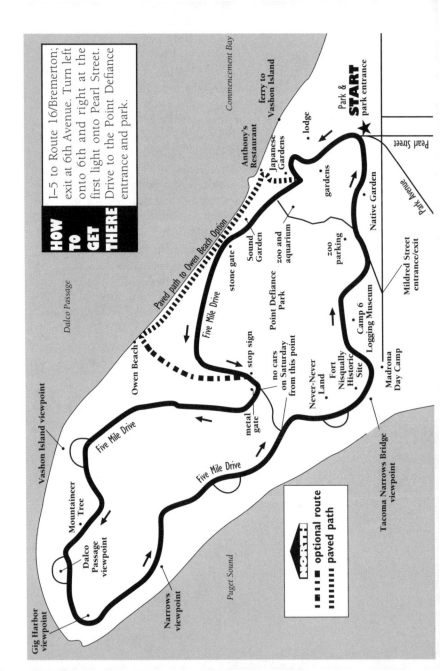

HOW TO GET THERE

I–5 to Route 16/Bremerton; exit at 6th Avenue. Turn left onto 6th and right at the first light onto Pearl Street. Drive to the Point Defiance entrance and park.

Commencement Bay

ferry to Vashon Island

Anthony's Restaurant

Japanese Gardens

• lodge

Park & **START** park entrance

Pearl Street

gardens

Native Garden

Park Avenue

Dalco Passage

Paved path to Owen Beach Option

• stone gate

• Sound Garden

zoo and aquarium

Point Defiance Park

zoo parking

Mildred Street entrance/exit

Five Mile Drive

• stop sign

no cars on this point

Owen Beach

Vashon Island viewpoint

metal gate

no cars on Saturday from this point

Never-Never Land

Fort Nisqually Historic Site

Camp 6 Logging Museum

Madrona Day Camp

Five Mile Drive

Mountaineer Tree

Dalco Passage viewpoint

Five Mile Drive

Narrows viewpoint

Tacoma Narrows Bridge viewpoint

Gig Harbor viewpoint

Puget Sound

NORTH

■ ■ ■ optional route
■ ■ ■ paved path

2.6	Tacoma Narrows Bridge/Gig Harbor viewpoint and picnic area.
3.6	Veer right toward Never-Never Land.
3.9	Fort Nisqually and viewpoint.
4.0	Madrona Day Camp.
4.2	Camp Six Logging Museum and 1929 steam train.
4.4	Pass Mildred Street exit.
4.6	Right and uphill past zoo parking lots.
4.7	Curve right at the road split. Zoo on left.
4.8	Native Garden.
5.0	Left to the parking area and ride's end.

Pierce County: Tacoma
Ruston Way Path

Distance & Rating:	2 miles each way; easy
Surface & Traffic:	Paved; none
Highlights:	Old Town, Historic Fireboat #1, fishing piers, waterfront parks and picnic sites, Puget Gardens
Eats:	Picnic or plentiful eateries
Sleeps, bikes:	See Ride 33

From an industrial mess a garden can grow. Ruston Way, once littered with lumber mills and a copper smelter, was reborn as a spectacular waterfront park along Commencement Bay. Currently, a path runs 2 miles from the Ruston Way overpass to 49th Street. Eventually, it will traverse the old Ruston Smelter site and connect to Point Defiance.

Joggers, walkers, in-line skaters, bicyclists, and dogs flock to exercise here. And why not? The paving is smooth, the views of Mount Rainier and the Olympic Mountains ideal, and the lapping water relaxing. Plus, boxes on poles hold doggie scooping bags; stiff fines for fouling the footway help keep the park clean.

When stomachs growl, there's everything from a hot-dog stand to fancy fish restaurants (with coffee, pizza, burger, and pasta establishments in between). Only Katy Downs (a bar) cannot allow children.

Don't miss the sidetrip to Puget Gardens (signs point the way), a tranquil, creekside specimen garden donated to Metropolitan Parks by its original owners.

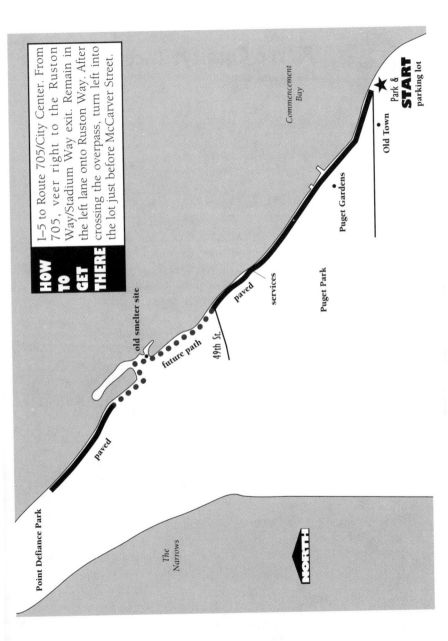

HOW TO GET THERE

I–5 to Route 705/City Center. From 705, veer right to the Ruston Way/Stadium Way exit. Remain in the left lane onto Ruston Way. After crossing the overpass, turn left into the lot just before McCarver Street.

Point Defiance Park

The Narrows

NORTH

paved

old smelter site

future path

49th St.

paved

services

Commencement Bay

Puget Park

Puget Gardens

Old Town

Park & **START** parking lot

35

Pierce County: Tacoma
Historical Loop

Distance & Rating:	15.8 miles (optional additional 5 miles); hilly
Surface & Traffic:	Paved; moderate
Highlights:	Point Defiance, Ruston Way Waterfront, Old Town, St. Peter's Church, Annie Wright School, Stadium Historical District, Stadium High School, Old City Hall, The Pantages, Tacoma Art Museum, University of Washington–Tacoma campus, Union Station Courthouse, Historical Society, Botanical Conservatory, Proctor District
Eats:	Old Town: Grazie, Starbucks, Spar; Downtown: Grounds for Coffee, Ravenous, Fujiya, Altezzo, Broadway Grill; Proctor District: Old House Café, Pomodoro, Starbucks, Queen Anne Thriftway; 6th Ave. District: Primo Grill
Sleeps:	On-line booking at www.tacoma.areaguide.net, Sheraton Tacoma, (253) 572–3200, and see Ride 33

Tacoma, some say, is the "armpit of Seattle." When Bruce Springsteen blamed the "Aroma of Tacoma" for his concert-stopping illness, locals laughed at the bad publicity. Pollsters rank Tacoma tops for livability.

Exploring Tacoma offers a different perspective. Quiet streets, city parks, historic sites. Stunning views. Gritty industrial areas. Friendly people. Espresso. Glass art. No odor—thanks to the Superfund Commencement Bay cleanup.

From Point Defiance's entrance head into Ruston, named for Tacoma Smelter Company founder William Rust. In the early 1900s Rust did the civic-minded thing; he employed locals. Little did they know that the processing of lead, silver, and gold ore spewed arsenic on their families. Amassing a tidy profit, Rust sold out to the American Smelting and Refining Company (ASARCO), which closed in the late 1980s. Its contaminated brick smelter stack, once a skyline landmark, was imploded in 1992 in an impressive, nationally televised procedure. Abandoned buildings and acres of poisoned, infertile land lie ripe for cleanup and recreational development.

Gliding down this eerie moonscape, a short, dark, wet tunnel bears a sign stating HONK. People do, startling the heck out of cyclists (don't try this after watching Heaven Can Wait). Tunnel removal and a waterfront path to Point Defiance are planned, but for now you take the tunnel to Ruston Way Waterfront. Along Commencement Bay are pocket parks, fishing piers, and restaurants that draw folks like flies to honey. The adjacent road, once a cruisers' paradise, has wicked curbs and no shoulder. Stick to the path that ends at Old Town. Mount Rainier looms over this industrial section.

In 1866 Morton McCarver purchased Job Carr's 320-acre waterfront land claim here, believing he had the inside scoop on the Northern Pacific (NP) Railroad's terminus. Naming the claim "Tacoma" (from *tahoma,* a Native American name for Mount Rainier), he foresaw big bucks. Alas, the Northern chose "downtown," dropping the bottom from McCarver's investment. In what became Old Tacoma (and later Old Town), the Hanson-Ackerson Steam Sawmill created a busy lumber town until it closed and left a tranquil residential neighborhood of Victorian and bungalow homes. Locals walk to Cicero's Coffee, Grazie's Restaurant, the Spar Tavern (choice watering hole), Starbucks, and the waterfront.

Off the main drag, St. Peter's Church (1874) is a wedding favorite. Its ivy-covered bell tower tops a massive tree stump, indicative of the old-growth trees that once blanketed this hill. In 1883 Old Tacoma was chosen as the site for a girls' boarding school. It struggled until 1924, when a $50,000 gift from Charles B. Wright paid for a charming brick Tudor that became known as Annie Wright School. A recent $2.5-million bequest has enabled the addition of a state-of-the-art performance center.

Nearby, in Tacoma's Historic District, stately turn-of-the-century homes were built big and to last—in English country, classic revival, sprawling Victorian, and turreted cottage styles. Sadly, some succumbed to the wrecking ball, but fortunately the building that is now Stadium High School escaped. Constructed in 1891 by Northern Pacific as an elegant French-château resort hotel, it never opened as the NP declared bankruptcy. Demolition was beginning as businessmen Conrad Hoska (a school board member) and Eric Rosling walked by on their way to work. Shocked, they dispensed with red tape, calling an architect and convening an emergency school-board meeting. By nightfall the board owned the six-acre site with its marvelous turreted and spired building—for $34,000. Stadium High School, opened in 1910, was named for its unique stadium, a bowl embedded in a ravine that garnered fame for utilizing "wasted" land. The stadium was destroyed by a 1980 water-main rupture and was replaced by the current concrete bowl. The school was the setting for the 1999 movie *10 Things I Hate About You*.

High above Stadium Way, with sweeping mountain and bay views, sits the 1890 Victorian-style home of William B. and Alice E. Blackwell. Entranced by a Harper's article extolling Puget Sound as "The Mediterranean of the Pacific," the Blackwells journeyed to Tacoma from Utica, New York, in 1873. Arriving in Tacoma, Mr. Blackwell built the Hotel Blackwell and became a banker, legislator, and president of the Washington State Historical Society. After he died and the house became home to the YMCA, it developed a reputation for being haunted by the ghosts of the Blackwells.

Downtown Tacoma, virtually abandoned during the 1960s shopping-mall exodus, sports colorful new structures juxtaposed against empty storefronts that whisper hauntingly of a bustling past. Restaurants come and go, though a recent trend of jazz clubs and cafés may alter that pattern—as well it should. The Theater District events deserve amenities.

Old City Hall (1885), in splendid ochre brick of Italian Renaissance style, had a go as an artsy mall in the 1970s, but evolved to office space. Its warm wood-and-brick interior is highlighted by a masterfully tooled staircase. A block away is the gray, spired, former Northern Pacific Headquarters (1888). Along Commerce fledgling art galleries are bringing ghostly storefronts to life.

On Broadway the Pantages Theater (1918), restored from sleaze, is an acoustical jewel. Nearby, big bucks retooled the Rialto Theater. Yet this Broadway lacks soul. Storefronts seem adrift, especially since the University of Puget Sound Law School slipped out to Seattle. A few sparks exist; Fujiya prepares top-notch sushi and the Sheraton Hotel's café and Altezzo Ristorante whip up quite respectable fare. An elegant glass sea-form installation by Dale Chihuly graces the hotel lobby. Catch his multicolored fantasias, floating like pond lilies on the arched windows of Union Station Courthouse (open weekdays for viewing) and his glass baskets and macchia forms at the Art Museum.

Northern Pacific's copper-domed Union Station (1911), designed by New York's Grand Central Station architects Reed and Stern, survived a planned demolition. The bridge over Thea Foss Waterway will cross to the Glass Museum, which is planned to open around 2002.

Along Pacific, once Brothel Row, praiseworthy stone and cast-iron architectural gems, such as the Carlton at South 17th Street, are undergoing restoration. Major renovations of turn-of-the-century warehouses and buildings for the new University of Washington–Tacoma campus have turned downtown Tacoma around. New shops and restaurants create a lively street scene. At

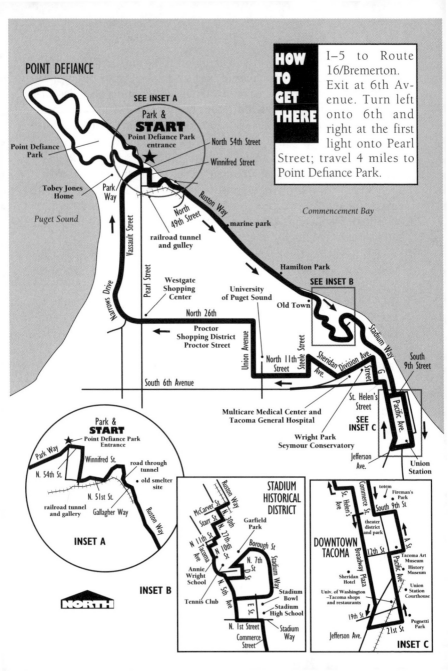

the newer Frank Russell Company, water cascades over a rose granite facade. Fireman's Park boasts the 105-foot totem dedicated in 1903 to President Theodore Roosevelt. On St. Helen Avenue an East Coast–style triangular building houses a café.

In Wright Park don't miss the glass-domed, 1907 Seymour Botanical Conservatory. Up the street is the Frisco Freeze. Known for its frying fat aromas (and booming car stereos), it's an institution that no self-respecting Tacoma teen (or adult) has forsaken—for more than thirty-five years.

Sheridan Avenue, lined with early Tacoma mansions, leads toward the University of Puget Sound and the Proctor Street Shopping District (not a strip mall), the liveliest neighborhood in Tacoma. Home to Queen Anne Thriftway, Starbucks, a bike shop, and more, it draws people on foot and bike.

Farther on, in the Westgate Shopping Center strip mall, is yet another Starbucks. On Vassault Street/Narrows Drive, stunning Puget Sound and Olympic Mountain views await. It's a fitting end to an eye-opening Tacoma day.

DIRECTIONS
FOR
THE RIDE

0.0	Park entrance. Left onto North 54th Street. To add the park's 5-mile drive, see Point Defiance Loop (Ride 33).
0.1	Right onto Winnifred Street.
0.3	Left onto North 51st Street. Downhill.
0.6	Tunnel (to be removed in future). Use flashers. RR tracks.
1.2	Left at 49th Street onto Ruston Way Waterfront path.
2.4	Marine Park. Historic fireboat. Restaurants.
3.0	Hamilton Park.
3.4	Right onto McCarver Street. Use pedestrian crosswalk. RR tracks. Uphill.
3.5	Left onto 30th Street. Cicero's Coffee, Spar Tavern, Starbucks.
3.6	Right onto Starr Street. St. Peter's Church. Uphill.

3.8 Left onto 27th Street, which becomes Park Drive.

3.9 Right onto 11th Street. Sawmill marker. Quick left onto narrow unmarked street that becomes 10th Street. Annie Wright School.

4.2 Left onto Tacoma Avenue.

4.5 Tacoma Historical District. Left onto North 5th Avenue.

4.6 Left onto D Street.

4.8 Left onto 7th Street.

4.9 Sharp right to Borough Street. Garfield Park. Curve right onto Stadium Way.

5.7 Left to parking lot sidewalk at North E Street. Stadium Bowl. Right at pool and gym building and left up ramp to Stadium High School plaza.

5.9 Cross North 1st Avenue onto North E Street, which becomes Stadium Way.

6.0 North 4th Street. Blackwell Mansion above YWCA.

6.6 Old City Hall. Stadium Way becomes Commerce Street. Kaperick Gallery. Commencement Art Gallery at South 9th Street.

6.8 Right onto South 9th Street; quick left onto Broadway Plaza. Ravenous Restaurant. Broadway Theater District; Pantages, Rialto, Theatre on the Square (Tacoma Actors' Guild).

6.9 Plaza park. Fountain. Stairs to Court C shops on right.

7.1 13th Street. Sheridan Tacoma Hotel.

7.5 Veer right as Broadway merges into Jefferson Street. Cross 19th Street. The Swiss Tavern; stop to see the Chihuly art glass. Rock Pasta Restaurant. Industrial area.

7.7 Left onto 21st Street. University of Washington–Tacoma campus. Bookstore. Starbucks.

7.9 Left onto Pacific Avenue. Pugnetti Park, antique stores, and espresso shops. Harmon Brewery & Restaurant.

8.1 Washington State History Museum. Courthouse in Old Union Station; Chihuly glass display. Bronze sculpture.

8.5 Right onto 12th Street. Tacoma Art Museum.

8.6 Left onto A Street. Frank Russell Company.

8.8 Left onto 9th Street. Fireman's Park. 1903 totem. Uphill.

9.0 Pass Broadway (home of Antique Row and Tacoma Farmers Market on summer Thursdays) on the right and veer right onto St. Helen's Street. Uphill.

9.3 Left onto 6th Avenue. Steep uphill for 1 block.

9.5 Right onto G Street. Wright Park. Botanical Conservatory.

9.8 Left onto Division Avenue.

10.2 Tacoma General Hospital. Frisco Freeze.

10.4 Right onto Sheridan Avenue.

11.0 Left onto Steele Street.

11.1 Right onto North 11th Street.

11.6 Cross Alder Street cautiously; no light.

11.9 Right onto Union Avenue, University of Puget Sound.

12.7 Left onto North 26th Street.

13.0 Proctor Shopping District; Starbucks, Rainier Cycles, Queen Anne Thriftway to left, Old House Café to right.

13.2 Westgate Shopping Center. Starbucks.

13.7 Right onto Narrows Drive, which becomes Vassault Street.

15.4 Right at curve onto Park Way. Bumpy street.

15.8 Left onto Pearl Street, returning to Point Defiance Park.

Pierce County: Steilacoom
Steilacoom, Lakewood, and DuPont

Distance & Rating:	26.4 miles or 14.6-mile shortcut; long flat stretches, several hills
Surface & Traffic:	Paved, trails in park; minimal to moderate
Highlights:	Fort Steilacoom Park, Steilacoom, Historical Museum, Tribal Museum, Bair Drug, DuPont, Chambers Creek
Eats:	Mimi's Kitchen, Bair Drug Cafe, E. R. Rogers, Affairs
Bikes:	Spoke & Sprocket Bike Shop (253) 564–1422
Sleeps:	Sally's Bear Tree Cottage, Thomewood Castle B&B and see Ride 33

Fort Steilacoom, the highest spot around, with its lake and farming fields, provided a safe haven for desperate Puget Sounders (non-natives) during the 1855 Indian Wars. Years later the old fort was converted into a mental hospital. When it outgrew its now-crumbling structure atop the hill, Western State Hospital was built on the flats below.

The dirt trails of Fort Steilacoom Park are perfect for fat-tire fun. A paved path circles Waughop Lake, named for John W. Waughop, the first superintendent (1880–1897) of Western State Hospital.

Outside the park, helter-skelter roads wend and change names as often as felons on the run. Keep a keen eye to the directions, especially for narrow Short Street from 104th. It leads into shoulderless Interlaaken Drive and the Lake Steilacoom bridge, where you can gape at Mt. Rainier. Lakewood's population boomed with the military bases. Its sole claim to fame, the 1937 Lakewood Colonial Center, was the first planned shopping center in the West (the route skips it).

Watch for the right onto Brook Lane, a downhill that circles left and climbs. Several quick turns go to a parking lot cut-through and Mimi's Kitchen (tasty Italian) on Gravelly Lake Drive. The lake is obscured by gated estates and landscaping. One home, the Villa Madera, 11,000-square-foot mansion of millionaire Joseph Carman, was where the lively upper crust of the 1920s and 1930s partied. Subdivided in 1978, it regained fame when actress Linda Evans moved in to live near New Ager J. Z. Knight of Ramtha fame.

Gravelly Lake is one of three major Lakewood lakes—the others being Steilacoom and American—that became hot summer property. Though most families later split their acreage, the Wagners held on, making their estate the last remaining ten-acre tract. Manicured and wild gardens on the property, bulging with Mrs. Wagner's worldwide specimen collection, are now Lakewold Gardens and well worth visiting.

In 1833, on another lake, Americans visiting the Hudson Bay Company held the Northwest's first Fourth of July celebration. Though the the Northwest Territories were not part of the United States, they roasted a pig, partied, and named the body of water, "American Lake." During World War I, it became Fort Lewis, the domain of the military. Popular with windsurfers and boaters, its north-end park also sports a seaplane launch.

A flat sprint along Fort Lewis bears headwinds that work your muscles. Above, bald eagles and red-tailed hawks float on the currents. Target practice noises resound as you head to the spanking new community of Northwest Landing, home to Intel, State Farm, and Historic DuPont. Located near the Hudson Bay Company's abandoned 1,500-acre prairie site and wharf, DuPont offered an isolated location for its explosives plant. Deer and cattle grazed, keeping vegetation and thus fire hazards down. DuPont's motto—"There's always time for safety"—and education programs allowed the company and town to survive over seventy years without a single house fire. Over a billion pounds of explosives produced here carved out the Northwest's roads, tunnels, and power dams, opened up mineral deposits, and were used during World War II.

Unlike company towns that gouged their workers, in the late 1800s and early 1990s DuPont rented out the homes but all other services were free-market enterprises. Attractive homes, stone walls, landscaping, stores, a club, a hotel, a playground, fire hydrants, a water system, sewers, and gas systems kept residents happy. The 350 employees and their families had dances, games, movies, a church, and a hospital with prepaid medical coverage. DuPont, however, lacked taverns. Men bicycled to Lakewood, hopped the train to Tacoma, and often forgot to return the next day. DuPont arranged incorporation and a liquor license, but the short-lived experiment ended with Prohibition.

During the 1930s, with better transportation available, families wanted to move. DuPont allowed employees to move their homes; the manager's home and granary were donated to the Depression-era development of Point Defiance Park and are now a favorite wedding site. In 1976 DuPont closed the plant, selling it lock, stock, and barrel to the Weyerhauser Company. During the early 1990s Weyerhauser platted Northwest Landing, leaving Historic DuPont smack in the middle and jettisoning its 600 residents from rural isolation; their lives changed as the economy switched from explosives to microchips. Visit the historic district as well as Northwest Landing, which re-creates the historic village's architectural styles, complete with front porches and alleyways leading to garages. It's a stunning change from standard tract homes.

Heading to Steilacoom, climb a mile-long, gradual uphill through a forest that is scoured by mushroom pickers in spring and fall. After the screeching descent to Gove Street, meander past colorful late-nineteenth-century homes—historic ones designated by plaques and charming gardens. A footbridge leads to Saltar Point

Beach Park, a tidal shore graced by its original stone shelter and rest room. Perkins Park, on Union Avenue, is named for Mary Fletcher Perkins, M.D., who served Steilacoom from 1902 to 1941.

A block downhill, at a triangle corner and picturesque maze frame house, read the Bryd Mill Road Historical Marker. Below, ferries run to Anderson, Ketron, and McNeil (State Penitentiary) Islands. Up Lafayette, the Oberlin Congregational Church (1903) houses the Steilacoom Tribal Museum in downtown Steilacoom, Washington's oldest incorporated town.

Founded in 1854 by Maine sea captain Lafayette Balch, the bustling frontier seaport was tucked perfectly into Puget Sound's low-bank coves. Balch planned Steilacoom well, providing amenities for residents and sailors in the form of a "hotel" (read brothel) and false-fronted stores. One such shop, Bair Drug and Hardware Store (1895), is a living museum filled with original hardware, medicine cases, a 1906 soda fountain, and post office. Now a touristy restaurant, Bair whips up classic American fare and no-nonsense desserts (forget low-fat or gourmet here). Balch had one quirk: It's a mystery why, in this timber haven, he imported a full precut-lumber house from New England.

Downhill 1 block, visit the 1891 Victorian E. R. Rogers Home. Restored as a restaurant in 1980, it uses its original rooms as dining areas. Hungry folk flock in, especially for the popular (big!) Sunday brunch. A park platform (four-star picnic spot) across the street details the views. Clustered on the next block and on Main Street are the Captain William Webster and Philip Keach homes and the Historical Museum, which focuses on the 1860–1900 period. Its outstanding scrapbooks of newspaper clippings can be addicting. Pick up a map of Steilacoom's thirty-two registered historic places. Uphill is the Nathaniel Orr Home (1857), a period gem that contained the original furnishings and artifacts of its furniture and wagon-maker owner. Unfortunately, in the rains of the spring of 1996, the house slid downhill 6 feet. Its precarious position has closed it to the public and leaves its fate undecided.

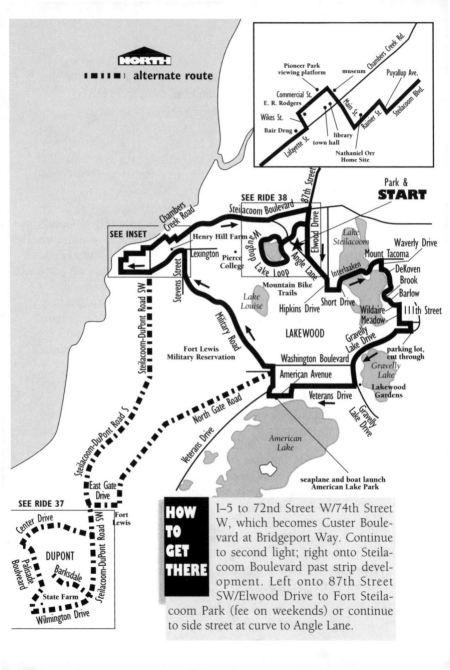

NORTH
▬▬▬▬▬ alternate route

INSET (top):
Pioneer Park viewing platform
museum
Chambers Creek Rd.
Puyallup Ave.
Commercial St.
E. R. Rodgers
Main St.
Steilacoom Blvd.
Wikes St.
Rainier St.
Bair Drug
library
town hall
Lafayette St.
Nathaniel Orr Home Site

MAIN MAP:
Park & START
SEE RIDE 38
Steilacoom Boulevard
87th Street
Elwood Drive
Lake Steilacoom
Waverly Drive
SEE INSET
Chambers Creek Road
Henry Hill Farm
Lexington
Wughop Lake Loop
Angle Lane
Interlaaken
Mount Tacoma
DeKoven
Brook
Barlow
Stevens Street
Pierce College
Mountain Bike Trails
Lake Louise
Hipkins Drive
Short Drive
Wildaire Meadow
111th Street
Steilacoom-DuPont Road SW
Military Road
Fort Lewis Military Reservation
LAKEWOOD
Gravelly Lake Drive
parking lot, cut through
Washington Boulevard
American Avenue
Gravelly Lake
Lakewood Gardens
North Gate Road
Veterans Drive
Veterans Drive
American Lake
seaplane and boat launch American Lake Park
East Gate Drive
Fort Lewis
Steilacoom-DuPont Road S

SEE RIDE 37 (inset):
Center Drive
DUPONT
Palisade Boulevard
Barksdale
State Farm
Wilmington Drive
Steilacoom-DuPont Road SW

HOW TO GET THERE
I–5 to 72nd Street W/74th Street W, which becomes Custer Boulevard at Bridgeport Way. Continue to second light; right onto Steilacoom Boulevard past strip development. Left onto 87th Street SW/Elwood Drive to Fort Steilacoom Park (fee on weekends) or continue to side street at curve to Angle Lane.

At Far West Drive SW, the primo finish is a dirt single-track slicing Fort Steilacoom Park's fields of tall, waving prairie grass. From this corner the firmly packed trail accommodates all but the skinniest tires. At its end, circle Waughop Lake Loop, heading back to the park entrance past the dairy barns, pastures, and sports fields. If you have racing wheels or prefer traffic, continue on Steilacoom Boulevard past Western State Hospital, using care to avoid dangerous storm drain grates.

DIRECTIONS
FOR
THE RIDE

0.0 Right onto Elwood Avenue from Fort Steilacoom Park.
0.6 Left curve onto Angle Lane SW.
1.0 Right onto Hipkins Road SW.
1.1 104th Street T-intersection. Left onto 104th Street SW.
1.3 Left onto Short Street SW. Becomes Interlaaken Drive (use caution crossing the bridge over Lake Steilacoom) and then Mt. Tacoma Drive SW. No shoulders.
2.3 Right onto Waverly Drive SW.
2.4 Left onto Lake Grove SW.
2.6 Veer right onto DeKoven Drive SW.
2.6 Right downhill onto Brook Lane; circle left and uphill.
3.1 Right at T-intersection onto Barlow Road.
3.2 Left onto Wildaire, and quick right onto Meadow Road.
3.5 Left onto 111th Street SW.
3.7 Right into parking lot. Mimi's Kitchen. Right onto Gravelly Lake Drive.
5.0 Lakewold Gardens. Right to Veteran's Drive.
6.0 Veer left past stores. American Lake North County Park.
6.5 Right onto Edgewood Drive SW.
6.7 Left onto North Gate Road SW (Winona on right).

Option (15.0 miles total): At 6.7 miles pass North Gate Road. Left onto Military Road, which becomes Stevens Street. Left at the T-intersection to Lexington Street, which becomes Sequalish Street. Right onto Union Avenue, rejoining basic route at 21.6 miles.

7.0 FORT LEWIS sign.

8.5 Right onto East Gate Drive at Fort Lewis.

8.9 Left onto Steilacoom-DuPont Road SW at T-intersection. Option (14.6 miles total): Turn right at 8.9 miles to skip the DuPont loop. Go to directions at 19.7 miles.

11.5 Right onto Center Drive. NORTHWEST LANDING sign.

11.7 Intel Headquarters.

12.8 Left onto Palisade Boulevard. Stone guardhouse.

13.6 Clock Tower and Northwest Landing office.

13.9 Left onto Wilmington Drive. State Farm Headquarters.

14.7 Left onto Barksdale Avenue. Historic DuPont. Museum.

15.0 Church. Old DuPont warning siren.

15.2 Haskell Street (pedestrian/bike connection to Northwest Landing).

15.3 Cul-de-sac. Backtrack.

15.6 Right onto Rapuno, left onto Brandywine.

16.0 Left onto Santa Cruz and right onto Barksdale Avenue.

16.1 Stoplight; left onto Wilmington Drive; becomes DuPont-Steilacoom Road.

19.7 Straight at East Drive. Climb 0.9 mile; downhill.

21.6 Road becomes Union Avenue. Left onto Gove Street.

22.0 Right at T-intersection to 1st Street, right onto Champion Street, left onto 2nd Street, right onto Martin Street. Saltar's Point Beach Park.

22.6 Left onto Union Avenue. Perkins Park. Espresso on the Bay.

22.7 Right onto Lafayette Street. Bryd Monument. Tribal Museum.

22.9 Bair Drug. Left onto Wilkes to E. R. Rogers restaurant. Right onto Commercial. Right onto Main Street to museum.

23.0 Cross Lafayette Street. Town hall and library on right. Uphill.

23.1 Left onto Rainier Street. Nathanial Orr Home site.

23.2 Curve right onto Puyallup Avenue and left onto Steilacoom Boulevard. Uphill.

24.1 Cross Sentinel Drive/Far West Drive to park's corner. Ride dirt trail through fields. Optional road finish (add 1 mile): Straight on Steilacoom Boulevard. Use caution—storm grates. Right onto 87th Avenue SW/Elwood Drive and right into park. Circle lake.

24.5 Straight at dirt-path intersection and curve right.

24.8 Right on paved path to circle Waughop Lake.

25.8 Right onto paved path toward barns.

26.4 Return to start at park entrance.

Pierce County: Dupont
Northwest Landing and Dupont

Distance & Rating:	4 miles +/-; easy
Surface & Traffic:	Paved; minimal
Highlights:	Top bike lanes and paths, DuPont Historical Museum
Link to:	Fort Steilacoom Park and Waughop Lake route (Ride 38).

Weyerhauser's new planned community sports separate bike paths and marked bike lanes in the roads. Designed with the curbside appeal of a friendly village, its small homes have front porches and landscaping provided. Garages are located off alleys, eliminating driveways and garages on the street side.

Few cars, flat land, and play lots make this area perfect for little ones. Use the map and follow the paths—you can't get lost. Visit historic DuPont and the DuPont Historical Museum, which explains the original village's past as a munitions-company town. This sleepy village of 600 had a rude awakening several years ago. It found itself surrounded by development in the form of headquarters for State Farm and Intel. The original town, however, remains much the same and is worth seeing.

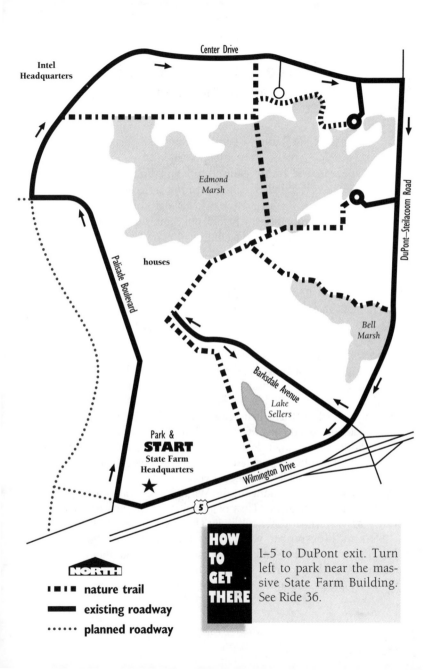

Center Drive

Intel
Headquarters

Edmond
Marsh

houses

Palisade Boulevard

DuPont–Steilacoom Road

Bell
Marsh

Barksdale Avenue

Lake
Sellers

Park &
START
State Farm
Headquarters

Wilmington Drive

5

NORTH

▪ ▪ ▪ nature trail

━━━ existing roadway

••••• planned roadway

HOW TO GET THERE

I–5 to DuPont exit. Turn left to park near the massive State Farm Building. See Ride 36.

Pierce County: Steilacoom
Fort Steilacoom Park and Waughop Lake

Distance & Rating:	1-mile circling lake plus trails; easy with optional hills
Surface & Traffic:	Paved path and dirt trails; no traffic
Highlights:	Birds, historic barns and farm site, grassy fields, blackberries, views
Eats & Amenities:	Picnic, honeybucket rest room facilities
Sleeps:	See Rides 33 and 36

Fort Steilacoom Park, once a dairy farm, is a favorite with locals. Hordes walk their dogs here (these seem the most well-behaved canine creatures around and are no problem to cyclists). Birders hang out with binoculars, peering at nesting and feeding ducks and geese at the lake. They might spot a blue heron, a woodpecker, or other birds. In spring, downy ducklings paddle contentedly after their mamas.

Packed dirt paths meander through flat, open fields and plateaus. Hill and forest trails tantalize big kids; runners, walkers, and mountain bikers flock to them like geese heading north. Young-uns can easily cycle the paved path, even on training wheels.

In spring and summer delicate prairie grass flourishes, rising 3 to 4 feet. Gliding along the single-track paths feels like flying though a chute. Sea breezes tickle the grasses' wheat-like tops, creating acres of gentle waves. Fans of Laura Ingalls Wilder's *Little House* books will sense the prairie's beauty *and* fear of a small child lost among the towering grass (as Wilder described in *By The Shores of Silver Lake*).

Striking blue-purple wildflowers bloom for months amid a changing array of white and yellow flowers and virtual mountains of untamed blackberry vines. Bring containers in late summer; these berries are plump and juicy.

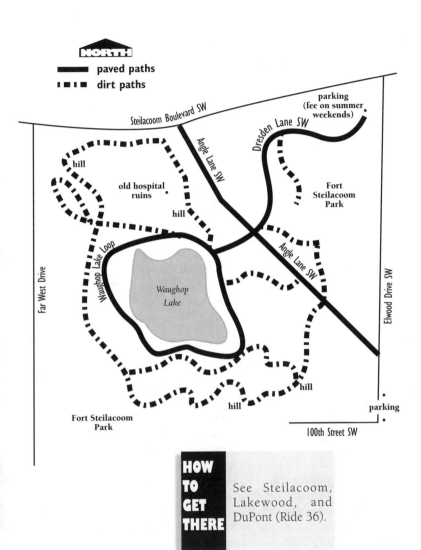

NORTH

— paved paths
▪▪▪▪ dirt paths

Steilacoom Boulevard SW

parking
(fee on summer
weekends)

Angle Lane SW

Dresden Lane SW

hill

old hospital
ruins

Fort
Steilacoom
Park

hill

Angle Lane SW

Far West Drive

Waughop Lake Loop

Waughop
Lake

Elwood Drive SW

hill

hill

Fort Steilacoom
Park

parking

100th Street SW

HOW TO GET THERE See Steilacoom, Lakewood, and DuPont (Ride 36).

Pierce County: Tacoma
Wapato Park/Puyallup Loop

Distance & Rating:	21 miles; all definitions of hills, lots of ups and downs
Surface & Traffic:	Paved; moderate traffic
Highlights:	Wapato Park, Washington State University Extension, Meeker Mansion, Farmer's Market in Pioneer Park
Eats:	See Ride 40
Sleeps:	See Ride 40
Etc.:	Chamber of Commerce (253) 845–6755, Valley Arts Walk
Note:	Avoid this ride during the Puyallup Fair in September

Driving to Puyallup on frenetic River Road doesn't inspire a bicycle trip. But a backroad path offers a pleasant surprise. The mileage may seem short, but the hills give you a run for your money.

Begin from Wapato Park through a quiet bungalow-lined neighborhood that evolves to less-populated rolling terrain. Near Waller Elementary School small produce farms, honey-producing beehives, and pastures flank the road, emitting earthy aromas. Use caution on this shoulderless downhill. Across the valley below, smoke plumes rise from the industrial Tide Flats. Cycling along Pioneer Way, Mount Rainier looms over the semirural Puyallup Valley's swampy wetlands, farms, and the railroad. Northern Pacific obtained this right-of-way, smack in the middle of the Puyallup Indian Reservation, in the late 1800s—after plying Indian representatives with liquor.

As in most semirural areas, all is not idyllic. Fertile fields are snapped up by developers. Dilapidated structures, such as Bulk Auto Parts, intrude on the landscape. On the more bucolic side, at the Pioneer Blueberry Farm (in season) you can hang a bucket from your waist and go for it. You're not truly a Northwesterner until you've picked millions more blueberries and strawberries than you need. It's addictive, until you get home and have forty pounds to freeze and turn into jam—then it feels like a bad hangover.

Other valley businesses include Grand Forks Auto Wrecking, Watson's Nursery and Gardens, and small farms. The immense farm buildings and spectacular gray and maroon farm mansion of the Washington State University Extension Center hail to another era. Across Pioneer Way learn a few tricks at the Master Gardener's Demonstration Gardens (April to September).

Puyallup could be a flat Midwestern gridiron town. Neatly maintained bungalows and cottages bear porches with swings and rockers; American flags and brilliant flower gardens adorn the yard. It warms a flatlander's heart. Downtown loks like part of a 1940s Hollywood movie set; storefront shops display needlework supplies, hardware, and furniture. Bakeries purvey old-fashioned goods, and old-timers sip coffee—not espresso—at Formica tables.

Puyallup owes its life to Ezra Meeker, an eccentric whose vision led him to diverse endeavors such as hops farming and joining the Gold Rush. The Meeker Mansion, at $4.00 a head, is worthwhile. Commercial development has impinged on its original acreage, but the Meeker Foundation hopes to repurchase the land for Meeker's dream Centennial Park. Wall signs provide basic information, but enthusiastic guides give the mansion personality. Ongoing restoration is undoing the damage wrought by three arson fires. Elegant painted ceilings, refinished wood, restored stained glass, and period furniture mix with stripped wood, tacky wallpaper, electrical wires, layers of institutional paint (twelve on some walls), and charred wood. Each room has cost a minimum of $10,000 to restore. The tour imparts a sense of this incredible undertaking.

Ezra Meeker selected different woods for each room: red oak, ash, cherry, black walnut, fir, Philippine mahogany, and redwood (your guide may remark, "I'm sorry Mr. Meeker, you shouldn't have used redwood because it's too soft to be refinished"). Original floor and fireplace tiles match the hand-tooled woods' tones. Each room contains a unique fireplace and ceiling painting, reproduced by a daughter of the man who began this painstaking project.

Upstairs, Eliza Jane Meeker's ball gown, in which she was presented to Queen Victoria in 1885, stands amid vintage clothing and memorabilia. Eliza Jane's husband, the original yuppie, wanted the latest gadgets. He installed speaking tubes and a telephone but couldn't make any calls, as no one else in the area owned a phone.

Circling back, the route passes the sprawling Puyallup Fairgrounds (once the site of the Northwest Japanese internment camp). On Saturdays from May through September, visit Pioneer Park and the farmer's market for abundant fresh produce, a plenitude of tasty fare, and crafts. Another serene spot and waterfowl haven is De-Coursey Park, where bathrooms are available before you assault the gentle and not-so-gentle hilly miles through pastures and encroaching development. Don't get discouraged by several "false summits." Remember, the Puyallup Valley (behind you) is flanked by foothills—and you're on them.

At Woodland Avenue the well-kept Fors Chicken Farm is owned by a longtime Tacoma family. They became known for more than chickens in the early 1980s when they became instrumental in pushing the government investigation for Vietnam POWs and MIAs. There is still no word of their missing son.

A power station, which gives birth to massive overhead power lines, clues you that the hills are over. Rolling farms lead to suburban and business streets. A historical marker at the Fernhill Library relates the Fernhill Boys' tale. Watch for the massive, yellow-brick Tacoma First Baptist Korean Church, which marks the turn to Sheridan Avenue.

At Wapato Park's entrance a white stone portico brings up visions of women in long dresses holding parasols and strolling to the lakeside. Fall is a favorite here for those who love charging through leaf piles. If your burning thighs can take it, wander the trails and footbridges through the park's marshy wildlife acres.

Then, head off to the Starbucks at 72nd Street and I–5. There's nothing like a steaming latte after a hard workout.

DIRECTIONS
FOR
THE RIDE

- 0.0 Left onto Sheridan Avenue from Wapato Park.
- 0.2 Right onto 64th Street; short steep hill.
- 1.0 Cross Pacific Avenue.
- 1.7 East Side Boys and Girls Club. Railroad tracks. Caution!
- 3.4 Left onto Waller Road at Waller Road Elementary School.
- 5.8 Right onto Pioneer Way at the T-intersection.
- 8.1 Pioneer Blueberry Farm.
- 8.9 Watson's Nursery. Filbert farm.
- 9.6 Veer left at the stoplight, staying on Pioneer Way. Caution.
- 9.7 Washington State University Extension Center. Garden.
- 11.2 Downtown Puyallup. Note public art.
- 11.4 Cross Meridian Street. Peace Lutheran Church.
- 11.5 Meeker Mansion.
- 11.7 Right onto 7th Street SE before Route 512.
- 11.9 Right onto 7th Avenue SW.
- 12.4 Cross Meridian Street. Fairgrounds.
  Option for Saturdays: Right onto 2nd Street SW to Pioneer Park and farmer's market. Return to 7th Avenue SW.
- 13.2 DeCoursey Park. Clark's Creek. Rest rooms.
- 13.5 Left onto Fruitland Avenue.
- 14.4 Right onto 84th Street before the crest. Uphill. Fors Chicken Farm.
- 15.8 Cross Canyon Road. Power station.
- 17.0 Cross Waller Road. 84th becomes 85th.

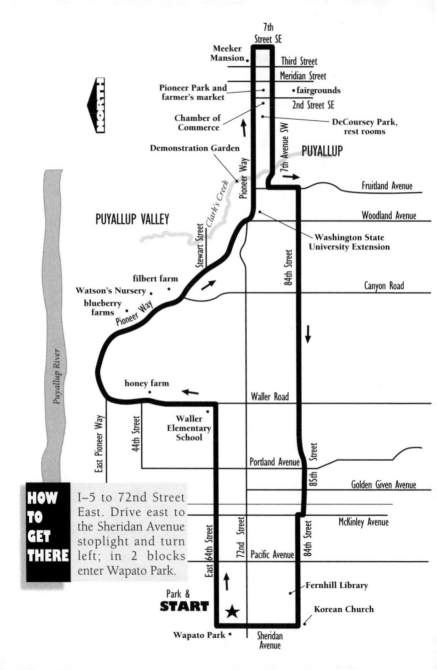

7th Street SE

Meeker Mansion

Third Street

Meridian Street

Pioneer Park and farmer's market

fairgrounds

2nd Street SE

Chamber of Commerce

DeCoursey Park, rest rooms

PUYALLUP

Demonstration Garden

Clark's Creek

Pioneer Way

7th Avenue SW

Fruitland Avenue

Woodland Avenue

PUYALLUP VALLEY

Stewart Street

Washington State University Extension

84th Street

filbert farm

Canyon Road

Watson's Nursery

blueberry farms

Pioneer Way

Puyallup River

honey farm

Waller Road

44th Street

Waller Elementary School

Portland Avenue

85th Street

East Pioneer Way

Golden Given Avenue

HOW TO GET THERE I–5 to 72nd Street East. Drive east to the Sheridan Avenue stoplight and turn left; in 2 blocks enter Wapato Park.

McKinley Avenue

East 64th Street

72nd Street

Pacific Avenue

84th Street

Fernhill Library

Korean Church

Park & **START**

Wapato Park •

Sheridan Avenue

18.5 Cross Golden Given Avenue. RR tracks.
18.7 Right onto McKinley Avenue.
18.8 Left onto 84th Street.
19.3 Cross Pacific Avenue. Fernhill Library historical marker.
20.0 Right onto Sheridan. First Baptist Korean Church.
21.0 Left into Wapato Park.

Pierce County: Puyallup
Puyallup Valley Tour de Pierce

Distance & Rating:	32.5 miles; flat except one steep hill
Surface & Traffic:	Paved; minimal except Orting Sumner Highway
Highlights:	Meeker Mansion, valley farmland, farmer's market, historic walking tour, downtown's Outdoor Gallery of public art
Eats	Lonzo's, Farmer's Market, Anna Maria's, picnic
Sleeps:	Chamber of Commerce (253) 845–6755, www.puyallupchamber. com, Murphy's Corner B&B, Tayberry Victorian Cottage
Note:	Avoid this ride during the Puyallup Fair in September

Thank you, Pierce County Parks, Foothills Rails to Trails, and the Tacoma Wheelmen for mapping out this delightful ride (slightly revised here). Starting at the Puyallup Fairgrounds, you wind through rural Pierce County towns of Puyallup, McMillan, and Sumner. Try a crisp autumn day.

Go south on 5th Street SW past the wooden roller coaster. You make your own, climbing up 15th Avenue SW and coasting down to the Department of Fisheries. This pleasant, flat neighborhood includes serene DeCoursey Park, a small gem cut by Clark's Creek and filled with waterfowl.

Across Fruitland Avenue orchards remain as a part of Western Washington's Extension University. Students learn about agriculture and the staff offers tons of consumer advice. Puyallup's flat, Midwestern-style ambience is at its best on Pioneer Avenue SW. Oldfashioned front porches face the street, garages are hidden behind, and flower gardens blossom. Meridian, Puyallup's main thoroughfare, is lined with small-town storefronts, still active despite the superstores. Visit the stately Meeker Mansion, squashed between encroaching buildings. (See Ride 39.) Car traffic diminishes as you approach the silty Puyallup River and almost disappears on Bentson Drive East, a shaded, winding country road. Rolling quietly through expansive farms growing berries, squash, and corn imparts a feel for the valley's once rural nature.

From the plenitude of antiques sold in this area, you'd think the Northwest had an 1800s population of some major East Coast city. Nearby, Coco Joe's marks the left across railroad tracks to West Valley Highway's fertile valley. Old homesteads and farms intersperse with encroaching development that increases as the West Valley Highway nears Route 167. Watch for broken glass beneath the overpass—there is always a fresh supply.

After this ride, when you pass the many Gordon trucks on I–5, you'll think about their massive storage yard at the north end of this route. Nearby, broad, flat farms produce vegetables and dairy products. At one red barn, you can stop and sample ice cream.

Before attacking the McCutcheon hill, stop at Riverside Park for rest rooms and hydration. If your energy is waning, take 96th Street E to the Orting Sumner Highway and avoid the struggle. Of course, that means you miss the spectacular downhill through a cool wooded road near the Puyallup River's wetlands. Choices, choices. If you pick McCutcheon, grit your teeth for the steep uphill.

You know you're at the top at a Y-intersection where Rhodes Lake Road veers left uphill—you don't have to go up. Virtually everyone rests at this Y-intersection (and many rest several times on the way up) before heading downhill. On 128th Street E a new bridge crosses the wide Puyallup River, a lovely rest spot for viewing the silty gray mountain runoff. The peacefulness evaporates in a few

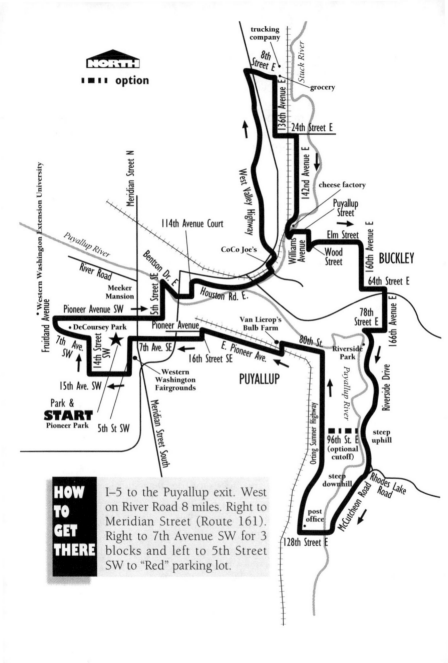

NORTH

▮▬▮▮ option

trucking company

8th Street E

Stuck River

136th Avenue E

grocery

24th Street E

142nd Avenue E

West Valley Highway

cheese factory

Puyallup Street

Elm Street

160th Avenue E

BUCKLEY

Wood Street

64th Street E

114 Avenue Court

Puyallup River

CoCo Joe's

Williams Avenue

Benson Dr. E

River Road

5th Street SE

Houston Rd. E.

Meridian Street N

Western Washington Extension University

Meeker Mansion

Pioneer Avenue SW

Pioneer Avenue

Van Lierop's Bulb Farm

78th Street E

166th Avenue E

Fruitland Avenue

DeCoursey Park

80th St.

Riverside Park

Puyallup River

7th Ave. SW

14th Street SW

7th Ave. SE

16th Street SE

E. Pioneer Ave.

PUYALLUP

Riverside Drive

15th Ave. SW

Western Washington Fairgrounds

96th St. E (optional cutoff)

steep uphill

Park & **START** Pioneer Park

5th St SW

Meridian Street South

Orting Summer Highway

steep downhill

Rhodes Lake Road

post office

McCutcheon Road

128th Street E

HOW TO GET THERE I–5 to the Puyallup exit. West on River Road 8 miles. Right to Meridian Street (Route 161). Right to 7th Avenue SW for 3 blocks and left to 5th Street SW to "Red" parking lot.

minutes as you hit Orting Sumner Highway at the McMillan Post Office. Stick to the wide shoulder; traffic speeds by. The good news is that you can rev up the endorphines on a fantastic flat sprint.

When turning left onto 80th Street E., you're almost home. In the Spring, Van Lierop Bulb Farm turns into a rainbow sea of tulips and daffodils. Finish up with a visit to Pioneer Park's Farmer's Market. Pick up a walking tour of Puyallup's unique public art and historical buildings.

DIRECTIONS
FOR
THE RIDE

0.0 Pioneer Park. South on 2nd Street SW.
0.5 Right on 7th Avenue SW.
0.8 Left onto 5th Street SW.
1.0 Western Washington Fairgrounds.
1.5 Right onto 15th Avenue SW.
2.2 Right curve onto 14th Street SW. Department of Fisheries.
2.8 Left onto 7th Avenue SW. DeCoursey Park.
3.2 Right onto Fruitland Avenue at T-intersection. Western Washington Extension University ahead.
3.4 Right onto Pioneer Avenue SW.
5.1 Cross Meridian. Meeker Mansion.
5.3 Left onto 5th Street NE. Cross RR tracks and Main Street.
5.5 Right onto Bentson Drive East after Puyallup River Bridge.
6.4 Left curve onto 114th Avenue Court E.
8.1 Right onto Houston Road E. Coco Joe's.
8.2 Left across the RR tracks and right onto West Valley Highway.
11.3 Right onto 8th Street E. Go under Highway 167.
11.5 Right onto unmarked 136th Avenue E. Small grocery.
12.8 Left onto 24th Street E. Cross the railroad tracks.
13.3 Right curve onto 142nd Avenue E.
14.7 Cross the Stuck River.
14.75 Left onto Puyallup Street. Cheese factory.
15.2 Veer right onto Williams Avenue. Cross the RR tracks.
15.5 Left onto Wood Street.

15.9 Veer right on Elm Street at the Y-intersection.

16.2 Right curve onto 160th Avenue E. Farms.

17.0 Left onto 64th Street E.

17.4 Right onto 166th Avenue E.

18.3 Right curve onto 78th Street E.

18.8 Left onto Riverside Drive. Riverside Park (rest rooms).

19.7 Right curve as Riverside merges with 96th Street E and immediate left onto McCutcheon Road.
Option: Continue on 96th Street E to avoid McCutcheon hill.

20.5 Steep uphill.

23.0 Veer right at top of Y-intersection, staying on McCutcheon. Steep downhill.

25.0 Veer right to 128th Street E. Cross the Puyallup River.

25.8 Right onto Orting Sumner Highway. McMillan Post Office.

26.6 Pass Old Military Road.

27.9 Cross 96th Street. Alderton.

28.6 Pass Pioneer Way stoplight.

28.8 Left onto 80th Street E just before Puyallup River bridge. Caution.

29.8 Left at T-intersection after Van Lierop Bulb Farm. Cross RR tracks.

29.9 Right onto E Pioneer Avenue. No shoulder.

30.1 Pass Shaw Road stoplight.

30.8 Left onto 16th Street SE. Pioneer Market.

31.0 Right onto 7th Avenue SE at stop sign.

31.4 Cross Route 512 overpass.

31.9 Cross Meridian Street. Fairgrounds.

32.0 Right onto 2nd Street SW.

32.5 Pioneer Park. Farmer's market (Saturdays May through early September). Chamber of Commerce (walking-tour maps). Rest rooms.

Pierce County: Orting
Daffodil Classic—Orting, Kapowsin, Eatonville, and Ohop Loops

Distance & Rating:	20, 30, or 51 miles; mixed flats and hills, one long uphill; 3.9- and 4.1-mile options to Northwest Trek and Eatonville
Surface & Traffic:	Paved; light to moderate
Highlights:	Orting, daffodils, Pioneer Farm Museum, views
Eats:	Picnic

In spring, they say, "A young man's fancy turns to love." In Pierce County a bicyclist's fancy turns to the Daffodil Classic—April's prelude to the end of gray. Usually the "Daffodil" misses the flowers. No matter; it also misses the rains. Proceeds from the group ride fund Sprocket Woman's school visits and club safety promotion. On your own you'll be charmed by spectacular Mount Rainier views and can cycle the optional side trips—and still make a donation to the Tacoma Wheelmen Bicycle Club.

Orting, where the route begins, was settled around 1850. It was temporarily abandoned during the Indian Wars of 1854, but four settlers returned, reclaiming their farming plats. With the 1877 construction of the Puyallup River bridge, these settlers could transport crops to the Tacoma market. Coal mining boomed briefly, along with hops. Frederick Eldredge, an entrepreneur farmer who platted Orting in 1880, became its first mayor. Desperately short of hops pickers, he enticed German immigrants from cane-picking jobs in Hawaii to Orting. In the late 1880s the hops failed due to infestation. Orting's fertile, volcanic soil, however, proved perfect for daffodil and tulip bulbs, the main industry after hops. Orting's population had a mild boom: In 1890 it was 623; now it's about 2,000.

Consisting of 20- and 30-mile intersecting loops, this route can be two moderate rides or a calorie-burning 50-mile jaunt (from Orting City Park). For the 30-mile route, begin at the Kapowsin Store at the loops' junction or in Eatonville. Terrain varies from thick, lush forests to rolling prairie and farmland.

Leaving Orting Park, the route goes quickly through town to rural countryside. After the Puyallup River it climbs rolling hills through forests, cresting to stunning Mount Rainier views. At Kapowsin, the 20- and 30-mile loops join. A store and tavern (motorcycle hangout) provide sustenance and rest rooms.

By some strange quirk of road planning, both Orville Road and Kapowsin Road bend at this Kapowsin corner. Be alert—for the 51-mile loop, turn left onto Orville Road, and for the 20-mile loop, turn right to Orting. In any case do not go straight. During the Daffodil Classic this is a checkpoint with food and honeybuckets (portable rest rooms).

On the 51-mile loop, pass Ohop Lake to Route 161. From this corner you can go to Eatonville (see option) or continue past the Pioneer Farm turnoff to stop at Dogwood Park. A historical marker here describes giant Mount Rainier. This is a perfect spot to contemplate the strength of Rainier and absorb its power—and have lunch, too. Right after Dogwood Park veer left onto Eatonville Cut-Off Road. To visit Northwest Trek Wildlife Park, continue straight 1.0 mile on Route 161/Clear Lake Highway. (See option.)

The basic route crosses Highway 7 (caution, it's a busy road!) onto Highway 702/McKenna-Tanwax Road. Angle right onto Kinsman Road, which becomes 8th Avenue East/Transmission Line Road. Turning onto 304th Street/Kapowsin Highway, pass a country store and recross Route 7. At Kapowsin, Orting Kapowsin Highway heads to Orting.

Watch for the Orting Cemetery. Wandering amid its old stones provides a snippet of history. Now for a great downhill: Hang onto your brakes, veering left at the Old Soldiers' Home. Established early in this century by the state government, it cares for veterans. Curve right as Orting Kapowsin Highway becomes Calistoga Street and return to Orting City Park.

Option to Eatonville

Thomas C. Van Eaton settled here in 1889, opening a trading post. As Scandinavians and Germans settled the Ohop Valley, Van Eaton supplied homesteaders by pack train. After the 1904 railroad arrived, the Eatonville Lumber Company boomed, employing 300 workers by 1910.

At the east end of town were the Depot and Depot Hotel. On Oak Street, workers were required to live in one-level company houses and shop at the company store. Behind the store and across the railroad tracks, the mill that was abandoned in 1954 looms—prime real estate ripe for development. The 1920s lumber baron's mansion serves as the Old Mill House B&B, whose rooms are named and decorated for famous folks—Isadora Duncan, Will Rogers, Bessie Smith, and F. Scott Fitzgerald. During Prohibition the home's secret library served the bad stuff.

As Oak Street E meets Mashell Avenue, a right turn leads downtown. To relax along the Mashell River, turn left to George Smallwood Memorial Park, then backtrack to this point. A historical marker on Mashell Avenue designates the original trading post, located near the 1915 bank building. On Rainier Avenue the Van Eaton family spread out from the sprawling home. Part of the original Van Eaton residence today serves as the Eatonville Clinic.

At the western end of town, visit the cemetery, taking time to view the graves of Japanese workers. Quite close together, they indicate the Japanese practice of burying the dead in a sitting position.

Pioneer Farm Museum in Ohop

Kids delight in this working farm—romping in the hayloft, riding the wagon, experimenting with tools, grinding corn, pounding horseshoes, or churning butter. They even get to dress up in old-fashioned clothing. As a big kid, you'll be fascinated by the perseverance it took to survive pioneer life here just a hundred years ago. Demonstrations of native crafts and a salmon hatchery give one an appreciation for living with nature. The museum is open daily in summer and on spring weekends.

Northwest Trek Wildlife Park

In this ecological park animals roam free, and people are caged for a one-hour tram ride. An interpretive center houses displays and special programs. In summer evenings rides (best time for wildlife viewing), salmon bakes, and tram are available. Consider parking here to ride the loop and return for dinner. The park is open daily February through October, weekends only other months.

DIRECTIONS

FOR
THE RIDE

0.0 Right from Orting City Park onto Route 162, also called Washington Street and Old Pioneer Way.

0.2 Right across RR tracks and quick left onto Route 162/Harman Way.

1.3 Right onto Orville Road.

4.8 Cross Puyallup River. Long uphill.

9.9 Kapowsin Recreation Area.

10.7 Left at intersection, staying on Orville Road as it makes sharp left between store and tavern. (Right for 20-mile loop, picking up directions at 41 miles.)

19.0 Ohop Lake.

20.0 Right onto Route 161. (To visit Eatonville go left 1 mile; see optional route, below.)

20.5 Pioneer Farm Museum.

21.6 Dogwood Park. Veer left onto Eatonville Cut-Off Road. (Straight 1 mile on Route 161/Clear Lake Highway for Northwest Trek Wildlife Park; see optional route below.)

26.5 Straight across Highway 7 onto Highway 702/McKenna-Tanwax Road.

28.7 Right at angled Kinsman Road, which becomes 8th Avenue E.

32.0 Right onto 304th Street/Kapowsin Highway.

35.1 Cross Route 7. Johnson's Corner.

41.0 Left onto Orting-Kapowsin Highway at Kapowsin.

49.0 Orting Cemetery. Downhill.

50.0 Veer left. The Old Soldiers' Home.

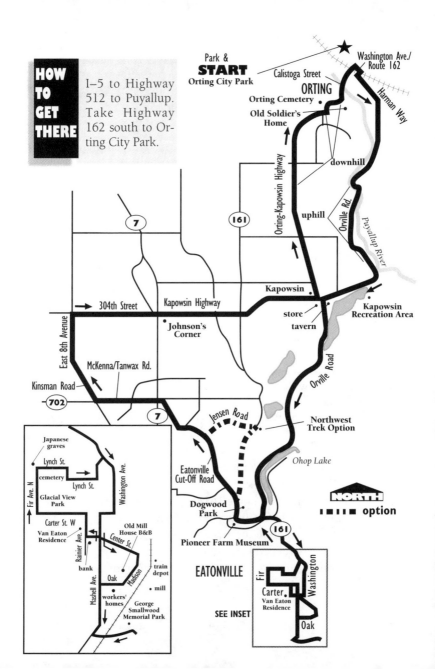

HOW TO GET THERE

I–5 to Highway 512 to Puyallup. Take Highway 162 south to Orting City Park.

Park & **START**
Orting City Park

Calistoga Street

Washington Ave./
Route 162

ORTING

Orting Cemetery

Old Soldier's
Home

Harman Way

downhill

Orting-Kapowsin Highway

uphill

Orville Rd.

Puyallup River

Kapowsin

Kapowsin Highway

store

tavern

**Kapowsin
Recreation Area**

304th Street

**Johnson's
Corner**

Orville Road

East 8th Avenue

McKenna/Tanwax Rd.

Kinsman Road

Jensen Road

**Northwest
Trek Option**

Ohop Lake

Eatonville
Cut-Off Road

Dogwood
Park

NORTH
option

Pioneer Farm Museum

EATONVILLE

Fir

Carter

Washington

Van Eaton
Residence

Oak

SEE INSET

Japanese
graves

Lynch St.

cemetery

Lynch St.

Washington Ave.

Fir Ave. N

Glacial View
Park

Carter St. W

Van Eaton
Residence

Rainier Ave.

Center St.

Old Mill
House B&B

bank

Mashell Ave.

Oak

Hadson

train
depot

mill

workers'
homes

George
Smallwood
Memorial Park

50.5 Right curve. Orting-Kapowsin Highway becomes Calistoga Street.

50.7 Right onto Washington Avenue/Route 162.

51.0 Right into Orting City Park. End of ride.

Option to Eatonville

0.0 Left onto Route 161.

1.1 Eatonville. Straight onto Washington Avenue.

1.3 Right onto Carter Street W.

1.4 Left onto Mashell Avenue.

1.6 Left onto Center Street.

1.7 Right onto Madison Avenue S at the Depot and Depot Hotel sites.

1.9 Right onto Oak Street E. Mill, Old Mill House B&B, store building, mill foreman's house, workers' homes.

2.0 Right onto Mashell Avenue. (Left to Smallwood Memorial Park.)

2.3 Left onto Center Street.

2.4 Right onto Rainier Avenue. Uphill. Van Eaton Residence.

2.5 Left onto Carter Street W.

2.7 Right onto Fir Avenue N. One block to log schoolhouse, Glacier View Park, and the cemetery; note the Japanese graves at the far left corner.

2.8 Right onto Lynch Street behind cemetery, following right and left jogs.

3.0 Left onto Mashell Street to Route 161.

4.1 Pass Orville Road, rejoining the basic route.

Option to Northwest Trek

0.0 Straight 1.0 mile on Route 161/Clear Lake Highway.

1.7 Right into Northwest Trek Wildlife Park.

2.7 Left out of park to Route 161.

2.9 Right to Jensen Road East. Mud Lake.

3.9 Right onto Eatonville Cut-Off Road, rejoining route.

Thurston County: Olympia
Priest Point Park, Boston Harbor, Historic Olympia

Distance & Rating:	37 miles; moderate, several steep hills
Surface & Traffic:	Paved; few to many cars
Highlights:	Priest Point Park, Budd Inlet, Boston Harbor, views, Tolmie State Park, historic homes, Percival Landing
Eats:	San Francisco Street Bakery, Sweet Oasis, Urban Onion, Ben Moore's, Olympia Farmer's Market arcade (April–December except Mondays) and demonstration garden, with ethnic market and organic-food stands, Mondo Shrimp, Louisa, Spar Café, Bulldog News & Coffee, Capitale, Buck's 5th Avenue
Sleeps:	Harbinger Inn B&B
Bikes:	Bike Tech (360) 754–BIKE

Congested downtown byways melt into agrarian pastures and dense timberland. Jam-packed mossy alders, cedars, vine maples, ferns, and ivy-entwined firs blanket this wet and placid peninsula. Tranquil marinas and secluded shoreline parks are juxtaposed against the sophisticated domed Washington State Capitol. Seagulls screech; wetland waterfowl feed silently. Sailboats glide serenely by; tugboat motors purr like cats, pushing or pulling log-loaded barges.

Peaceful Priest Point Park once served as spiritual sanctuary for the Oblate Catholic Mission (1848). Here, in the damp, fern-ensconced hills, beneath nature's luxuriant canopy, the priests opened a residential school for Native American converts. Cycle the leaf-carpeted, cathedral-like 0.5-mile oval lane to reach East Bay Drive's bike path.

Crossing a muddy inlet, as if being transported into a time warp, catapults you from urban to rural. East Bay Drive becomes Boston Harbor Road NE, passing Gull Harbor Mercantile, an old-fashioned shop stocked with packaged snacks and assorted sundries. After Adams Creek glide effortlessly between broad pastures, which end abruptly at densely wooded hills. Midway on the left (marked by a DEAD END sign), Inlet Drive's sprawling fields once blossomed with the fruit of Sunny Bay Plantation, a 300-acre ranch owned by West Coast Grocery Founder Mark Ewald. Nearby, Burfort Park is a lovely spot with beach trails.

Make brief side trip to Boston Harbor, a modest marina with a grocery, rest rooms, and a spectacular view. Backtracking, climb to farmland plateaus and pastures and zoom down to Libby Road NE and Dickenson Point's secluded cottage- and mansion-edged shore.

Be alert for the left to Woodard Bay Road NE (66th Avenue NE on the right). Glide down across algae-green and muddy Henderson Inlet, a tidal waterway snaking through wooded wetlands replete with waterfowl. The character of the Northwest woods is revealed by graceful, soft-boughed cedars, spiring firs, red-trunked madronas, and gray-barked alders. Maple and alder leaves insulate the forest floor. Classic red barns and white farmhouses anchor serene meadows.

Traditional Western, weathered-wood fences enclose grazing horses and a Christmas tree farm. On South Bay Road NE, stick to the shoulders. Veer left onto Johnson Point Road, edging a swampy slough; take care not to head straight onto Hawks Prairie Road.

Along 63rd Avenue NE farms nestle on sloping pastures, depictions of life as it was—and still is, except for targeted development. One area that remains untouched is the spectacular Tolmie State Park, a 0.9-mile jaunt that descends to the park and shore.

Honoring Dr. William Fraser Tolmie (1812–1866), the park bespeaks of this gentle man who spent sixteen years as the physician, botanist, and fur trader for the Hudson's Bay Company at nearby Fort Nisqually. His grasp of native languages enabled him to trade, provide medical care, and interpret the Indian War settlement. Enthralled with nature, he pioneered mountain climbing as the first white man to ascend Mount Rainier, where he is commemorated at Tolmie Peak. Awed by the unmatchable beauty of Nisqually's prairies, wetlands and Mount Rainier, he captured their essence in detailed natural history journals, writing in one, "When tired of the shade wood, you can emerge into the boundless prairie to which any nobleman's park cannot be compared, neither in size, beauty or magnificence."

A park map details trail access. The protected cove harbors waterfowl; a spit and footbridge lead into the slough from which you can view the Nisqually Reach, Case Inlet, Key Peninsula, Anderson Island, and the Nisqually Delta. Backtrack, climbing the punishing hill; walking is okay.

Behind a veneer of roadside trees, logging operations have shorn forests like a giant razor's swath. Ready your thighs for more uphill on Hawks Prairie Road NE, but then soar down toward developments plopped in former farmland and across the slough bridge.

Commanding a broad plateau to the left is the 1885 Bell-Bennett House. After Woodard Creek semirural 26th Avenue NE suburban at John Rogers School and Olympia Junior Academy.

At San Francisco Street NE, don't pass up the San Francisco Bakery—hearty, whole-grain breads, muffins, and New York–style bialys. In this densely populated area, the turns come as fast as TV commercials. In 1 block turn left to Tullis Street NE's cottages and climb to the 1882 Queen Anne–style Hale House at number 902 and Bigelow Park. Across busy Puget Street NE picture-book frame cottages flank Quince Street and Glass Avenue. Tucked into this charming hillside, Victorian gingerbread homes nestle like a museum display; brass plaques denote their origins, such as the Bailey-Bigelow cottage and the impressive 1854 Gothic Revival Bigelow House at 918 Glass. From this pretty neighborhood, a right from Glass onto East Bay Drive will take you back to Priest Point Park.

If you have time, you might want to explore downtown Olympia. Don't miss the impressive State Capitol, Percival Landing, and the recently constructed Olympia Farmer's Market and surronding shops.

DIRECTIONS
FOR
THE RIDE

0.0 Follow the NORTH EXIT signs around Priest Point Park's 0.5-mile oval lane.
0.5 Right onto East Bay Drive's bike path.
0.9 Cross Ames Road. East Bay Drive becomes Boston Harbor Road.
3.0 Gull Harbor Mercantile. Fire station.
4.0 Cross Adams Creek.
4.4 Pass County Park and 66th Avenue NE. Curve left.
4.5 Pass angled Zangle Road NE.
5.3 Burfort Park.
5.7 Left onto 73rd Avenue NE. Backtrack and cross Boston Harbor Road.
7.0 Left onto Zangle Road NE. Boston Elementary School and fire station. Steep uphill.
7.9 Right onto 81st Avenue NE. Steep downhill.
9.0 Left onto Libby Road to Dickenson Point.
9.4 Pass Fishtrap Loop Road NE.
11.5 Left at the dead-end sign onto unmarked Fishtrap Loop Road NE.
12.2 Right at the T-intersection to unmarked Libby Road NE.
13.0 Left onto Woodard Bay Road NE (66th Avenue NE on the right). Henderson Inlet.
13.9 Pass Lemon Road NE.
14.2 Veer right onto unmarked Shincke Road NE.
14.8 Left onto 56th Avenue NE, curving right onto Sleater-Kinney Road NE.
16.8 Left onto South Bay Road NE. Caution; traffic.

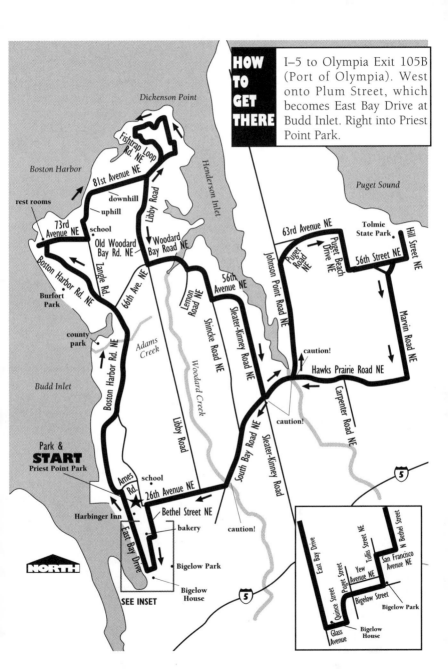

HOW TO GET THERE

I–5 to Olympia Exit 105B (Port of Olympia). West onto Plum Street, which becomes East Bay Drive at Budd Inlet. Right into Priest Point Park.

Dickenson Point

Fishtrap Loop Rd. NE

Boston Harbor

81st Avenue NE

Henderson Inlet

Puget Sound

rest rooms

downhill

uphill

Libby Road

73rd Avenue NE

school

Old Woodard Bay Rd. NE

Woodard Bay Road NE

63rd Avenue NE

Tolmie State Park

Hill Street NE

Puget Road NE

Puget Beach Drive NE

56th Street NE

Boston Harbor Rd. NE

Zangle Rd.

66th Ave. NE

56th Avenue NE

Johnson Point Road NE

Marvin Road NE

Burfort Park

Lemon Road NE

Shincke Road NE

Sleater-Kinney Road NE

caution!

county park

Adams Creek

Woodard Creek

Hawks Prairie Road NE

Budd Inlet

Libby Road

South Bay Road NE

Sleater-Kinney Road

Carpenter Road NE

caution!

5

Park & **START** Priest Point Park

Ames Rd.

school

26th Avenue NE

Harbinger Inn

Bethel Street NE

bakery

caution!

NORTH

East Bay Drive

Bigelow Park

Bigelow House

SEE INSET

5

East Bay Drive

Tullis Street NE

N Bethel Street

Quince Street

Puget Street

Yew Avenue NE

San Francisco Avenue NE

Bigelow Street

Bigelow Park

Glass Avenue

Bigelow House

17.2 Pass Hawks Prairie Road NE. South Bay Road becomes Johnson Point Road NE.

17.7 Right onto Puget Road NE.

19.8 Right onto 63rd Avenue NE. Pass Marvin Road on the left.

20.5 Right at the T-intersection onto unmarked Puget Beach Drive NE. Road curves left.

21.5 Triangle intersection. Veer left onto 56th Street.

22.4 Left onto Hill Street NE.

23.0 Tolmie State Park. Backtrack to triangle intersection.

24.6 Left onto Marvin Road NE.

26.5 Right onto Hawks Prairie Road NE. Pass Carpenter Road NE.

29.4 Bridge. Left onto South Bay Road NE. Caution; busy road.

30.1 Cross Sleater-Kinney Road NE. Bell-Bennett House.

32.3 Cross Woodard Creek. Right to 26th Avenue NE. School.

33.7 Left onto Bethel Street NE.

33.9 Right at T-intersection onto San Francisco Avenue. Bakery.

34.0 Left onto Tullis Street NE. Hale House at Yew Avenue NE.

34.1 Bigelow Park. Right onto Bigelow Avenue NE. Cross Puget Street NE.

35.0 Curve left onto Quince Street.

35.1 Right onto Glass Avenue. Bigelow House.

35.8 Right on East Bay Drive.

36.9 Priest Point Park.

Thurston County: Olympia
Chehalis Railroad/Woodard Bay Trail

Distance & Rating:	6.2 miles one way; easy to moderate
Surface & Traffic:	Mostly paved, few dirt sections remain; paving planned
Highlights:	Farmland, wetlands, forests, Woodard Bay Natural Resources Conservation Area
Eats, Bikes:	See Ride 42

Running up the abandoned Chehalis Western Railroad track, this path traverses wetlands and ponds, rolling farmland, and dense mossy woods. Float along the paved area until the short dirt and gravel sections test those mountain-biking skills—less than a mile's worth.

Continuing beneath a bridge, the trail splits. Straight ahead you can go around the fence, over a few logs, and out to an old railroad bridge (no access to bridge). To the left a short path leads to a parking lot. To return, backtrack.

Option
Right from parking lot to unmarked Woodard Bay Road for 0.3 miles. Cross Woodard Bay and turn right to Woodard Bay Natural Resources Conservation Area. No pets or bicycle riding—lock up and walk the road or trail 1 mile to an abandoned house and log boom loader. Great bird-watching and picnic spot.

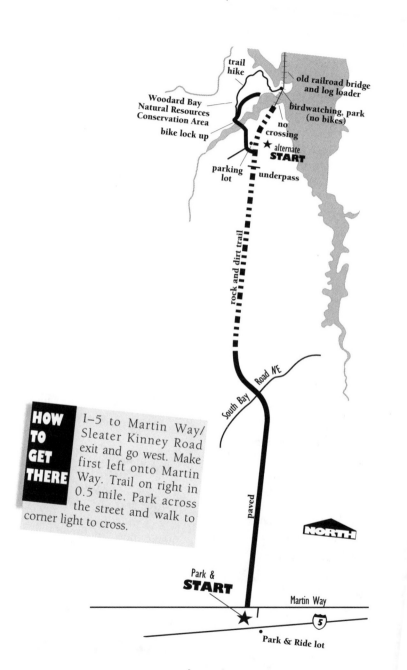

trail hike

old railroad bridge and log loader

Woodard Bay Natural Resources Conservation Area

birdwatching, park (no bikes)

bike lock up

no crossing

★ alternate START

parking lot

underpass

rock and dirt trail

South Bay Road NE

HOW TO GET THERE I-5 to Martin Way/ Sleater Kinney Road exit and go west. Make first left onto Martin Way. Trail on right in 0.5 mile. Park across the street and walk to corner light to cross.

paved

NORTH

Park & **START**

Martin Way

⑤

Park & Ride lot

Thurston County:
Millersylvania
Olympia, Mounds, Wolves, and Sandstone

Distance & Rating:	44 miles; easy
Surface & Traffic:	Mostly flat (really!) paved road; minimal cars except Route 507
Highlights:	Millersylvania State Park, Mima Mounds, Tenino's Sandstone, Wolf Haven
Eats:	Picnic; Blue Heron Bakery (not on ride; nearby off Route 8 at Mud Bay exit)
Etc.:	Thurston County Chamber of Commerce (360) 357–3362, see Ride 42

Flat Northwest workout rides are rare—here's one. Well, it does sneak in a few inclines, but don't let that or the 44 miles put you off. Enveloped in misty fog or squinting against a hot sun, you'll find the miles evaporate. Glide by pastoral fields, forested boggy valleys brimming with yellow-flowered skunk cabbage, moss-laden trees, or summer's wildflower and berry patches.

At Millersylvania noisy mallards and honking Canadas graze along Deep Lake, adjacent to the 841 acres Squire Latham homesteaded in 1855. A later owner, John Miller, deeded the land for a park in 1921. Developed as a 1930s Civilian Conservation Corps project, it remains a natural wilderness of towering firs and cedars and abundant wildlife and Miller's home, now the Environmental Learning Center. Creeks and wetlands harbor beavers, ducks, geese, squirrels, and native birds. Hiking trails meander past Miller's orchards, remnants of a narrow-gauge logging railroad, notched stumps of logged trees, and wetlands. Winding, tree-canopied roads humble your spirit. Alas, booming hot-rod stereos shatter the peace.

But you came to ride, so head out. Along the route swampy pastures and farmlands emit rich, rural manure odors. Bald eagles nest in tree snags. They do not appear on demand; be alert. Horses and cattle graze, Christmas trees and luxurious green turf grow, and abandoned farm buildings weather and crumble.

Rhodie fan alert! At Down's Rhododendron Nursery, a plethora of thriving rhodies and azaleas tantalize blossom lovers from March through June. Though located in Littlerock, a pip-squeak of a town, crowds scurry in. Otherwise, this is not a tourist area, and road signage can be poor.

Up Waddell Road the 445-acre Nature Conservancy's Mima (pronounced MY-muh) Mounds has been designated a National Natural Monument. At the first parking lot, scraggly ponderosa pine falter, an experiment in growing native Eastern Washington trees in Western Washington. From the second lot (rest rooms here), trails meander a 0.5- or 3.0-mile interpretive loop. Climb the observatory for an eerie overview of this otherworldly phenomenon. As far back as the Wilkes Expedition, visitors have labeled the landscape with such designations as the million mounds, pimpled plains, baffling bumps, hillocks, and hogwallows. Despite extensive study the mounds' origins remain baffling.

Waddell Creek Road becomes Mima Road, traversing the Black Hills Valley. Swampy bogs and moss-covered trees evolve to broad fields of grassy, lumpy mounds and clear-cuts. The Black Hills Cattle and Timber Company shines in stark contrast to locals' worn shacks and appliance-littered yards. Immense expanses of green saplings blanket the black earth, mired in the white irrigation systems of Weyerhauser Mima Forest Tree Nursery. Morkey's Violin Shop appears suddenly, a curiosity amid this country setting.

Near the Gate City School (1910–1941), a boarded-up, yellow-and- white relic, flocks of waterfowl cluster at the Black River, whose winding path borders acreage quilted by the red-barked blueberry bushes of Drew's Farms. Next door, Overlake Products' harvests and processes Drew's berries (advertising leads you to believe Overlake grows the berries). Across the road miles of silky grass compose the Black River Turf Farm. Thank goodness they, and not we, have to mow it.

Watch for narrow Schooland Road, just before a red fake brick house. Your nose identifies the Briarwood Poultry Farm's gray henhouses. Oddly, at Wolf Hill Feed and Fertilizer, odors seem locked up. The red-brick, yellow-trimmed Rochester Primary School clues you to turn left at the stoplight onto Route 12.

Rochester is a no-nonsense town of loggers, offering basic food in simple diners. Still, along with massive log-storage lots, it sports an espresso stand and the tasty treats of Chehalis Mint Candy. Though traffic on Route 12 rushes past, an ample shoulder provides safety. The only tough spot on this ride is the left from Route 12 to 183rd Avenue (after the green Rochester Home Center). Wait for a traffic break and walk across Route 12 and the railroad tracks leading to a Christmas tree farm.

At 25 miles Fort Henness makes a perfect picnic spot. Two hundred pioneers camped here during the 1855–1856 Indian War. Chimney- and well-stone piles mark the fort's existence while a map depicts its cramped quarters. Across the road Grand Mound Rochester Cemetery includes raised crypts, New Orleans–style graves laid well above the high-water table. Older graves and fenced family plots, many holding infants and young children, offer sad historical browsing.

South Sound Speedway marks the heavier traveled Old Route 99 (wide shoulders). A town with the charming, literary-style name of Violet Prairie produces log-home packages near dairy farms and DanDar, one of the state's largest thoroughbred breeders. In spring young colts and calves cavort.

More mounds, like erupting bubbles, dot these pastures until Tenino (population 1,400). Though the directions sound complicated, you follow winding Route 507 as it enters town and crosses the railroad. Here it's lined by laborers' cottage homes and a turn-of-the-century, fish-scale–faced, yellow church that's now a locksmith shop and ceramic studio. In a more prosperous town, this would be snapped up as hot restaurant real estate.

Note the 1910 Russell Building (owners of the Tenino Stone Company) with its decorative floral and sunburst panels. Between Howard and Olympia Streets, six early twentieth-century sandstone buildings harken to Tenino's bustling past. Three house the Saddle Company, the Tenino Deli (salad bar, sandwiches, and cookies), and the 1906 corniced State Bank building that purveys antiques. In the late 1800s Tenino prospered with the national demand for sandstone for fireproof construction. Around 1920 the advent of concrete brought quarrying's demise, and Tenino's economy evolved to farming and logging.

A side trip down Olympia Street leads to the Quarry House, City Park, and the 1914 sandstone Depot Museum. In the quarry behind this yellow-trimmed museum, waterfalls cascade over moss-covered block cuts into a unique public pool alongside landscaped gardens. Its serene beauty inspires hope for dying industrial areas.

The Depot harbors years of smoky wood-stove odors. Structurally unchanged, the building's original wood floors, bathrooms and ticket windows make you long for old-fashioned, civilized travel. Displays of quarry work, railroad memorabilia, and medical and household supplies illustrate Tenino's golden era. Don't miss the beautifully crafted Washington Centennial Quilt. The museum is open mid-March through mid-October, Thursday through Sunday afternoons.

Watch for the Tenino Stone Carver at the 1913 quarry headquarters, now City Hall. Leaving Tenino on Old Route 99 (uphill), pass Tenino Elementary School, a creek, and Pederson's Acme Cattle Company. In summers prolific wild sweet peas and tiger lilies edge the road.

At Wolf Haven strutting peacocks, jumping rabbits, and waddling ducks have the right-of-way. Wolf enclosures house dozens of these stately creatures, all too domesticated for release to the wilds. Displays, $5.00 tours (May through October), and Friday/Saturday "Howl Ins" detail this endangered species' future.

Though the Old Route 99 downhill looks tempting, turn left to McCorkle Road. Gear way down for a steep incline (don't complain, you're on the homestretch) before the final left to Millersylvania Park. Now it's okay to lie like a sloth next to the lake.

DIRECTIONS
FOR
THE RIDE

0.0	Left onto unmarked Tilley Road South.
0.2	Region 1 Park Headquarters and trail heads.
1.0	Left onto 113th Street.
3.3	Cross Case Road and the I–5 over-pass.
4.5	Left at the T-intersection onto Littlerock Road/Route 121.
5.5	Down's Rhododendron Nursery.
6.5	Littlerock. Littlerock Elementary School.
6.7	Right onto unsigned Rochester Road/128th Street (Route 121).
6.8	Follow sign to Capital Forest. Cross railroad tracks.
7.8	Right at T-intersection onto Waddell Creek Road.
8.8	Left into Mima Mounds to second parking lot.
9.8	Return to entrance. Right onto Waddell Creek Road.
10.8	Cross 128th. Waddell Creek Road becomes Mima Road.
12.0	Black Hills Cattle and Timber Company.
14.0	Weyerhauser Mima Forest Tree Nursery. Morkey's Violin Shop.
17.5	Curve left across RR tracks and veer right.
17.6	Curve left onto unmarked Moon Road. Gate City School.
17.8	Black River. Drew's Farms. Overlake Products. Turf Farm.
19.3	Left onto Schooland Road. Briarwood Poultry Farm.
20.6	Cross Forstrom Street. Wolf Hill Feed and Fertilizer.

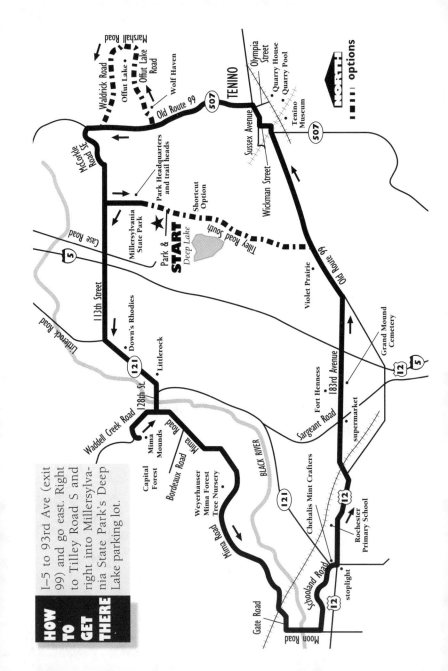

21.0 Curve right as Schooland Road joins Route 121.

21.8 Left onto Route 12. Stoplight. Rochester Primary School.

22.2 Chehalis Mint Candy Crafters Store.

23.0 Left onto 183rd Avenue, crossing Route 12 and RR tracks. Caution!

23.1 Veer right as 183rd Avenue turns.

24.6 Cross Sargeant Road. Supermarket. Caution.

25.0 Grand Mound Rochester Cemetery and Fort Henness.

27.5 Cross I–5.

28.1 Left at T-intersection onto Old Route 99. Violet Prairie.

33.5 Tenino. Curve left onto Wickman Street (Route 507).

34.2 Right onto Sussex Avenue (Route 507). Historic Tenino.

34.5 Right onto Olympia Street. Cross RR tracks.

34.7 City Park, Quarry House, and Depot Museum.

35.9 Backtrack and right onto Sussex Avenue. STONE CARVER sign.

36.4 Left onto Old Route 99/Route 507 toward Olympia and Offut Lake.

39.0 Right onto Offut Lake Road for 0.1 mile to Wolf Haven.

39.2 Ride 4-mile Offut Lake Option or backtrack to Route 99 and turn right.

40.2 Left onto McCorkle Road SE before downhill.

43.2 Steep uphill and left onto Tilley Road S.

44.0 Right to start.

Lewis County: Chehalis
Historical Lewis County Loop

Distance & Rating:	14.8 or 45 miles; long flat stretches, several hills
Surface & Traffic:	Paved; minimal to moderate
Highlights:	Historic Chehalis, farmer's market, Lewis County Historical Museum, scenic countryside, Mount St. Helens views, Chehalis River
Eats:	Picnic, Mary McCrank's
Sleeps:	Chehalis: Howard Johnson's; Centralia area: Shephard's Inn (25 miles east in Salkum); Castle Rock: Blue Heron Inn (south of Chehalis)
Etc.:	Visitors Bureau (800) 525–3323, Southwest Washington Tourist Info (360) 425–1211

Step back in time at the Lewis County Historical Museum. When you ask to park your car in the lot, the elderly docents love to describe the hordes of cyclists who wend through the steep hills on the Lewis County Park Historical Ride. Don't be scared off; the hills are not bad and the solitude away from the "madding crowd" soothes the soul.

Chehalis (pop. 6,100), which gets its name from a Native American word for "shifting sand," began as a way station for the weary and hungry traveling between Portland and Tacoma/Seattle. Today, I–5 strip development continues the way-station tradition. Noted for its flooding and mud, Chehalis was originally called Saunders Bottom after founder Schuyler Saunders. Roads still flood; check before cycling here after severe rainy weather.

Once away from the I–5 corridor, delightful bicycling through dairyland, verdant farmland, thick forests, and logged hillsides awaits. Reforestation and wild regrowth please the eye, while dilapidated, decaying homesteads make you ponder what quirks of fate ended their owners' hopes and aspirations. The start of your ride, the Lewis County Historical Museum, housed in the 1912 National Historic train depot, gives a few hints, featuring Chehalis Indian heritage and turn-of-the-century life. Nearby, stroll through the Saturday Farmer's Market in summer for fresh produce and baked goods.

Head out on West Street, crossing the first set of railroad tracks, into an industrial area of feed warehouses. Several turns lead you to Pennsylvania Avenue's historic district. Elaborate, porticoed carriage-era homes ("fixer-uppers" in real estate terms) grace streets lighted with 1920s fixtures.

Rejoining West Street, you pass Westside Park, crossing I–5. West Street becomes Airport Road, passing the Chehalis-Centralia Airport (since 1927) and the Riverside Golf Course. Farms spread across this flat countryside. Hamilton's Farm, near the interstate, has gained fame for its politically conservative billboard philosophizing, such as: IF YOU EARNED ENOUGH FOR THREE SQUARE MEALS, THE GOVERNMENT ATE YOUR LUNCH. The farm itself, in ill repair, is inhabited by woolly sheep and lambs.

Back in 1919 at the Chehalis River's Old Hangman Bridge, patriotic American Legionnaires hanged an unfortunate I.W.W. union member, or "Wobblie," following an Armistice Day clash. Believing that "the working class and the employing class have nothing in common," the Wobblies clashed with the individualistic Northwest spirit. After repeated lynchings they lost power and disbanded.

Cutting through a suburban area on Cooks Hill Road, pass Providence Hospital. A left onto Schueber Road takes you past rural farms and uphill. From the crest the valley farms appear as a green checkerboard. An early-twentieth-century brick silo towers amid sweet- smelling, freshly mown hay and lazy cattle. If you're lucky, you may spot a deer bounding and crashing through roadside thickets—despite encroaching development. Porch-rimmed, yellow-and-white farmhouses harken to a disappearing self-sufficient past in a spot where modern civilization has intruded. Two behemoth mansions, secured behind electronic gates, loom like English castles. Ahead, herds of sheep graze near the Lewis County Adventist School.

Joining unmarked Highway 6 at a T-intersection and stop sign, turn right to the Claquato Historic Marker. The town of Claquato, Native American for "high ground," sits above; you must climb up a hill to the church and cemetery. Why the marker was erected at the hill's base is a mystery; perhaps, on the highway, it's a convenient tourist spot.

Claquato Church, a sturdy 1858 pioneer building topped with a louvered belfry and "crown of thorns" steeple, doubled as the schoolhouse. As the first Protestant church north of the Columbia River, it remains the oldest still holding services. Backtracking, return to Stearns Road and the Claquato Pioneer Cemetery. Here, beneath its towering fir Pioneer Tree, settlers huddled for protection from inclement weather. What stamina! Would you have forsaken your warm Eastern digs for a hardy, uncertain homesteader life? When most of us came West, all we needed to do was buy a house. Now, we're out in inclement weather by choice—usually for outdoor fun. Times have changed.

For the 14.8-mile ride (see option), backtrack down Stearns Road. For the hardy 45-mile jaunt, head left at the cemetery, gliding downhill. On N McLaughlin Road's rolling hills, Littell's mill town thrived from 1896 to 1898 during the Northern Pacific Railroad's construction. Pumping uphill past a shake mill, inhale the sweet cedar odors of fresh-cut wood. Turning to Chilvers Road, climb uphill. On the downhill glide, be careful not to soar by the left to Dieckman Road. You don't want to miss its steep incline to the elementary school, where you can catch your breath and slide down to sleepy Adna. After crossing the Chehalis River on Highway 6, take a quick left onto Twin Oaks Road, which leads to Pleasant Valley Road (aptly named); a wondrous, flat 6 miles through a fertile, velvet-green valley. Flanking hills, logged to submission, vary from neglect to tended tree farms. Fireweed, berries, and mountain ash beautify immense clear-cuts. Luxuriant Queen Anne's lace and prickly purple-pink bull thistles crowd roadside ditches. Abundant, tart salmonberries quickly pacify your insistent stomach. Passing thick virgin-forest stretches, one marvels at the tenacity of settlers attempting to tame this valley.

After the Lewis County Public Works Department, cycle Highway 603's shoulder past the Evaline School. Originally formed in 1883, the present 1925 structure is the last two-room schoolhouse in the state. Then, escape onto Avery Road West's gentle rollers to the Mustard Seed Restaurant, a greasy-spoon lunch spot with picnic tables on a square patch of grass patch next to I–5. On the overpass prepare for blow-you-away Mount St. Helens views. Just imagine the force that blew its top.

Passing Spiffy's (acceptable food), visit the Fruit Warehouse and Shell Station for rest rooms and refueling. Continue 1 block on Route 12 and cross cautiously onto lightly traveled Avery Road. In another mile, from behind an unfenced red farm and warehouse, a huge German shepherd may mistake you for lunch. Stop, freeze, and yell "NO"; then walk. At "Loggers World" head right onto Jackson Highway, part of the Oregon Trail. Across Highway 12 visit the 1845 log cabin known as Jackson House. Peer in the windows, flop beneath a cherry tree, and munch an overdue lunch. John Jackson's home, run by his wife, Matilda (who, unlike ladies of her day, ran the Columbia River rapids in a canoe), served as the first territorial courthouse, an inn for politicians, a grocery store, and a post office. John, a mover and shaker, had his fingers in many pies, including the Washington Territory creation. It's hard to imagine squeezing such variety into this compact space.

Backtrack past Avery Road and Matilda Jackson Park. After a large barn and silo, Jackson Highway becomes a well-traveled, shouldered road that slips through farmland. Watch for the Lewis

County Road Department Shop and turn left to Forest-Napavine Road for a last fleeting bit of rural ride. After the Newaukum River, you are ejected from rural solitude to an I–5 McDonald's and Rib-Eye Cafe.

Crossing under I–5 to Hamilton Road, the country flavor is lost, but at least the road is flat and relatively free of cars. Recross I–5 on Labree Road, going left onto unmarked Bishop Highway. Before the railroad crossing take a left onto Interstate Avenue, heading to an I–5 intersection with a plethora of fast-food stops and cars blasting loud music. Escape to SW Parkland, crossing the tracks and edging the Chehalis Recreation Park.

At the park's end turn to unmarked SW William Avenue and curve right to Cascade Avenue into a residential neighborhood of small frame homes. On Market Street enter laid-back downtown Chehalis where, if you crave non–health-food baked goods, you can indulge in The Bakery's gooey apple squares. Or wander into Sweet Inspirations for a sandwich or Oreo-shaped Chehalis Mint. Continue on Market Street to the museum.

Option of 14.8 Miles

From the cemetery backtrack downhill on Stearns Road. Go left onto Highway 6, which leads to Main Street and downtown Chehalis.

DIRECTIONS
FOR
THE RIDE

0.0 Lewis County Historical Museum (599 NW Front Street). Left onto West Street.

0.1 Cross first set of RR tracks.

0.2 Left to unmarked State Street before the second set of RR tracks.

0.4 Right onto Prindle Street.

0.5 Angle right onto St. Helens Avenue.

0.7 Right onto Pennsylvania Avenue. Historic District.

0.9 Left rejoining West Street.

1.1 Pass Westside Park. Cross I–5 and Louisiana Avenue.

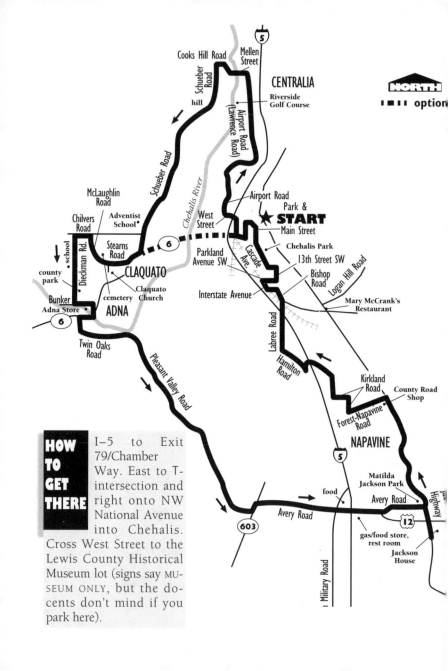

NORTH
∎ ▪ ▪ ▪ option

CENTRALIA

Cooks Hill Road
Mellen Street
Schueber Road
hill
Riverside Golf Course
Schueber Road
Airport Road (Lawrence Road)
Chehalis River

McLaughlin Road
Adventist School
Chilvers Road
Airport Road
West Street
Park & **START**
Main Street
Chehalis Park

Stearns Road
6
Parkland Avenue SW
Cascade Ave.
13th Street SW
Bishop Road
Logan Hill Road

Dieckman Rd.
school
CLAQUATO
cemetery Claquato Church
Interstate Avenue
Mary McCrank's Restaurant

county park
Bunker
Adna Store
ADNA
6
Labree Road

Twin Oaks Road
Hamilton Road
Kirkland Road
County Road Shop

Pleasant Valley Road
Forest-Napavine Road

NAPAVINE
5

Matilda Jackson Park
Avery Road

food
Avery Road
603
12

gas/food store, rest room
Jackson House

Military Road

HOW TO GET THERE I–5 to Exit 79/Chamber Way. East to T-intersection and right onto NW National Avenue into Chehalis. Cross West Street to the Lewis County Historical Museum lot (signs say MUSEUM ONLY, but the docents don't mind if you park here).

1.4 West Street curves right and left, becoming St. Helens Avenue. Veer right onto Lawrence Road/Airport Road. Riverside Golf Course.

5.1 Veer right onto Cooks Hill Road. Providence Hospital.

5.4 Left onto Schueber Road. Uphill.

9.3 Pass the Lewis County Adventist School.

10.4 Right onto Route 6 (Ocean Beach Highway) at the T-intersection. Left for option (see below), but first visit Claquato Church.

10.5 Right onto Brockway Road and quick left onto Stearns Road. Historic Marker. Uphill.

10.9 Left onto Waters Street. Claquato Church.

11.0 Backtrack. Left onto Stearns Road. Pioneer Cemetery. (Right for 14.8-mile route, see option below).

12.0 Right onto McLaughlin Road. Cedar mill.

12.9 Left onto Chilvers Road. Up and down hill.

14.0 Left onto Dieckman Road. Adna and Black Memorial County Park.

14.8 Left onto Bunker Road.

15.2 Curve right after the Adna Store onto Highway 6. Cross Chehalis River.

15.5 Left onto Twin Oaks Road.

17.0 Right onto Pleasant Valley Road.

25.0 Left at T-intersection onto Highway 603.

25.6 Right onto Avery Road.

28.5 Cross I–5. Heavy traffic. Use shoulder.

29.0 Left onto Avery Road as Route 12 veers right.

30.2 Right at T-intersection onto Jackson Highway.

30.4 Jackson House. Backtrack to T-intersection and straight.

33.2 Matilda Jackson Park on left.

35.6 Left onto Forest-Napavine Road. Lewis County Road Shop.

36.8 Right onto Kirkland Road.

38.8 Left under I–5. Quick right onto Hamilton Road South.

40.8 Right onto Labree Road, recrossing under I–5. Railroad tracks.

41.2 Left at first stop sign, onto unmarked Bishop Road. (Right 1.0 mile to Mary McCrank's restaurant.)

42.5 Left onto Interstate Avenue. Enter Chehalis city limits.

42.7 Right onto Parkland Road (curves left into 13th Street).

42.8 Cross RR tracks. Chehalis Recreation Park.

43.0 Left at park's end onto unmarked William Avenue.

43.8 Curve right onto Cascade Avenue.

44.6 Right onto Main Street. Routes join here.

44.8 Left onto Market Street.

45.0 Lewis County Historical Museum starting point.

Option for 14.8-Mile Ride

11.0 Right onto Stearns Road from Claquato Church.

11.5 Right onto Brockway Road.

11.6 Left onto Highway 6/Ocean Beach Highway. Good shoulder.

14.0 Cross the Chehalis River, I–5, and RR tracks.

14.3 Highway 6 becomes Main Street.

14.5 Left onto Market Street.

14.8 Lewis County Historical Museum on Front Street.

Cowlitz County: Woodland
Covered Bridge and Cedar Creek Grist Mill

Distance & Rating:	18.9 or 24.7 miles; hills: moderate to challenging
Surface & Traffic:	Paved roads, short gravel stretch; Mountain bike best; moderate to low traffic
Highlights:	Covered bridge, Cedar Creek Grist Mill
Eats:	Oak Tree Restaurant
Etc.:	Woodland Info Center (360) 255–9552, Mount St. Helens info (360) 750–3900, Grist Mill (360) 225–5832, Chamber of Commerce (360) 423–1211

For a romantic jaunt to the past, cycle up the Lewis River Valley to the Cedar Creek Grist Mill. During its Saturday and Sunday openings, visitors watch the grain processing of pioneer days and take home a bit of cornmeal or whole-wheat flour. No charge, but the mill appreciates donations.

Adjacent to Clark County's rebuilt covered bridge, the mill perches on a high bank of Cedar Creek's canyon. Its reconstructed 650-foot flume diverts creek water to an interior turbine wheel that powers the millstone. The clean water, known as "tailrace," returns to the creek. Here, where town folk once gathered while their grain was milled, you can picnic and take photos. You might choose to walk up the steep gravel lane to the Spurrel Road decision point.

The optional country lane loop wanders up and down along forested ravines and high-plateau Christmas tree and dairy farms first settled by Finnish immigrants. Lacking a rail link for quick milk transport, the settlers made high-quality cheese that would keep over long periods. Here cows graze lazily on verdant fields. In forests tree limbs draped in chartreuse moss shade bountiful ferns and trillium. The foothills, Mount St. Helens, and clear-cuts rise above the powerful, broad Lewis River. Tinged muddy brown, it reflects the mountain runoff of volcanic soil.

From Woodland pick up Route 503 and *drive* east to Mount St. Helens; cycling is risky on this narrow, highly traveled road. Get directions in Woodland for the viewpoints and four visitor centers. If you overnight at the Lewis River Inn, eat at the fine Oak Tree Restaurant.

DIRECTIONS
FOR
THE RIDE

0.0 Cross bridge.

0.4 Left onto NW Hayes Road (becomes NE Hayes). Wide shoulder.

4.0 Cemetery. Shoulder ends. Uphill.

6.2 Veer right at Y-intersection; becomes NE Cedar Creek Road. Uphill.

8.8 Left onto NE Grist Mill Road/Cedar Creek Fishway; gravel and dirt, downhill.

9.1 Covered bridge and grist mill. Steep gravel grade.

9.6 Left at T-intersection with Spurrel Road. Right for longer loop—see option.

10.4 Veer left onto NE Etna Road.

11.4 Cross Cedar Creek; uphill.

12.6 Pass Cedar Creek Road. Etna becomes NE Hayes Road.

18.5 Right onto North Fork Lewis River Bridge.

18.9 Return to parking lot.

Optional Longer Loop

0.0 Right onto Spurrel Road at 9.6-mile point. Hills.

2.1 Left onto NE Pup Creek Road at T-intersection.

2.8 Left onto NE Etna Road; Grinnell Road and Green Mountain School to the right.

5.8 Straight onto NE Etna Road at Spurrel Road, joining the shorter loop.

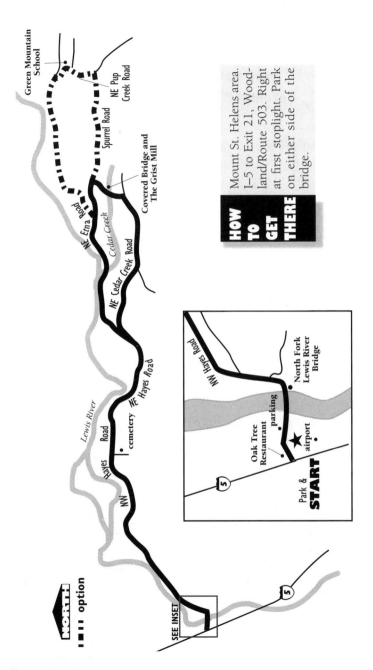

NORTH

- - - option

HOW TO GET THERE

Mount St. Helens area. I-5 to Exit 21, Woodland/Route 503. Right at first stoplight. Park on either side of the bridge.

Green Mountain School

NE Pup Creek Road

Spurrel Road

Covered Bridge and The Grist Mill

NE Etna Road

Cedar Creek

NE Cedar Creek Road

NE Hayes Road

Lewis River

Hayes Road

cemetery

NW

SEE INSET

NW Hayes Road

Oak Tree Restaurant

parking

North Fork Lewis River Bridge

airport

Park & START

Cowlitz County: Woodland
Columbia River Delta

Distance & Rating:	17.4 miles; flat, easy
Surface & Traffic:	Paved roads; mountain bike for optional dirt-bike trails; light traffic
Highlights:	Holland Bulb Farm, Lewis–Columbia Rivers merge, Hulda Klager Lilac Gardens
Link to:	Covered Bridge and Cedar Creek Grist Mill, Ride 46
Eats:	See Ride 46

Mother Nature designed floodplains to accommodate a river's high water during heavy rains and mountain runoffs. "Reclaiming" those wetlands for farming and housing requires a system of dikes (levees) and pumping stations like those invented by the Dutch. Circling this delta on dikes protecting it from the confluence of the Columbia and Lewis Rivers clarifies what "reclaiming" means. See what you think as you glide lazily along this flat delta.

Ride this route seperately or combined with the Covered Bridge-Grist Mill route. Sprawling fields of tulips and produce share the wide open space with wetland wildlife and a motley assortment of riverbank shacks, trailer homes, and migrant-labor housing. And then there are the pulp-mill plumes across the Columbia. Nevertheless, it's pleasant cycling. Flocks of waterfowl and shorebirds nibble in lush marshes brimming with alder and cottonwood trees, dogwood, berries, and grasses. Fishermen set up RVs and cook over fires while praying for salmon. Farmed berries proliferate on staked vines between pastures. April brings colorful tulip displays at the

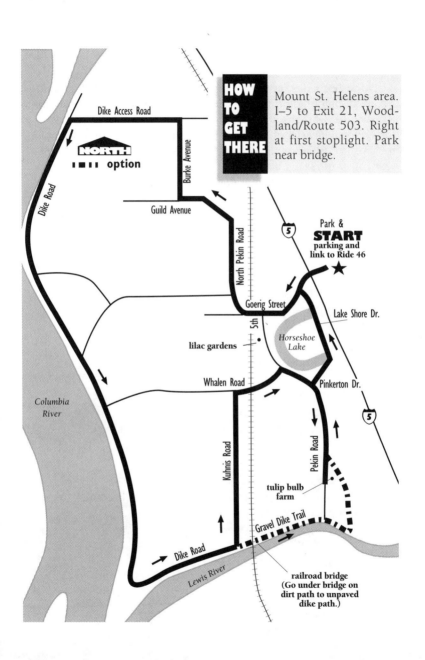

Dike Access Road

Burke Avenue

NORTH
▬▬▬ option

Dike Road

Guild Avenue

North Pekin Road

HOW TO GET THERE
Mount St. Helens area. I–5 to Exit 21, Woodland/Route 503. Right at first stoplight. Park near bridge.

5

Park & **START**
parking and link to Ride 46

Goerig Street

Lake Shore Dr.

5th

lilac gardens

Horseshoe Lake

Whalen Road

Pinkerton Dr.

Columbia River

Kuhnis Road

Pekin Road

5

tulip bulb farm

Gravel Dike Trail

Dike Road

Lewis River

railroad bridge
(Go under bridge on dirt path to unpaved dike path.)

Holland Bulb Farm on S Pekin Road—reached from Whalen Road or the dirt-bike path.

Horseshoe Lake Park offers picnicking and swimming, but amid a convention of motor homes. For a quieter moment visit the Hulda Klager Lilac Gardens at a charming Victorian farmhouse listed on the National Register of Historic Places. Klager, reading during an illness, picked up horticulture tips. Her new interest grew into a fifty-year career of raising lilacs and producing internationally renowned strains. There's no charge, but donations are accepted.

One warning: There's no shade on this ride—use sunscreen in sunny weather.

DIRECTIONS
FOR
THE RIDE

0.0 Cross under I–5 on Route 503; becomes Goerig Street and veers right.
1.0 Right onto N Pekin Road.
2.0 Left onto Guild Avenue.
2.6 Right onto Burke Avenue.
3.3 Left onto Dike Access Road.
4.5 Left onto Dike Road.
11.2 Railroad bridge. Left as road turns to Kuhnis Road. Or go right under bridge for option onto dirt/gravel dike trail that exits onto Pekin Road.
12.5 Right onto Whalen Road. Cross RR tracks.
13.0 Right onto S Pekin Road to bulb farm and backtrack.
14.5 Right onto Pinkerton Drive; becomes Lake Shore Drive at Horseshoe Lake.
15.5 Left onto Goerig Street; becomes Davidson Road.
16.1 Left onto 5th to Hulda Klager Lilac Gardens. Backtrack to Goerig Street and turn right.
17.4 Cross under I–5 and return to start.

Pacific County: Long Beach Peninsula

Historic North Peninsula/Leadbetter Point Loop

Distance & Rating:	46.6 miles; flat and easy
Surface & Traffic:	Paved with bike lanes most of way; little traffic
Highlights:	Cranberry bogs, Willapa Bay, Washington State University (WSU) Research Unit, Leadbetter Point Wildlife Refuge, The Ark Restaurant, Nahcotta, Ocean Park, Oysterville, oyster processing, waterfowl, rhododendrons
Eats:	Long Beach: Dooger's Seafood & Grill, My Mom's Pies, Milton York; Park/Nahcotta: The Ark Restaurant, The Dunes; Seaview/Ilwaco: Shoalwater Inn, 42nd Street Café, Sanctuary, Bubba's Pizza
Sleeps:	Long Beach: Boreas B&B, Edgewood Inn, Land's End B&B, Scandinavian Gardens Inn; Ocean Park/Nahcotta: Moby Dick Hotel, Caswell's on the Bay, DoveShire B&B, Whalebone House B&B; Seaview/Ilwaco: China Beach Retreat, Shelbourne Inn
Etc.:	Peninsula Visitor's Bureau and Festival Info (800) 451–2542 in WA or (800) 451–2540 out of WA, www.funbeach.com

Beating this weekend bike tour would be tough. It's a getaway extravaganza with countless sidelights: hiking, birding, historic sites, kite flying, horseback riding, fishing, clamming, whale watching, beach- combing, antiquing, and festivals—just to name a few. To top it off there are gourmet food and funky B&Bs.

Flatlanders see this 25-mile sand spit as paradise. Separating Willapa Bay from the Pacific Ocean, the peninsula is a treasure trove of spectacular scenery. Roads meander through forests and along the sea, most requiring only one-gear pedaling. Bike lanes edge main roads, though in busy sections they are shared with in-line skaters and surreys. Don't limit yourself to summer; try other seasons so long as you're wrapped in warm clothing and rain gear. Lodging locations vary, so rides begin at arbitrary points. Adjust as needed.

"Beach driving," an unusual Long Beach phenomenon, arouses bitter controversy. During Long Beach's infancy a hundred years ago, stagecoaches traveled the low-tide, firm sand to meet ferries and steamships in Ilwaco. Following this never-outlawed custom, cars cruise the beach, infuriating conservationists. In 1990 the state legislature began limiting car traffic, but bicyclists are welcome. Nothing beats a low-tide, shoreline ride (mountain bike required). Check the tide tables and begin on an outgoing tide (or you'll be lugging your bike back through deep, soft sand). Reduce your tire pressure to about forty pounds and sail along the surf's edge. It's a unique high.

For this route pack walking shoes, mosquito repellent, and extra clothing for Leadbetter Point. As with the Lewis and Clark Loop (Ride 49), begin at Rutherford Field; its water tower makes it an easy find. Cycle north on Washington Street past frame cottages to a grassy, fir tree–edged acre and go right onto Pioneer Road. Stop at WSU's visitor center to garner a historical view of the cranberry business.

In 1881 San Franciscan Robert Chabot purchased this marshy acreage, noting its native cranberries. Out to make a buck, he planted cranberries from Cape Cod. White women, children, Chinese, and Native Americans harvested the crop, working long hours packing boxes with the tiny berries. After a decade Chabot closed the bogs, overcome by shipping costs, mildew, and pest attacks on the non-native vines. For twenty years the land lay fallow until its purchase by WSU, when D. J. Crowly developed pest sprays and frost- and heat-protecting overhead sprinklers. The cranberry industry was reborn. Blooms peak in June; harvesting of more than three and a half million pounds occurs in October.

Sandridge Road, on the Willapa Bay side, is flat and uncrowded. Head up it from Pioneer Road, gliding by the electric substation, scenic pasturelands, cranberry and blueberry farms, and the Ocean Spray Cooperative (parent to twenty-six of the peninsula's twenty-eight growers). In spring don't miss Clark's Rhododendron Nursery in bloom.

Dense trees and wild rhododendrons obscure the bay until Nahcotta, just past the Shoalwater Cove Gallery where Marie Powell (a bicyclist) displays her pastels and lithographs of the area. The view opens at Moby Dick Hotel B&B, a unique accommodation that was formerly a coast guard station. Fritzi and Ed Cohen, spunky Washington, D.C., natives, remodeled it using a 1940s beach motif and opened the inn in 1991. Home-cooked breakfasts, a casual living room, shelves brimming with books, a piano, and an organic garden paint an idyllic picture. Nearby, the Nahcotta Natural Food and Cafe offers tasty grub, baked goods, and an outdoor wall of history. Next door, watch the handmaking of Spartina paper at the Nahcotta Paperworks.

Willapa Bay's calm waters draw kayakers for exquisite paddling, often to trek in Long Island's Willapa National Wildlife Refuge, home to elk, bears, bald eagles, pileated woodpeckers, grouse, and otters. Hiking its 274-acre, first-growth western red cedar and hemlock groves humbles the soul. You need your own water transport (trips and rentals available) and must hike a few muddy roads alongside clattering log trucks. Bring water.

Nahcotta, namesake of Indian Chief Nahcati, was the terminus of the Ilwaco Railway narrow gauge "Clamshell," used for oyster and tourist transport. Although much of the original town burned in 1915, summer residences, many now historic landmarks, can be seen as you ride. On the 273rd Street wharf, the Willapa Bay Interpretive Center describes the bay's oystering history. Displays detail the spread of Spartina, a non-native cord grass that crowds out native eelgrass required by native creatures. Jolly Rogers and Bendixin's purvey fresh and smoked fish. Mountains of oyster shells tempt kids, but—fair warning—you'll need to chuck their smelly shoes.

Nahcotta's Ark Restaurant and Bakery, a regional favorite, purveys scrumptious herb breads, melt-in-your mouth chocolate chip cookies, chocolate-covered garlic (!), and sinful bearclaws. Owners Nanci Main and Jimella Lucas whip up gourmet food worth savoring as much as the view. With three cookbooks and well-deserved fame (James Beard was a big fan), they remain dedicated to innovative, tasty fare using seasonal, fresh, local ingredients. Offerings vary with the seasons; go for sturgeon in May and June. Don't miss the decadent bread pudding any time. The Ark closes during January.

Visiting the peninsula without experiencing the Oysterville National Historic District would be like an ice-cream sundae without the hot fudge. Settled in 1854 after Chief Nahcati shared his succulent oyster beds with R.H. Espy and I. A. Clark, Oysterville rollicked with hardworking hard drinkers. As a wealthy town, it became Pacific County's seat, only to lose its power when "kidnapped" city records and furniture surfaced in South Bend. Overharvested, the oysters waned. Tides wrought further decline, washing away shoreline, homes, and oyster beds. Yet many 1860s and 1870s graceful wood residences remain, enhanced by front porches, gingerbread scrollwork, fish-scale shingles, eaves, gables, and picket fences. The 1892 Baptist Church reveals small-town simplicity at its best. Dark, worn, wood benches and floors elicit quiet contemplation. Pick up a historical guide map at the church.

Before leaving Oysterville you might want to loop past the miniature Oysterville Fire station to the Oysterville Sea Farm. Owner Dan Driscoll, who claims the "avoid oysters in 'r' months" rule is hogwash, handpicks the succulent creatures daily. West on Pacific Avenue, the Oysterville Store stocks basics and silly signs. The cemetery headstones hint at the joys and sadnesses endured. From Pacific Street/Oysterville Road, cycle paved, bumpy Stackpole Road to Leadbetter Point/Willapa National Wildlife Refuge. Lock up at the road's end and walk to the sandy beach. Slather on insect repellent and recline against a hunk of driftwood, picnic, and birdwatch. In this salt marsh preserve's wetlands, dunes, and woods live 256 resident and migratory species. Blue herons, kingfishers, terns, black brants, diving ducks, loons, grebes, bitterns, snowy plovers, hummingbirds, woodpeckers, finches, and sandpipers abound. Hawks and eagles soar regally. If your energy is high, hike the 4-mile trail. You wanted to do a biathlon, didn't you?

Back on Oysterville Road head to the ocean, pedaling up a short steep hill. Plunge to Surfside, a community battered by gusty sea winds that scatter sand and form gnarly pines. A tough pull up 295th Street climbs over the hill to the less windy side and the south return on Vernon Avenue/Route 103.

At Pacific Pine State Park on 274th Place, escape to Ocean Park's backstreets. On Park Avenue/L Place note the historic 1883 weathered, shake Lambertson Cottage and the 1914 United Methodist Church. The town evolved from the still active Methodist Church Camp. Across it, on lushly wooded Park Avenue, a motif of enchanting log and frame homes is reminiscent of a North Woods hideaway. One austere exception, the 1895 Pilot House (260th Place) designed for Portland Judge L.B. Sterns, bears a broad open porch with white railings.

At Vernon Avenue/Route 103, you could turn right to Long Beach—if you fancy abhorrent traffic. Or, be sensible (yes, do this) and turn left to ride across the peninsula and retrace Sandridge Road. Pass the local school and "The Wreckage," a 1912 National Register house constructed from salvaged beach materials. Jog around the park to Bay Street and the Tokeland Oyster Station Mural. Once the address of note, it retains remnants of a richer time, such as the 1908 Loomis House and the 1891 Whalebone House. Both are on the Washington State Register of Historic Places. Last but not least is the elegant 1897 Victorian home of Hinrich Weigardt (a pioneer oyster farmer) that holds its original charm as the Potrimpos Art Gallery. A block off Bay Street, across from Oakie's and behind the Ramblin Rose, visit the Petite Maison Country Restaurant and Bakery.

Near Willapa Bay retrace Sandridge Road to unmarked Pioneer Road. Cross Route 103 at the Anchorage Resort, cycling quiet North Boulevard. Bolstad Street crosses Pacific Highway/Route 103 to return to Rutherford Park.

DIRECTIONS
FOR
THE RIDE

0.0 Culbertson Park/Rutherford Field. Head north on Washington Avenue North.

1.0 Right onto Pioneer Road. WSU Research Unit, gift shop, and museum.

1.8 Left onto unmarked Sandridge Road at the T-intersection. Electric substation.

3.5 Cranguyma Cranberry and Blueberry Farms.

4.1 Ocean Spray Cooperative.

5.7 Clark Rhododendron Nursery.

11.0 Nahcotta. Moby Dick Hotel, Caswell's, and Our House B&Bs, Nahcotta Cafe, Nahcotta Paperworks.

11.8 Right onto 273rd Street toward the wharf. The Ark Restaurant, Willapa Bay Interpretive Center, and oyster growers. Backtrack.

12.8 Right onto Sandridge Road. Harborview Motel.

15.4 Veer right at the Y-intersection to Oysterville National Historic District.

15.5 1892 Baptist Church. Oysterville School. Oysterville Sea Farms.

15.9 Left onto Pacific Street toward the Oysterville Store (or straight and loop right to Oysterville Sea Farms).

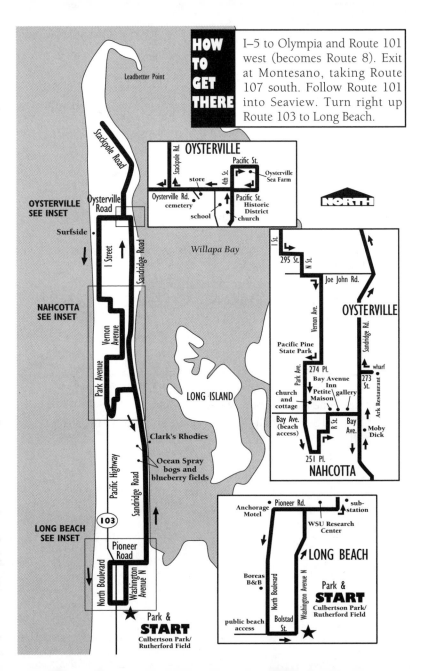

HOW TO GET THERE

I–5 to Olympia and Route 101 west (becomes Route 8). Exit at Montesano, taking Route 107 south. Follow Route 101 into Seaview. Turn right up Route 103 to Long Beach.

Leadbetter Point

Stackpole Road

OYSTERVILLE SEE INSET

Oysterville Road

Surfside

I Street

Sandridge Road

Willapa Bay

NAHCOTTA SEE INSET

Vernon Avenue

Park Avenue

LONG ISLAND

Clark's Rhodies

Ocean Spray bogs and blueberry fields

Pacific Highway

Sandridge Road

103

LONG BEACH SEE INSET

Pioneer Road

North Boulevard

Washington Avenue N

★ **Park & START**
Culbertson Park/ Rutherford Field

OYSTERVILLE

Stackpole Rd.

Pacific St.

4th St.

Oysterville Sea Farm

store

Oysterville Rd.

cemetery

school

Pacific St. Historic District church

NORTH

I St.

295 St.

N St.

Joe John Rd.

Vernon Ave.

OYSTERVILLE

Pacific Pine State Park

Sandridge Rd.

274 Pl.

wharf

Park Ave.

Bay Avenue Inn

273 St.

church and cottage

Petite Maison

gallery

Ark Restaurant

Bay Ave. (beach access)

R St.

Bay Ave.

Moby Dick

251 Pl.

NAHCOTTA

Anchorage Motel

Pioneer Rd.

sub-station

WSU Research Center

LONG BEACH

Boreas B&B

North Boulevard

Washington Avenue N

Park & START
Culbertson Park/ Rutherford Field

public beach access

Bolstad St.

★

16.5 Oysterville Cemetery. Right onto Stackpole Road.

19.3 Leadbetter Point/Willapa National Wildlife Refuge (NWR).

21.2 End of road. Lock bike and walk. Backtrack.

25.5 Right onto Oysterville Road. Up and down steep rise.

26.5 Left onto I Street in Surfside.

29.0 Left onto 295th Street. Uphill.

29.3 Right curve onto N Street.

29.4 Left onto unmarked Joe Johns Road at the T-intersection.

29.5 Right onto unmarked Vernon Avenue/Route 103.

30.2 Right onto 274th Place. Pacific Pine State Park, Ocean Park.

30.4 Left onto Park Avenue/L Place.

30.6 262nd Place. 1883 Lambertson Cottage. United Methodist Church.

30.7 Cross Bay Avenue onto Park Avenue.

31.0 1895 Pilot House. Left curve onto 251st Place.

31.3 Left onto Vernon Avenue/Route 103.

31.9 Right onto 256th Place. "The Wreckage."

27.3 Left onto R Street.

32.4 Right onto Bay Street.

32.9 1908 Loomis House, Oyster Station Mural, Petite Maison.

33.8 Whalebone House—now Bay Avenue Inn.

34.0 Z Street. 1897 Hinrich Weigardt Home/Potrimpos Art Gallery.

34.5 Right onto Sandridge Road.

42.8 Right onto unmarked Pioneer Road.

44.2 Cross Route 103 and left onto North Boulevard.

45.9 Boreas B&B. Left onto Bolstad Street. Cross Pacific Highway/ Route 103.

46.6 Return to Park.

Pacific County: Long Beach Peninsula

49

South Peninsula/Lewis and Clark's Loop

Distance & Rating:	20 miles; half flat, half moderately hilly
Surface & Traffic:	Paved; light to moderate
Highlights:	Ilwaco Boat Basin, Baker Bay, Columbia River, Historic Seaview, North Head Lighthouse, Fort Canby State Park, Cape Disappointment, Ilwaco fishing fleets, cannery
Eats, Sleeps, Etc.:	See Ride 48

When interminable rain and fog blanket the Northwest, you can feel the chilling, damp winter that Lewis and Clark endured at the mouth of the Columbia River. Savoring summer seashore weather might have elevated their depressed spirits. Who knows? Rather than returning east for accolades, they could have settled this tempestuous coast.

During that 1805 stay the explorers failed to discover the 25-mile long, 2.5-mile-wide, magical sand spit that separates Willapa Bay from the Pacific Ocean. Teeming with birds, abundant wildlife, bountiful clams and fish, and luxuriant plant life, it provided exquisitely for Native Americans, like an overzealous mother. Northwest homesteaders, eager to share the riches, founded fishing, canning, and logging communities in Ilwaco and Chinook. The military, hot to guard the Natives' usurped land on the Columbia, constructed Fort Clatsop, Fort Canby, and Fort Columbia.

In 1880 Henry Tinker developed Tinkerville (now Long Beach) and drew vacationers like a magnet. A wanderlust from Ellsworth, Maine, Tinker knew he'd have a hit when he glimpsed the flat beaches that would offer wading, fishing, clamming, and kite-flying, as well as rural solitude for the city's masses. You have to wonder at what his thoughts would be about the amusement parks, wax museums, and tourist shops.

Don't scoff at the low mileage on this route; the extras fill up time. Choose a gloriously clear day to savor the sights. Head out toward the ocean, passing vintage beach cottages that huddle near the town center. Before the Beach Access Arch (*do not* use the raised boardwalk; biking it risks a $500 fine), head down South Boulevard, where you'll pass motels, riding stables, and dunes, to enter historic Seaview. Founded in 1881, Seaview catered to Oregonians who arrived at Ilwaco via Columbia River steamers and to Seaview by the Clamshell Railroad. Local hotels, such as the historic Shelburne Inn (home of the excellent Shoalwater Restaurant), offered a resort array of parties and trips.

Well-heeled vacationers resided in charming, palatial, gingerbread- trimmed Victorian homes. Loving restorations of fish-scale shingled cottages slumber in shaded yards. Wraparound porches beckon, eliciting images of turn-of-the-century lazy, carefree summers of swimming, crabbing, razor clamming, and fishing. Soak up the architecture and atmosphere.

Near the Seaview Beach Access, the turn-of-the-century Hewitt House is representative of upscale summer homes and gardens. Across the street a rambling red structure marked "office" houses the historic Sou'wester Lodge, built by Senator Winslow-Corbett in 1892. Now an overnight facility, it hosts Fireside Evenings, workshops, and cultural events. Note the historic mural on a planted mobile home, the Heritage House B&B, and several Victorian homes. Farther south on K Street delightful, colorful cottages seem like part of a movie set. At Holman Road/30th Street, Seaview fades away as you traverse and climb forested Willows Road.

Catching your breath at the top, head toward the ocean. Purple bull thistle and gnarly trees edge the road as you climb to a panoramic ocean and marsh viewpoint. Drifting downhill, peruse old clear-cuts before struggling up to the North Head Beach Lighthouse

Road. Take binoculars—from the promontory you might catch sight of migrating whales (best chance is March to May or December to January). Lock your bike in the parking area or ride the gravel, wild rose–surrounded trail to the 1898 lighthouse. Nonstop views of the ocean, rocky cliffs, soaring birds, screeching seagulls, and crashing surf mesmerize and dissolve city tensions. Makes it tough to leave. Below is Beard's Hollow, a surf-fishing hot spot.

Backtrack and follow Fort Canby and Lewis and Clark Interpretive Center signs for 1 mile on Robert Gray Drive. Coast down to the fort, named after General Canby, an officer killed in the Modoc Indian Wars. A grocery store and rest rooms sit at the base. Request a hiking trail guide at the guard station.

Cruise out to the North Jetty on a smooth road that slices flat, shoreline, scrub land. Pass Waikiki Beach's gorgeous, protected cove (what a Northwest dreamer must have named this!). At the road's end lock up and wade the soft sand to the jetty wall, a popular fishing and picnicking spot. Scanning the coastal cliffs, you'll see the Cape Disappointment Lighthouse that guarded the Columbia River's entrance from 1862 until World War II. Returning to Fort Canby's entrance, climb to the Lewis and Clark Interpretive Center. Ride or walk up the dirt path to the old Coast Guard gun emplacements. The pictorial center re-creates the 8,000-mile (for which Congress allocated $2,500), two-year expedition that ended in this glorious ocean view (though it probably rained). Guided by Sacajeweah, the expedition arrived in 1805 and set up camp across the Columbia River at what is now Fort Stevens State Park. The restoration is definitely worth the trip (by car). During the Civil War these companion forts flanked the river, protecting its 4-mile opening.

From the Interpretive Center walk 0.75 mile to Cape Disappointment Lighthouse or cycle 1.3 miles from the parking lot. Named in 1788 by Captain Meares, the cape pays homage to his unsuccessful search for the Northwest Passage. Today the lighthouse provides a beacon above the treacherous, ship-eating river mouth and frequent impenetrable fog. Its Coast Guard Motor Lifeboat Station and training school are the West Coast's busiest. Nevertheless, nearly 2,000 vessels have been wrecked, stranded, or sunk here in the "Graveyard of the Pacific." Buoy 10, the salmon-season fishing marker, floats below.

From Fort Canby's entrance backtrack uphill to the first intersection. Head right onto unmarked Robert Gray Drive, a forested, cliffside road perched high above scenic Baker Bay. From Point Adams Fish Packing Company, view the Port of Ilwaco. Here, the road descends, surrounded by abundant berries, thistles, and wild roses, to a fenced boat-repair yard and right onto unmarked Eagle Street and Ilwaco.

At England Marine Supply turn to the 300-slip fishing port, crossing the *do not* enter (for cars) barrier. Ride along the boardwalk, noting the day's catch posted on the derby shack. Wander the piers checking out such colorful boat names as *High Hopes*, *Hustler*, and *Coho Sally*. Inhale mouthwatering smoked-fish aromas at the cannery—take a few cans along. Coast by restaurants, charter boat offices, and empty storefronts, all sad signs of tough economic times.

Ilwaco was originally called Unity, marking the Civil War's end. Settled by a group evicted from the army, the town prospered around lumbering. Renamed Ilwaco in 1870, it honored the Chinook Indian Chief Elowahka Jim. An 1880 influx of Midwestern fishermen shifted the economy to fishing, canning, sportfishing, and tourism. Competing with local and Indian gillnetters, these Great Lakes settlers used a permanent net and piling system that resulted in the 1884–1910 Gill Net Wars.

The 1974 Boldt decision severely cramped the fishing industry by reinstating Indian rights and severely limiting the non-Indian catch. Nevertheless, charter and commercial fishing for salmon, tuna, and sturgeon remains as Ilwaco's economic base. Ocean fishing requires crossing the rough bar, but the calm river fishing can easily hook you if you reel in a monster sturgeon. Try a trip; you'll love it, despite the pre-sunrise departures and nausea. You'll then understand Alfred Lord Tennyson's "Crossing the Bar." Sticking to the saddle for now, exit the boardwalk's end to Elizabeth Street.

On Spruce Street vintage gingerbread homes built by early fishermen display widow's walks. A block up Williams Avenue, in an old church, is the funky Inn at Illwaco B&B and its theater. In the business district a railroad mural depicts the Clamshell Railroad. Turning right onto North Route 101, note a salmon-seiner mural and pass the Ocean Beach Hospital. Veer right at the Y-intersection past a war memorial and lily-padded Black Lake to unmarked, less-traveled Sandridge Road, passing Cran-Mac Cranberry Farm's extensive bogs. Summer's yellow berries ripen to autumn's dark reds in readiness for Turkey Day.

A left onto 10th Street and a right onto Washington Street South deliver you to the start. Wander around Long Beach; grab a delicious espresso and snack at Pastimes, a cottage shop strewn with newspapers and games, comfy chairs, and old-fashioned charm (except for some of the help). For yet another tasty option, detour right on Pacific 0.5 mile to My Mom's Pie Kitchen. Delicious, flaky-crust fruit pie (be forewarned; split one piece) and coffee won't disappoint. Decisions, decisions.

In town peruse the Book Vendor, buy a kite, sample Milton York's sweets, explore the gift shops and museum, and steer clear of the amusements.

DIRECTIONS
FOR
THE RIDE

0.0 Begin at Culbertson Park/Rutherford Field. Left onto Bolstad Street.
0.2 Cross Pacific Highway/Route 103.
0.3 Left to South Boulevard, before arch.
0.7 South Boulevard becomes K Street.
0.8 Right onto 38th Street at the T-intersection and quick left onto Jade Place.
    Seaview Beach Access, Hewitt House, and Sou'wester Lodge.
0.9 Left curve. Heritage House B&B.
1.0 Right onto unmarked K Street.
1.3 Right onto Holman Road/30th Street at the T-intersection.
1.4 Left onto Willows Road.
2.8 Uphill. Right onto unmarked North Head Road at the T-intersection.
3.6 Crest. Panoramic viewpoint.

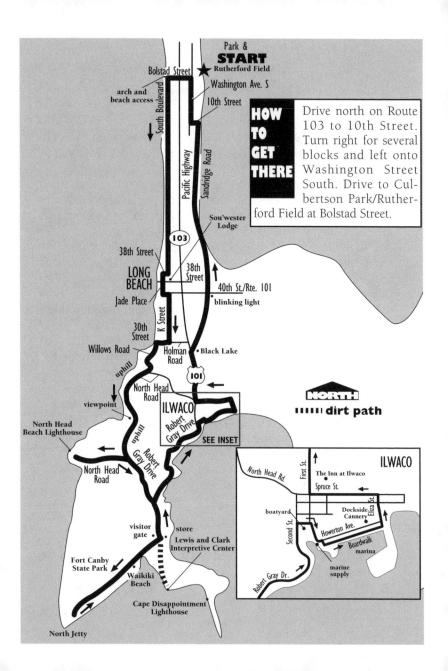

Park &
START
Rutherford Field

Bolstad Street
Washington Ave. S
arch and
beach access
10th Street

South Boulevard
Pacific Highway
Sandridge Road

HOW TO GET THERE

Drive north on Route 103 to 10th Street. Turn right for several blocks and left onto Washington Street South. Drive to Culbertson Park/Rutherford Field at Bolstad Street.

Sou'wester Lodge

103

38th Street

LONG BEACH

38th Street

40th St./Rte. 101
• blinking light

Jade Place

30th Street

K Street

Willows Road

uphill

viewpoint

North Head Beach Lighthouse

uphill

North Head Road

Holman Road

• Black Lake

101

North Head Road

ILWACO

Robert Gray Drive

SEE INSET

NORTH
dirt path

Robert Gray Drive

visitor gate •

store •
Lewis and Clark Interpretive Center

Fort Canby State Park

Waikiki Beach

Cape Disappointment Lighthouse

North Jetty

ILWACO

North Head Rd.
First St.
The Inn at Ilwaco
Spruce St.
Eliza St.
boatyard
Dockside Cannery
Second St.
Howerton Ave.
Boardwalk
marina
Robert Gray Dr.
marine supply

4.5	Right to the North Head Beach Lighthouse and trailhead.
5.0	Parking. Walk or ride to the lighthouse. Backtrack to the road.
5.5	Right, following Fort Canby and the Lewis and Clark Interpretive Center signs. Road becomes Robert Gray Drive.
6.5	Grocery store. Right to Fort Canby Park's North Jetty.
7.0	Waikiki Beach.
8.8	Road ends—lock your bike. Cross sand to the jetty wall. Return to Fort Canby's entrance.
10.2	Right to the Lewis and Clark Interpretive Center.
11.0	Glide down to Fort Canby's entrance. Backtrack up Robert Gray Drive.
12.2	Right to Ilwaco onto unmarked Robert Gray Drive at first intersection.
13.5	Point Adams Fish Packing Company and Port of Ilwaco view.
13.9	Right to unmarked Eagle Street after a fenced boat-repair yard.
14.0	Right in 1 block at the T-intersection onto unmarked First Street.
14.1	Left curve onto unmarked Howerton Avenue to Ilwaco's port.
14.2	Right at the first corner after England Marine Supply.
14.3	Left at the DO NOT ENTER (for cars) barrier onto boardwalk.
14.5	Cannery. Left onto Elizabeth Street at the broadwalk's end.
14.8	Left onto Spruce Street.
15.0	Williams Avenue. Inn at Ilwaco. Murals.
15.1	Right onto First Street/Route 101. Murals. Hospital.
15.5	Black Lake. Veer right onto unmarked Sandridge Road at the Y-intersection. Cran-Mac Cranberry Farm.
16.6	Cross 40th Street/Route 101 at the blinking light.
17.6	Left onto unmarked 10th Street (second street).
18.1	Right onto Washington Street South.
20.0	Return to start of ride.

Pacific County: Long Beach Peninsula
Ilwaco—Fort Columbia Loop

Distance & Rating:	19.8 miles; steep hill to Fort Columbia
Surface & Traffic:	Paved; moderate
Highlights:	Ilwaco fishing marina, Fort Columbia, wetlands
Eats:	The Sanctuary

Early in the 1900s fishing for salmon was akin to striking gold. At the Columbia River's mouth, each angler caught thousands of pounds a day, giving Chinook the wealthiest population per capita in the United States. How times change as we use up resources and alter the habitat. Yet the awesome scenery and fishing fleets remain a palpable reminder of Western discovery and self-sufficiency.

Part of this ride shares Route 101 with heavy automobile use. A bike lane eases the stress, however, and the scenery makes the cycling caution worthwhile. Starting from Ilwaco's marina parking lot, the route travels Spruce Street/Business Route 101 briefly. It escapes onto little-traveled Stringtown Road, edging the Columbia River's tranquil Baker Bay, making you feel you own the place. The airport (basically mowed grass) is barely noticeable.

Turning onto Route 101 leads to the town of Chinook, named for the same Indian tribe that gives its name to the Chinook salmon. The historic village remains home to its largest employer, the Chinook Packing Company. Return for dinner at the Sanctuary Restaurant, housed in a late-1800s Methodist Church. Beneath vaulted ceilings relax in church pews wedged around tables laden with fresh fish, Swedish meatballs, and tasty desserts, served down-home style.

Restored 1890s and 1900s fishermen's homes and a false-fronted store offer glimpses of a well-heeled past. Scattered pilings emerge eerily from the river, remnants of turn-of-the-century net anchorings that trapped eighty-pound salmon. The traps were outlawed in 1935 due both to the diminishing size and numbers of salmon and because of objections from Native Americans.

Earlier, in 1895, Alfred Houtchen and fishermen similarly distressed by diminishing wild salmon founded the first state-run salmon hatchery on the Chinook River. Every local fishing family donated a day's catch to stock it. Now known as the Sea Resources Hatchery Complex, a nonprofit organization, it is on Houtchen Street.

Chinook County Park hovers along the Columbia River's bay, where blue herons feed. Near the Chinook Tunnel, Fort Columbia State Park presides at the hilltop. Now composed of an Interpretive Center, the Columbia House Museum, and a youth hostel, the land was once home to the Chinook Indians. Step back in time to the 1903 life of this coastal fort. Audiovisual displays depict Northwest exploration and trade, Chinook Indian history, and fishing practices. Tour the commander's elegantly restored home and walk up Scarborough Hill for breathtaking views. Backtrack to Chinook.

If you feel gutsy, a sidetrip south on Route 101 leads to a few interesting sites. The catch is that to reach them you must negotiate the long tunnel. Activate the flashing yellow bike sign, alerting drivers you're in the tunnel. If your heart pounds as visions of Warren Beatty in *Heaven Can Wait* flash, this might not be for you. Wear a reflective vest or neon or white clothing and use flashers. Emerging along the water, pass Fort Columbia Park on a knoll overlooking the Columbia River's mouth. In the cannery town of McGowan, adjacent to the 1904 St. Mary's Catholic Church, is another "Lewis and Clark slept here" marker. Easterners have George Washington tourist spots; Westerners have Lewis and Clark. This marks the explorers' campsite enroute to Cape Disappointment (November 1805).

Though their vista was undisturbed, your view is commandeered by the Astoria-Meglar Bridge spanning the Columbia to Astoria's cliffs, where the movie *Short Circuit* was filmed. Completed in 1966, the bridge replaced a forty-five-minute choppy ferry ride and calmed many a stomach. The $24.5-million bridge, at 4.1 miles in length, is the longest continuous-truss bridge in North America (unlike three other Washington bridges, it hasn't fallen once). Bridge critics feared its construction would burden taxpayers, but the $2.2 million collected in tolls each year has proved them wrong. Bicycles cross the bridge for 50 cents, a terrific bargain for a spectacular ride—but not for the faint of heart. Just past the bridge, a viewpoint (with rest rooms) overlooks the powerful river. It's a stunning place to rest before returning up Route 101 to Chinook Valley Road, which meanders through farmland and sloughs along the Chinook River. It's a serene, flat interlude before cycling Route 101 back to Ilwaco.

DIRECTIONS
FOR
THE RIDE

0.0 Left from the Ilwaco Marina Parking Lot onto unmarked Howerton Street.

0.2 Left onto Elizabeth Street at the T-intersection.

0.5 Right onto Spruce Street/Route 101 toward Astoria. Hill.

1.9 Right onto Stringtown Road after the downhill at AIRPORT sign.

2.1 Veer right at the Y-intersection. Baker Bay. Landing strip.

4.5 Right onto Route 101. Cross inlet. Bike lane/shoulder.

6.6 Enter Chinook. Sanctuary Restaurant. Wall murals.

7.8 Pass Chinook Valley Road.

8.2 Sea Resources Hatchery Complex to left.

8.6 Chinook County Park.

9.4 Right before the tunnel to Fort Columbia State Park. Uphill! Interpretive Center, Columbia House Museum, Youth Hostel. Scarborough Hill. Views. Backtrack.

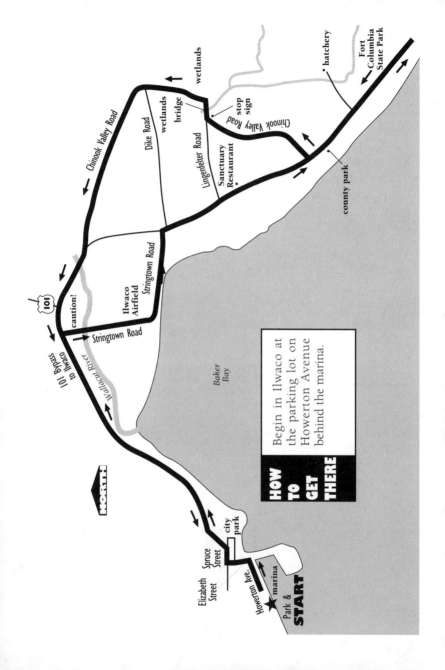

10.4 Left onto Route 101.

12.0 Right onto Chinook Valley Road.

12.8 Right at stop sign. Cross bridge.

15.5 Straight past unmarked Dike Road.

17.5 Right onto Route 101.

17.7 Veer left at intersection toward Ilwaco/Route 101. Uphill.

19.4 Enter Ilwaco as Route 101 becomes Spruce Street.

19.5 Left onto Elizabeth Street.

19.8 Right onto Howerton Avenue, returning to the parking lot.

Wahkiakum County: Grays River

Grays River Covered Bridge

Distance & Rating:	9.1 miles; easy to moderate hills
Surface & Traffic:	Paved; few cars
Highlights:	Grays River Bridge, dairy valley
Eats:	Picnic

Rolling bike tires may lack the romantic reverberations of clopping horse hooves, but gliding through a barn-like structure spanning the placid Grays River softens the most hardened city slicker. A National Historic Landmark, it is one of two covered bridges in Washington State. Its restoration bears evidence of the hardy pioneering spirit and pride required to settle and farm the Grays' soggy floodplain. Built (and rebuilt) by locals, the bridge demonstrates the power of communal effort, already practiced here at Rosburg's cooperative creamery. This joining of forces enabled the community's survival.

Serene backroads, luxuriously forested undulating hills, and fragrant hay and pungent dairy aromas greet you on this rural jaunt. Gray morning mists float above valley pastures. Well-kept farms and the meandering river evince a soggy English countryside chill. Massive aluminum silos, towering like Gothic cathedrals, anchor this settlement. Roadside pull-offs provide ringside photo spots to record a piece of history.

The pièce-de-résistance hovers above the Grays River, 158 feet long and 14 feet wide. Constructed as an open bridge in 1905, it was covered in 1910 to protect its support timbers from rot. Inside, when the skies gush, raindrops pounding against the weathered wood echo like thousands of drumbeats. Note the huge support beams, replicated from the original construction. Restored and rededicated in 1989, it's a peaceful path to the past. The original bridge cost $2,615: inflation hiked its restoration price to $350,000.

Beyond the bridge the lush valley floor and dense forests provide a haven for elk and deer herds (except in hunting season). Criss-crossing burbling streams abound, as do wildflowers. On spectacular sunny days traffic may increase, but this route remains a serene interlude of cycling. Visit the village of Grays River after the ride but avoid cycling on Highway 4 as it's busy with logging trucks.

DIRECTIONS
FOR
THE RIDE

0.0 Junction of Ocean Beach Highway 4 and Route 403 in Rosburg. Right from store, past Rosburg Community Hall.

0.3 Cross Grays River and left onto Barr/Durrah Road.

2.8 Right onto Loop Road. Historic Site.

4.2 Right onto Covered Bridge Road.

4.4 Cross the Grays River Covered Bridge. Picnic site on right.

4.7 Veer right onto Worrell Road.

7.0 Left at T-intersection onto unmarked Barr/Durrah Road.

9.0 Veer right.

9.1 Right onto Route 403. Cross Grays River.

9.5 Return to start.

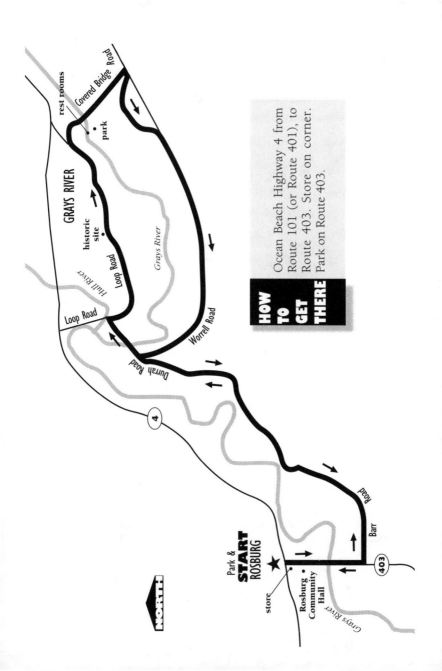

NORTH

GRAYS RIVER

Covered Bridge Road

rest rooms

park

historic site

Hull River

Loop Road

Loop Road

Grays River

Worrell Road

Durah Road

Route 4

Barr Road

Route 403

Park & START
ROSBURG

store

Rosburg Community Hall

Grays River

HOW TO GET THERE

Ocean Beach Highway 4 from Route 101 (or Route 401), to Route 403. Store on corner. Park on Route 403.

Kittitas County: Ellensburg
Wild West Weekend

Distance & Rating:	31 or 62 miles; first half: hilly and battering head-winds; second half: tailwinds and rolling hills
Surface & Traffic:	Paved; few cars except in towns
Highlights:	Kittitas and Yakima Valley, Yakima River, Yakima Canyon, Cle Elum, historic Ellensburg, Central Washington University (CWU), Labor Day Weekend rodeo
Eats:	Ellensburg: The Valley Cafe, Cafe Rose Espresso Bar, Frazzini's Pizza Place; Cle Elem: Mama Vallone's, The Cottage Cafe
Bikes:	Recycle Bicycle (509) 925–3326
Etc.:	Chamber of Commerce & Information (509) 925–3137, Rodeo Tickets (800) 637–2444, State Fair (509) 248–7160, Recreation Center (509) 962–7211

Big sky country. Beef cattle. Sagebrush. The Marlboro Man. Dry, dusty side roads. Sleek horses. Rodeos. Shimmering cottonwoods. Weathered barns and cool metal silos. Farm aromas. "Bonanza!" Deep blue skies. You get the picture—now come and see it.

Slide over the pass from western Washington and escape to Kittitas County's bucolic, rough-around-the-edges world. Rodeo is the hot tourist event: Go at least once. But for ideal bicycling visit in spring or fall to soak up the real, cowboy-college, small town ambience. Avoid summer's intense heat, or carry a lot of water.

Ellensburg, the heart of this irrigated agricultural valley, sprouted in 1870 with Splawn and Burch's trading post, jokingly called "Robber's Roost." Purchasing it two years later, along with 160 acres, enterprising John Shoudy platted a town and named it for his wife, Mary Ellen. Population exploded when the railroad came, providing transportation for local iron ore, coal, and produce and forever shifting the ranching focus to farming and dairying. Amid such prosperity disaster struck on July 4, 1889, when fire destroyed 200 homes and nine downtown blocks. True to the optimistic Western spirit, the citizens dug in, rebuilding in brick. Many of those charming structures still grace the historic downtown area.

Ellensburg boasts well-rated Central Washington University. Awarded to city fathers as a booby prize when Ellensburg lost its 1889 state capitol bid, its parklike campus, architecture, art gallery, anthropology museum, and diverse cultural events supplement your ride. On Labor Day Weekend the Ellensburg Rodeo and alcohol-free fair brings the Old West to life—or at least what has been marketed as the Old West. Cowboys, America's mythical heroes, drove cattle (even Teddy Roosevelt, Lyndon Johnson, and Ronald Reagan got into the act). They didn't spend days riding bucking broncos or throwing steers to the ground, but it's great entertainment. To get in the spirit, stay in CWU's dorms—cheap, clean, and noisy.

On to the ride. Try it alone or head out on the organized Manatash Metric Century sponsored by the Ellensburg Recreation Department. To begin, turn left from the Fire Station onto 2nd Street and left onto Main Street at Dean's Muffler, adorned with colorful, spare-part, whimsical sculpture. Pass fast-food city and turn right onto Damman Road. Immediately, you're transported to rural western America on a rich-smelling farm road. You also get whacked with your first taste of the notorious Kittitas County head winds.

Pedal under I–90, passing massive, fetid, muddy cattle feedlots and the Yakima River's Irene Rhinehart County Park. Cross the bridge and turn right up Brown Road to an open, high plateau; brown, treeless hills on the left and gray, jagged, barren Cascade Mountains on the right. Magpies dart about hay fields, while a soaring hawk hunts hidden prey.

Battering head winds rein your speed, virtually yanking you back like an elastic band. Scattered, low-sprawling ranch homes, so unlike two story, Eastern-style, porched farm homes, impart a distinctly Western flavor. White plastic tubing emerges from slender irrigation canals, like arteries pumping life to these dry, dusty plains. Tall, shimmering poplars stand like soldiers at attention, forming windbreaks and marking property lines. Long-needled scrub pines lean east, permanently bent from the relentless wind. Endless barbed-wire fences, invented in 1874, enclose enormous acreage and mooing herds. Signs of preparation for the icy, chill winds of winter are the threshed fields, plowed acres, and immense stacks of hay squeezed into open-sided bars like books on an English professor's shelves.

Marine blue, cloudless skies and a brilliant sun contrast sharply with ominous, gray cloud banks suspended over the Cascade Divide. Protected from the brutal sun by weeping willows and white-barked birch is Murphy's Country Inn B&B, a charming stuccoed and stone porched country home. Shortly, the velvet green Ellensburg Country Club and Golf Course sticks out like a sore (but green) thumb in this naturally golden plateau.

Weathered, brown-stained barns depict ranching's past—warm and friendly compared to today's sleek, metal-sided and -roofed structures. These ranches are all business, with no gentlemanly kitsch or gingerbread fluff. A single, ostentatious, red Victorian exception is copiously adorned with sparkling white gingerbread, column porches, and a *Better Homes and Gardens* yard complete with a white curlicued walking bridge across the irrigation canal. Like a plantation master's domain, it reigns over the surrounding plains. You expect to see Scarlett.

Flat terrain in this stretch would be a piece of cake were it not for the incessant wind. Cattails and flowers carpet roadside ditches. Veering right onto Killmore Road, you cross Route 90, pass Thorp Fruit and Antique Mall and Iron Horse State Park, and enter rural Thorp (its name an archaic synonym for "village"). Its sleepy streets are flanked by timeworn, shingled homes whose rickety front porches and unmanicured yards are replete with ancient stoves, ratty couches, and rusting cars. Cordwood, stacked sky-high, hints at a woodstove– warmed winter.

Next to the railroad tracks, a lumberyard dominates the town center, its heyday shown by the historic 1883 Thorp Mill. Here, Kittitas County farmers delivered grain, receiving flour and livestock feed in exchange. Powered by a waterwheel, the mill ceased production on Monday and Tuesday evenings, diverting its electric energy for housewives' laundering and children's homework lights. Thorp Mill closed in 1946.

As Killmore Road comes to a T-intersection, it marks the short and long ride dividing point. For the 31-mile loop, continue on Killmore Road 1.5 miles to Route 10, where you join the longer ride at its 44.5-mile point. For the 62-mile loop, turn left onto Tanneum Road. (To ride the second half another day, park in Thorp. Follow the basic route from Thorp, returning on Route 10 and cutting right to Killmore Road after the Yakima Canyon.) Undulating terrain rolls by—cattle graze on sloping hillsides and working-ranch homes lie tucked below rising hills. Rusting cars and broken farm machinery clutter yards. The debris is put out to pasture like the animal herds and strewn as haphazardly as a teenager's chaotic bedroom.

This is Wild West cowboy country, where ranches are named. There's Springwood Ranch and the most famous of all, Stuart Anderson, adorned with its aqua- and gold-lettered sign. At the I–90 overpass and right up Thorp Prairie Road, don't get rubbery thighs at the daunting hill ahead. An energy drink and rest will reinvigorate you for the gravity-defying climb.

Gusty winds may make you feel like a spent salmon swimming upstream. Reminiscent of a Western movie set, the dry, pale brown, windswept prairie grass and sweet-smelling sage blanket otherwise parched, tree-barren rounded hills. This arid plain gathers no moss. Circling hawks zero in on unsuspecting field mice, the only sign of life up here. Garner your second wind against the persistent external tempest. Crest after a mile, feeling as exuberant as Rocky summiting the concrete steps. Spectacular vistas, interrupted only by a Jack and the Beanstalk–sized, white erector-set structure, reward your efforts. As if a lost space ladder, the skinny structure signed FLOW goes nowhere and hides its mysterious purpose.

Now, the downhill. Keep pedaling. What wind! Below, in this open valley, a black-topped road and sparkling irrigation canals crisscross brown prairies like fluttering velvet ribbons. Scattered, abandoned, crumbling shacks highlight the prairie's harshness. A single frame home proudly dominates a small rise, its few trees forever wind bent. As Bob Dylan sang, "You dont need a weatherman to know which way the wind blows."

Pedaling adjacent to I–90, traffic noise whines intrusively. After Elk Heights (elevation 2,359 feet), soar down past bushy long-needle pines, laden with giant, reddish-brown pine cones. Immense power lines, buzzing like swarming locusts, traverse the road, shooting electricity to the hungry West. Craggy Cascade peaks float on the horizon as the road veers over I–90, where a freeway rest area is reachable via a dirt path (rest rooms on this ride are rare). Just ahead cross, for the first of many times, the wide, blue-green, swiftly moving Main Canal—deliverer of sustenance to thirsty eastern acreage. Here, like a man-made Continental Divide, we see our needy consumption fulfilled; electricity flows west, and water flows east. Defying such control is the wind, which slows you to the pace of a reluctant bachelor.

Scraggly pines on dry, dusty-smelling sandy earth diminish as the greener valley evolves. Pass Watson Cut-Off Road and hang onto your handlebars! Notorious battering wind gusts (30 or more mph) slow riders to a demoralizing crawl, a pace akin to Senate hearings. But talk about waving wheat. It looks ready to sing "Oklahoma!"

Greenish-black Cascade foothills mark the dry east's end and topographical shift to wet. Settled in this evolving terrain, Cle Elum is an "integrated neighborhood" of eastern pines and cottonwoods interspersed with western fir. On First Street, Cle Elum's main thoroughfare, Mama Vallone's Italian restaurant serves up hearty fare. Glondo's Sausage Company aromas beckon. Most cyclists descend like buzzards on the Cle Elum Bakery (First and Peoh Streets) for fatty, old-fashioned baked goods. Try the torchetti—flaky, sugar-coated breadsticks. Yum.

Toward the end of town, The Cottage Cafe, a crowded locals' favorite, smells of frying fat and dishes up everything banned from the American Heart Association list, although they do have salads. Housed in a yellow frame cottage, its noisy, 1950s smoke-filled atmosphere, augmented by knotty pine walls and silver-posted, red-topped counter stools, went the way of corsets in a recent remodel to American bland. Still no hanging ferns.

At the Y-intersection watch to veer right onto Route 903. Escape the heavy traffic by turning off in 0.3 miles onto Airport Road, looping back to Route 903 on West Masterson Road. A left and quick right lead to Route 10 East/Ellensburg at a wooded parking area and railroad tracks. Get ready for take-off—tailwinds eject you like a slingshot.

Route 10 climbs uphill along the rippling, gravel-bedded Yakima River that carved the scrub- and pine-flanked valley below.

Killmore Road (44.5 miles) is where the shorter ride joins in (or marks your right turn if doing only the second half). From here you cycle between the river and an abandoned irrigation flume for several miles. Like an oasis, the River Farm Produce stand, with crunchy apples and fresh cider (in season), materializes to quench your thirst. Shimmering aspen groves surround a river rafters' put-in and rental shop. At 50.5 miles watch on the left for McManamay Road, tranquillity away from Route 10. Dust, whipped up by wind gusts, swirls in plowed fields.

Sprawling farms reveal rich, fertile soil in plowed, furrowed fields. Cattle, grazing on distant fields and ridges, stand like Hollywood Indians ready to charge down the short, but intimidating, hill (last one) near Walking Horse Ranch. After the T-intersection with unmarked Look Road, soar off to flat farmland and Ellensburg's outskirts. Passing a cemetery at 60 miles, enter Ellensburg City Limits. Pass the City Recreation Center and Pool next to the Rodeo Fairgrounds, returning to the Fire Station. Congratulations!

Historic turn-of-the-century Ellensburg and CWU, better known as Central, are best explored on foot. For a small fee you can refresh with a swim and shower in the Recreation Center! BYOT (bring your own towel). For dinner try The Valley Cafe on 3rd Street: delicious pastas, salads, fish and Ellensburg lamb served in a relaxed, 1930s bistro complete with wood-paneled high mahogany booths.

Don't miss John Clymer's *Saturday Evening Post* covers at the downtown Clymer Museum and Gallery. Other than lamb he's Ellensburg's claim to fame.

DIRECTIONS
FOR
THE RIDE

0.0 Left from the Fire Station onto 2nd Street.
0.1 Cross Pearl Street.
0.2 Left onto Main Street at Dean's Muffler.
1.2 Right angle onto Damman Road.
1.8 Go under I–90.
2.7 Cross the bridge. Yakima River's Irene Rhinehart County Park.
3.1 Right sharp curve onto Brown Road.
3.5 Continue right on Brown Road, called Brunt Road to left, at the T-intersection.
3.8 Left onto Barnes Road.
4.4 Right onto Hansen Road at stop sign.
5.3 Left onto unmarked Thorp Road at T-intersection.
6.4 Murphy's Country Inn B&B.
6.7 Ellensburg Country Club and Golf Course.
10.0 Veer right onto Killmore Road across Route 90. Thorp Fruit and Antique Mall. Iron Horse State Park.

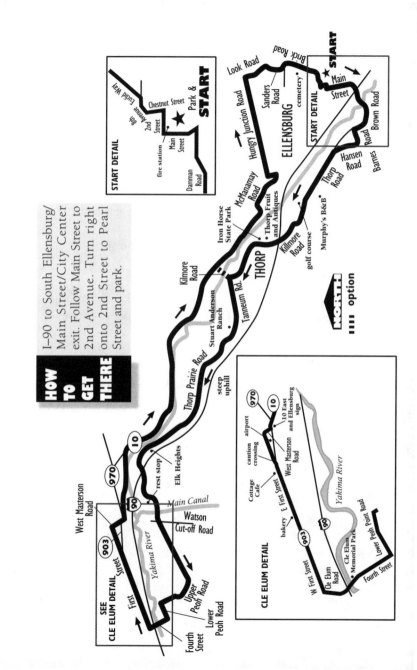

HOW TO GET THERE

I-90 to South Ellensburg/Main Street/City Center exit. Follow Main Street to 2nd Avenue. Turn right onto 2nd Street to Pearl Street and park.

START DETAIL

Euclid Way
8th Avenue
2nd Street
Chestnut Street
Park & START
fire station
Main Street
Damman Road

START DETAIL

Look Road
Brick Road
START
Sanders Road
cemetery
Main Street
Brown Road
ELLENSBURG
Hansen Road
Thorp Road
Barnes Road
Hungry Junction Road

McManamy Road
Iron Horse State Park
Thorp Fruit and Antiques
THORP
Killmore Road
golf course
Murphy's B&B
Tanneum Rd.
Kilmore Road
Stuart Anderson Ranch

Thorp Prairie Road
steep uphill
Elk Heights
rest stop
970
10
Main Canal
Watson Cut-off Road
Yakima River
West Masterson Road
903
First Street
Upper Peoh Road
Lower Peoh Road
Fourth Street
SEE CLE ELUM DETAIL

NORTH •••• option

CLE ELUM DETAIL

W First Street
903
bakery
E First Street
Cottage Cafe
caution crossing
West Masterson Road
airport
970
10
10 East and Ellensburg sign
Cle Elum Road
Cle Elum Memorial Park
Fourth Street
Lower Peoh Point Road
Yakima River

10.4 Enter Thorp.

12.3 Left onto Tanneum Road at T-intersection. (For 31-mile loop option, continue straight on Killmore.)

14.0 Stuart Anderson Ranch.

15.0 Right onto Thorp Prairie Road at the I–90 overpass.

16.0 Crest uphill.

18.6 Pass a freeway exchange.

20.0 Cross Elk Heights (elevation 2359).

23.0 Cross I–90. Towering pines.

23.6 Freeway rest area on right, reachable by a dirt path.

24.0 Cross Main Canal.

24.2 Pass Watson Cut-Off Road. Battering wind gusts.

27.0 Views of Cascade foothills. Cle Elum.

28.4 Right curve onto Upper Peoh Road.

29.3 Left to Lower Peoh Road at stop sign and T-intersection.

30.3 Right curve onto Cle Elum Road/Fourth Street (Moore House B&B sign).

30.5 Cle Elum Memorial Park. Cross the Yakima River. Go under I–90.

30.8 Veer right onto First Street. Cle Elum. Cle Elum Bakery. First Street and Route 903 join.

32.0 The Cottage Cafe.

32.1 Veer right onto Route 903 at the Y-intersection.

32.3 Left to Airport Road. Caution!

33.0 Airport.

34.0 Veer right onto West Masterson Road.

34.5 Left onto Route 903. Quick right onto Route 10 East/Ellensberg at Y-intersection. Tailwinds.

36.0 Yakima River.

44.5 Pass Killmore Road. Shorter ride junction (right if doing only the second half).

48.0 River rafters' put-in and rental shop.

50.5 Veer left onto McManamay Road.

52.0 Left onto unmarked busy road at T-intersection. Quick right onto Hungry Junction Road.

54.5 Cross Reecer Road.

56.0 Pass Walking Horse Ranch.

57.0 Right onto unmarked Look Road at the T-intersection.

58.8 Left onto unmarked Sanders Road at the T-intersection and Ellensburg.

59.5 Right curve as Sanders Road becomes Brick Road. Cemetery.

60.0 Ellensburg City Limits.

60.5 Right onto 10th Avenue/Euclid Way at the T-intersection.

60.7 Left curve as street becomes 8th Avenue.

60.9 Left onto Chestnut Street, crossing 8th Avenue. Caution!

61.0 City Recreation Center and Pool. Rodeo Fairgrounds.

61.2 Left onto 2nd Street.

62.0 Pearl Street Fire Station. Congratulations!

Option of 31-Mile Loop

12.3 Continue straight on Killmore Road.

13.8 Right onto Route 10. Joins longer route's end at 44.5 miles.

Kittitas County: Yakima
Donald and Zillah Orchard and Wine Loop

Distance & Rating:	39 miles; half flat, half easy hills
Surface & Traffic:	Paved; few cars in rural areas, heavier in towns
Highlights:	Donald's Fruit & Mercantile, Mexican bakery, hop barns, Yakama Nation Cultural Heritage Center, Toppenish murals, El Ranchito, Covey Run and various wineries
Eats:	Donald's Fruit & Mercantile, El Ranchito, Deli de Pasta, Grant's Pub/Micro Brewery, Gasparetti's, Santiago's, The Greystone
Etc.:	Yakima Chamber of Commerce (509) 248–2021, Visitors Bureau (509) 575–3010 (Yakima bike map available free), Wine Growers Association (509) 786–1000, Toppenish Chamber of Commerce (509) 865–3262 (map of 52 murals), www.yakima.net

Wine. Visions of stomping grapes. Intriguing dinner conversations. Skid-row denizens slurping brown-bagged jug wine. Medicinal values. Religious use. Wine plays big since time immemorial. Bacchus (Dionysus), the god of wine, grasped its virtues and dangers, vacillating between being man's benefactor and man's destroyer. Uplifting his worshippers, he imparted gaiety and power, exultantly revealing their hidden strengths but then slipping them into a drunkenness that destroyed their spirited confidence and inspiration. Yet hope springs eternal, and we sample again. No wonder wine tasting is big business.

Winery touring doesn't require an educated nose, palate, or verbiage, but learning does enhance the experience. Make this a "Wine 101" weekend. Tour, question, and taste (tasting and spitting into counter containers is acceptable). Once you inhale wine's earthy, robust, fermented aroma, you're hooked. You know it instantly, like a whiff of broiling steak. Suddenly you're spewing the words: acidity, tannin, aroma, bouquet, clarity, vertical tasting, oaky, must.

"A wine before its time" characterizes Washington's wine business; young in age and amenities compared to sun god California but spirited and growing. Though the valley is more Wild West than California's stylish wine country, B&Bs are opening and restaurants maturing. Long, warm days and cool nights enhance varietal grape flavor, balancing natural sugars and acids. Aged in traditional oak barrels, some maturing premium reds have won accolades and awards. Tastes foretell further success. Besides, the price is right.

Beer drinkers will appreciate the valley's bounty, too. Central Washington's hops comprise three-fourths of the U.S. crop (one-fifth of world production) supplied to beer makers. Ideal conditions lengthen vines 25 feet per season. Most beer production occurs elsewhere, but microbreweries are cropping up. World-class Grant's Ale remains a Yakima favorite.

Beer and wine are not all the valley produces. Delectable fruit garners its own fame: Delicious apples, pears, cherries, berries, peaches, apricots, melons, mint, pumpkins, and other vegetables. The agricultural industry requires tremendous seasonal help, drawing Mexican workers (a third of the valley's population). It wasn't always so. Beginning around 1915 Japanese contract laborers tended orchards, leased land, and made production skyrocket. But the 1921 and 1923 Alien Land acts prohibited leasing, forcing many Japanese to "act" as hired hands, using verbal agreements with white owners. A second blow followed Pearl Harbor, when the 1,200 Yakima

Valley Japanese were interned in Wyoming. Few returned. Offensive NO JAPS WANTED signs greeted those that tried. During World War II desperate valley farmers began the Bracero Program. Allowing Mexican laborers temporary U.S. entry during harvest season begat the migrant-worker phenomenon and their ethnic influence in Yakima.

In the valley arid plateaus, slashed by blacktop roads and life-sustaining irrigation canals, give way to lush green orchards, fertile vineyards, and aromatic wineries. Crisp red apples dangle like Christmas ornaments, wetting your appetite for sugary autumn pies, cinnamon-baked brown betty, and an old-fashioned apple squeeze. In September, bulging fragrant grape clusters cling to trellised vines. Tangled hop vines with maturing cones snake along arbor-like, wire-strung posts. Crush Weekend festivals at September's end occur during perfect bicycling weather, but late fall cycling offers cool, sunny weather and uncrowded tastings. Spend a weekend. In years ahead when you drag mature Washington wine from your cellar, you can say "I was there when . . ."

Hit the road from Donald's Fruit and Mercantile, crossing I–82 and the meandering, forested Yakima River tributaries. Emerge to sun-drenched fields and orchards, in view of massive Mount Adams. Long-tailed black-and-white magpies, the valley's nemesis, dart about in a feeding frenzy. Growers install automatic shot and predator bird call devices to ward off these birds, who can pick a tree clean in ten minutes.

The town of Wapato (a native term for starchy root plants and potatoes), serves as the valley's major fruit-packing community. A half-block off the route, bicyclists zero in like heat-seeking missiles to Barajas Mexican Bakery & Restaurant (closed Saturday). Grab an orange plastic tray and tongs, plucking out puffy sugary pastries and mysterious fat, frosted cookies from behind sliding-glass and wood-doored cabinets.

After traversing Wapato's shopping area, you'll see the highway road is flanked by down-at-the-heels farms and produce stands. Escape to quieter, flat Ashue Road at the Krueger Pepper Farm sign.

Hampering enjoyment are barking attack dogs. Halt and walk (they do turn tail when you freeze). These sentries are just doing their job.

Panoramic vistas reveal the barren, brown Rattlesnake Hills, undulating Toppenish Ridge, Mount Adams, and expansive valleys—so unlike wet, fecund Western Washington. Rusty smudge pots stand like infantry anxious to defend against killing frosts. Down a gravel lane off Branch Road, Krueger's grows peppers of every kind.

On South Wapato Road off-duty crop dusters, fighters of the insect front, rest. Hop fields surround weathered, abandoned hop barns topped with distinctive sentry-like roof cubicles. From the late 1800s to the mid-1900s, hop cones were spread on burlap in second-story "kilns," drying above first-floor wood-stove heat. Women, children, and Native Americans picked hops, the others joining in on weekends for gatherings and dances. Today gas-burnered aluminum structures replace the venerable wood hop barns, and automatic pickers abound. Fortunately, old buildings remain as proud reminders of a less mechanized, more community-spirited past.

On Oldenway Road orchards bask in the warm sun. A stark, silvery metal barn dominates the box-like migrant-worker shacks—plagued by peeling paint, broken steps, cracked or missing windows, and junkyard cars—the scene is a 1990s version of *Grapes of Wrath*. Use caution turning onto Fort Road/Route 220—traffic picks up.

Don't miss the exceptional Yakama Nation Cultural Heritage Center. Luckily for the Yakamas and us cyclists, Nipo Strongheart acted in motion pictures for forty years. Feeling a great tribal and historical sense, he amassed the largest American collection of Indian artifacts. His generous will made this evocative museum possible.

Yakama, a Native American word used by distant tribes to describe local inhabitants, has no clear interpretation. Loosely, it means a growing or expanding family. The museum, with its distinctive roof line replicating a tule lodge, teaches "The Challenge of Spilyay"—a legendary trickster disguised as a coyote. He taught others to survive by living with nature. Embracing his advice, the fourteen tribes of the Confederated Yakama Nation (grouped at the 1855 treaty signing) flourished. Foragers, they believed that land is loaned in trust for future generations. "Take only what is necessary, leave no remains to upset other creatures, refuse to lay a green bough on the campfire." Now relegated to one and a half million acres of reservation land, the Yakama Nation bases its economy on natural resources, furniture making, agriculture, and the museum.

Inside the museum recordings of chirping birds and trickling water enhance expansive dioramas of food gathering, fishing rights, tribal beliefs, and housing. Tule shelters and mats, sweathouses, "anutash" winter housing, clothing, and beadwork provide vivid native life insights.

After riding through strip-mall Toppenish, head to Historic Toppenish, where high-quality artists' murals grace false-fronted buildings. The community's pride and the first of a proposed set of thirty, the murals depict freight and stage lines, clearing the land, Haller's Battle, and local history. Nearby, railroad tracks pass an abandoned train station. Situated halfway between Yakama and Pasco, Toppenish swarmed with eastward-bound cattle and horses in the late 1800s. The adjacent run-down neighborhood ends abruptly at a T-intersection and farmland, beyond which Myers Road leads to the Yakima River's wetlands.

Across Route 82 is Zillah Oakes Winery and a bike-lane hill to Zillah. Namesake of the Northern Pacific Railroad president's daughter, Zillah edges the former railroad holding yard on First Street. Colorful storefronts, in the tourist mode, face deteriorating fruit shipping plants. Veer right uphill to a unique lunch at El Ranchito, a tortilla factory, restaurant, bakery, gift and food shop. This gregarious, vibrant, folksy gathering spot serves up mouth-watering enchiladas, soups, and tortillas to a boisterous Spanish-speaking crowd. Stopping here is like walking into a foreign country. Lumber up to the counter, order, get a number, and wait. *Números* are called in Spanish and English. A recent remodel slightly Americanized El

Ranchito, but there's still a dazzling array of Mexican crafts that entice you to part with *dinero*.

Leaving El Ranchito, you pass a freeway entrance Lucy Road soars downhill, a prelude to the afternoon rollers. Lush, trimmed orchards and velvet pastures, fed by the Roza Canal, feel luxuriant in contrast with the browner morning. Looming on the horizon are the brown, sage-covered Rattlesnake Hills, snowy Mount Adams, and a sliver of Mount Rainier. On Highland Drive, designated "Fruit Loop Road," grapes and fruit proliferate, starting with Portteus Vineyards.

Though Vintage Road is hilly and partially gravel, don't miss Covey Run Vintners. Angled orchards, cattle ranches, and vineyards carpet the valley, forming an incredible crazy quilt. Covey Run, a trendy, California-style, upscale winery, presides like a castle. The cedar deck, floating above the sloping valley, can't be beat for views—a feast for the eyes, like a dazzling Hockney painting. Inside, metal fermentation tanks, visible behind glass walls, demonstrate modern techniques, but lusty wine aromas hint at traditional taste. You won't be disappointed with the smooth reds, dry whites, and friendly staff.

Highland Drive's rolling terrain is flanked by mature, gnarled apple trees and vineyards, including Hyatt Vineyards and the lovely Bonair Winery. Don't get complacent here: Prepare for the "bloody" dogs that may require the "halt and walk" bit repeatedly. Mature orchards, dotted with ancient smudge pots and three-legged picking ladders, ramble down the sloping valley. Cresting a curving hilly mile, pass a bustling fruit-packing plant, its grounds stacked high with heavy wooden crates. Below, as Lombard Loop Road jogs left, a striking home atop a poplar-edged bluff commandeers a stunning view.

Crest the day's last, but steep, hill on Clark Drive, curving left to a T-intersection at Yakima Valley Highway and turing right to return to Donald's Fruit & Mercantile. Quench your thirst with crisp apple cider.

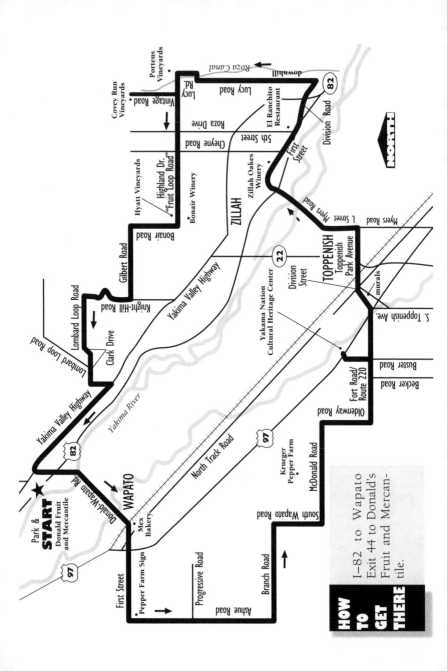

DIRECTIONS
FOR
THE RIDE

0.0 Right onto Donald-Wapato Road. Cross I–82 and the Yakima River.

2.0 Enter Wapato. Cross RR tracks. Veer right onto First Street. (Barajas Mexican Bakery straight ahead).

2.5 Cross Route 97.

4.0 Left onto Ashue Road at the Krueger Pepper Farm sign.

6.0 Cross Progressive Road.

7.0 Left to Branch Road. Ashue Grange and Purina Chow.

9.0 Right onto Wapato Road.

10.0 Left onto McDonald Road. Watch for dogs. Hops.

12.0 Right onto Oldenway Road.

13.0 Left onto Fort Road/Route 220.

14.5 Left onto Buster Road. Yakama Nation Cultural Heritage Center.

15.0 Return to Fort Road. Cross Route 97. Pass a flea market and Route 22.

16.0 Veer left onto angled Toppenish Avenue as Fort Road becomes 1st Avenue. Historic mural map. Depot.

16.3 Left at the stoplight to Division Street. Historic Toppenish murals.

16.5 Cross RR tracks, veering right onto Toppenish Avenue.

17.0 Left onto L Street at the T-intersection.

18.0 Veer right onto Myers Road.

18.5 Cross the Yakima River wetlands and Route 82.

19.0 Zillah Oakes Winery. Straight on E 1st Avenue into Zillah.

19.5 Pass Cheyne Road and 5th Avenue. Veer right uphill.

20.3 El Ranchito tortilla factory, restaurant, bakery, and gift shop.

21.3 Cross I–82 entrances and Yakima Valley Highway, veering left onto Division Road.

22.0 Left onto Lucy Road.

23.0 Right at stop sign. Cross Roza Canal bridge.

23.1 Left onto unmarked Lucy Road.

24.1 Left onto Highland Drive/"Fruit Loop Road." Porteus Vineyards.

24.7 Right onto Vintage Road to Covey Run Vintners. Backtrack.

28.0 Right onto Highland Drive. Orchards and vineyards.

29.0 Cross Roza Drive and Cheyne Road. Hyatt Vineyard.

30.5 Right onto Bonair Road. Bonair Winery to the left.

31.5 Left onto Gilbert Road and quick right onto Knight-Hill Road.

32.5 Orchards; wooden crates at packer.

33.0 Left at the T-intersection onto Lombard Loop Road.

35.0 Pass Lombard Loop Road onto Clark Drive. Uphill.

36.0 Curve left.

37.5 Right onto Yakima Valley Highway at the T-intersection.

38.7 Left onto Donald-Wapato Road. Abandoned Moxee Fruit
Plant.

39.0 Donald's Fruit and Mercantile.

Kittitas and Benton Counties:

Sunnyside/Prosser Wine Loop

Distance & Rating:	40 miles; easy (provided you only sip wine . . .)
Surface & Traffic:	Paved; light to moderate
Highlights:	Yakima River Winery (1978), one of the region's wine pioneers, vineyards, wineries, orchards, Yakima River, cheese factory, dairyland, Farmer's Market at City Park (Saturdays, June–October)
Eats:	Prosser: The Blue Goose, Chucker Cherries Store, The Wine Country Inn
Sleeps:	The Wine Country Inn B&B, Best Western Prosser Inn
Etc.:	Great Balloon Rally (509) 786–1298, September Wine and Food Fair (800) 408–1517; Sunnyside Chamber of Commerce (509) 837–5939

A simple park entrance sign stating NO HORSES IN THE PARK lends credence to Sunnyside's ranching endeavors. Livestock empires predominate now, but the area's 1880 roots stemmed from farming made feasible by Walter Granger's irrigation canal. Dug in return for a railroad land gift, the canal led to swift Sunnyside expansion. Growth was cut short, however, by the 1893 panic and terminated completely in 1898 due to failure and receivership.

New life began when three Midwestern entrepreneurs purchased the beleaguered canals and Sunnyside, creating the Christian Cooperative Colony, a city of codified values, including land deeds with forfeiture clauses precluding saloons, Sunday desecration, dancing, horse racing, gambling, and other sundry vices. Nicknamed "Holy City," it flourished by the sweat of several hundred hardworking families. The only problem was that the ill-managed canal seeped, sinking Sunnyside in mud. Salvation arrived via the railroad and the U.S. Reclamation Service, which straightened out the canal mess.

Choose a crisp, sunny fall day to embark on this ride. Starting from South Hill Park, you may feel you're in Mexico amidst vivacious, Spanish-speaking children. Heading out, catch a whiff of Cascade Estate's hearty wine aromas and grab picnic grub in Sunnyside (left off Lincoln Avenue to 6th Street and Decatur Avenue shops).

Past a honey producer, as cornfields emerge, Lincoln Avenue becomes Factory Road. At Yakima Valley Highway, pick up the bike path, gliding along to Grandview. Eventually it will run to Prosser, but only sections between Grandview and Prosser are complete. Stop at Tucker Fruit Stand and Wine Cellars for fresh fruit or juice. After crossing under I–82 onto "Wine Country Road"/Main Street, the rest is pure joy—wanderings through Grandview and into magnificent rural fields of bounty.

Grandview retains much of its commercial and residential districts of 1906, when irrigation and rail service stimulated fruit farming and cattle ranching. At prohibition's end Château St. Michelle, one of the state's earliest wineries (1941), opened. Savor wine tastes on the return trip. Traversing the industrial areas takes you past the sprawling Snokist fruit-packing plant, a huge employer of locals.

Wire-strung, wood poles provide an extensive arbor support system for hops in fields that alternate with vineyards. This is not genteel wine country. Rather, it is flat, arid, hard-edged, working-class agriculture sustained by irrigation canals and interspersed with car wreckers, cattle pastures, and migrant shacks. Nevertheless, sweet grape aromas fill the air at harvest time.

Entering Prosser, a green sign proclaims A PLEASANT PLACE WITH PLEASANT PEOPLE. Meet a few at Chucker Cherries and munch on dried and chocolate-covered cherries, blueberries, and cranberries. Delicious.

Veer left at the "Y" island onto Sherman Avenue/"Wine Country Road." A short side trip on the first street leads to the Benton County Historical Museum and the tasty Blue Goose Restaurant. A residential area, it is heavily populated by farm workers and filled with the aromas of savory Mexican food.

Hinzerling Winery sits on the edge of town, just before the railroad underpass. Orchards, vineyards, and processing plants share this sprawling valley beneath the Horse Heaven Hills. Picnic and fritter time away at Chinook Winery's lovely garden. Sample their excellent, crisp whites. Across the road earthy grape wine aromas pervade the Hogue Cellars winery, which sits amid 200 vineyard acres. Try the smooth, soul-satisfying reds and mellow whites. Next door, the huge Seneca fruit-processing plant emits sweet, fruity odors.

Though a wine center now, Prosser began in 1887 with the Hinzerling flour mill at the river's falls, once a traditional Yakama native fishing site. The gristmill served wheat farmers from the Horse Heaven and Rattlesnake hills. Various crops, fruit orchards, ice making, and the railroad enhanced Prosser's economy, which is celebrated each August at the Prosser Wine and Food Fair. Crowds arrive for extensive tastings and events; you need reservations well in advance. No one under twenty-one is admitted.

In downtown Prosser, on 6th Street, is the brick train depot and Visitor's Center plus tasty authentic Mexican cuisine. Crossing the Yakima River bridge, head left onto North River Road and down to its river view stretch. Be careful not to continue straight to Buena Vista Road.

Nestled at the river's edge, an array of herb and produce farms can be reached by gravel roads. Homesteaded by Welsh immigrants and continued by their descendants, the farms are lush and prolific.

Here, also, the Yakima River Winery (1978) opened as one of the region's wine pioneers. Old Prosser Road heads into industrial Grandview. Pointed white silos, the Yakima Valley Grape, and the brick Port of Grandview/Chamber of Commerce line the railroad tracks. Nearby, hone in on your last winery, Château St. Michelle—the Northwest's oldest and most famous (its castle-like Woodinville home is north of Seattle). Powerful, fruity aromas sweeten the air as you sip unexpected pleasures among the auto-touring tasters (typically awed at bicyclists' athletic prowess) and ubiquitous fruit flies.

After Dykstra Park, Putterbaugh Road slices downhill through prolific apple orchards. On Forsell Road the Hillvale Dairy's mammoth haystacks await their role as winter feed for the black and white milk-maker cows. Between hop fields L1 and L2, enter unmarked, smooth Midvale Road. After Murray Road prepare your nose! Ahead are the enormous, muddy, powerfully odiferous feed lots, where corralled cattle mull about like amusement park mobs. Ascend and descend through more feedlots. Hold your breath. You may rethink your meat-eating habits.

The Dairigold Dairy Fair (closed Sundays), a short trek down Alexander Road, produces award-winning Gouda. Enjoy mellow, smooth-tasting samples—plain, smoked, peppered, and double cream (only 8.5 fat grams per ounce!). Cross under I–82 to return to South Hill Park.

DIRECTIONS
FOR
THE RIDE

0.0   Left onto Midvale Avenue from South Hill Park.

0.5   Right onto Lincoln Avenue. Cascade Winery.

0.6   Optional sidetrip to shops: Veer left onto 6th Street to Decatur Avenue and return.

1.2   Pass 16th Street, where Lincoln Avenue becomes Factory Road.

2.0   Cross RR tracks, veering right onto Yakima Valley Highway and onto the parallel bike path. Path ends in Grandview and picks up near Prosser.

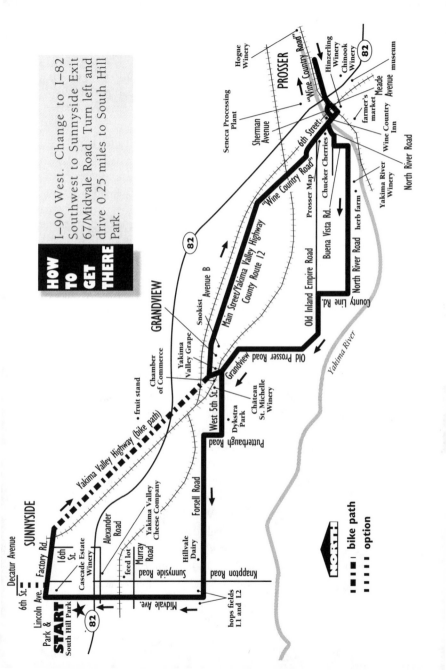

HOW TO GET THERE

I-90 West. Change to I-82 Southwest to Sunnyside Exit 67/Midvale Road. Turn left and drive 0.25 miles to South Hill Park.

NORTH

bike path
option

SUNNYSIDE

Decatur Avenue
6th St.
Lincoln Ave.
Park & START
South Hill Park
Factory Rd.
16th St.
Cascade Estate Winery
feed lot
Alexander Road
Murray Road
Yakima Valley Cheese Company
Hillvale Dairy
Sunnyside Road
Knappton Road
Midvale Ave.
hops fields L1 and L2
Forsell Road

Yakima Valley Highway (bike path) · fruit stand

GRANDVIEW

82

Avenue B
Snokist
Yakima Valley Grape
Chamber of Commerce
West 5th St.
Château St. Michelle Winery
Dykstra Park
Putterbaugh Road
Grandview
Grandview Road
Old Prosser Road
Old Inland Empire Road
County Line Rd.
North River Road
Yakima River

Main Street/Yakima Valley Highway County Route 12

"Wine Country Road"

Prosser Map
Chucker Cherries
Buena Vista Rd.
North River Road
herb farm

PROSSER

82

Hogue Winery
Hinzerling Winery
Chinook Winery
"Wine Country Road"
Seneca Processing Plant
Sherman Avenue
6th Street
farmer's market
Meade Avenue
museum
Wine Country Inn
Yakima River Winery
North River Road

2.6   Tucker Fruit Stand and Wine Cellars.

6.3   Cross under Route 82, following WINE COUNTRY road signs.

6.5   Grandview. Veer right to paved path. Go through parking lot and right onto "Wine Country Road"/Main Street.

7.4   Pass the Snokist plant.

7.7   Cross Avenue B. Main Street becomes Yakima Valley Highway/County Route 12.

13.0   Go under RR tracks to paved path on right.

14.0   Enter Prosser, edging 6th Street/"Wine Country Road."

14.2   Sign: A PLEASANT PLACE WITH PLEASANT PEOPLE.

14.5   Cross Old Inland Empire Road. Prosser map. Chucker Cherries.

14.8   Cross Yakima River Bridge and Grant Avenue (walk your bike). The Wine Country Inn B&B.

15.0   Veer left at the Y-intersection onto Sherman Avenue/"Wine Country Road." Benton County Historical Museum to right.

15.5   Hinzerling Winery.

16.0   RR underpass. Cottage Court Market and B&B.

16.7   Cross I–82 to the Chinook Winery. Seneca processing plant.

17.4   Hogue Cellars. Backtrack across I–82.

19.0   Veer left onto Meade Avenue/City Center at the Y-intersection.

19.1   Downtown. Right onto 6th Street. For farmer's market continue straight, curving left to Market Street, right to Park Avenue to City Park. Visitor's Center.

19.3   Left, remaining on 6th Street at the Y-intersection.

20.0   Cross the bridge. Quick left onto North River Road.

20.5   Follow North River Road left onto unmarked Nunn Road. (Do not go straight on Buena Vista Road).

21.6   Yakima River Winery on gravel road.

23.0   Herb and produce farms on side roads.

25.1   Right onto County Line Road at the T-intersection.

26.0   Left onto Old Inland Empire Road at the T-intersection.

27.0 Right curve onto Old Prosser Road.

29.5 Bear left onto Grandview at the Y-intersection.

29.7 Yakima Valley Grape. Port of Grandview/Chamber of Commerce.

29.9 Straight onto W 5th Street. Château St. Michelle Winery.

30.5 Dykstra Park and the Grandview School.

31.6 Right onto Putterbaugh Road.

32.0 Left before railroad tracks onto Forsell Road.

34.8 Hillvale Dairy.

35.5 Cross Knappton/Sunnyside Roads.

36.0 Right between hops fields L1 and L2 to unmarked Midvale Avenue.

36.5 Cross Murray Road.

37.0 Odiferous feed lot!

39.5 Right onto Alexander Road. Yakima Valley Cheese Company.

39.7 Backtrack and cross right under I–82.

40.0 Return to South Hill Park.

Skamania/Klickitat Counties
Columbia River Gorge: White Salmon Loop

Distance & Rating:	28.6 miles from Bingen Park, 21.7 miles from White Salmon River; one long uphill, headwinds
Surface & Traffic:	Paved roads; minimal cars except on Route 14
Highlights:	Bingen, Mont Elise Winery, orchards, Mount Adams and Mount Hood views, rural countryside, fish hatcheries, Columbia River Gorge, windsurfers
Eats:	The Wild Mushroom, Loafers Bakery, Mother's Marketplace
Sleeps:	The Bingen School Inn

Roll on, Columbia, roll on.
Roll on, Columbia, roll on.
Your power is turning our darkness to dawn,
So roll on, Columbia, roll on.

Woody Guthrie earned $266 for that catchy ballad and twenty-six other songs written for the Bonneville Power Administration's (BPA) slick promotional movies. Back in 1941 private companies ran the nation. Though power-hungry customers considered the damming and harnessing of the Columbia modern, necessary, noble, and humanitarian (Native American protesters saw the situation differently), folks did worry about transferring hydroelectric power from private control to a government arm. What foresight they had.

Nevertheless, the BPA won. The ditties caught on, their upbeat tunes and lyrics popularized by Woody, a sort of down-and-out, one-of-the-people, guitar-strumming wanderer. The electorate joined the bandwagon voting for the BPA. The government got the cheapest deal ever in paying Woody. Hardly just due for a song that rollicks in your head as you ponder this magnificent river's shore.

Although altered forever by dams and hydroelectric plants, the Columbia River remains an impressive, powerful sight. Carving, over eons, a seaward channel, it and its surrounding forests have provided fertile ground for wildlife. Most famous are the wild Columbia River salmon, a flavorful, endangered, and now pricey fish. Impeding its upriver trek to spawn, the dams have diminished its survival. Fish hatchery–spawned stock fares worse than nature's heartier wild stock. Enjoy them while you can.

Unsurpassed beauty and rural solitude make this ride. Luxuriant orchards, vineyards, and woods appeal to any spirit. Be prepared for rain—this is on the cusp of Washington's western side. Also, bring a warm layer for downhill and river portions.

Begin from Daubenspeck Park with a Loafer's Bakery (on Route 14) stop. Bingen, though pronounced "BEAN-gan" in German and named after Bingen-on-the-Rhine, is called "BIN-gan" by locals. So much for cultured ways. Cross the White Salmon River, treatied to Columbia River Indians for steelhead and salmon fishing. Dilapidated fishing shacks, reminiscent of Cannery Row, line the shore. Start here for a shorter ride. Climbing forested Cook Underwood Road requires low gearing. Don't be intimidated. Though it climbs a mile to an altitude of 1,200 feet, it's a gradual slope. Needless to say, the payback comes in a screeching descent to the Columbia.

On the upper plateau beneath Mount Adams, orchards and vineyards abound. Views of the Gorge, Mount Hood, and orchard blossoms in spring are heart stoppers. Stacked Mount Adams Orchard's crates mark the downhill, but stiff head winds can overpower gravity. At the ravine's bottom the pristine Little White Salmon River cascades in rumbling waterfalls adjacent to the Willard National Fish Hatchery.

Mill A and Cook, former logging towns converted to pastures, orchards, and tree farms, are inhabited by hardy farming folk—the kind who build clever covered-wagon mailboxes and who manicure yards with toy windmills, pioneer statues, and extensive Easter displays of plastic bunnies and chicks. Leave the liberal politics at home. Dropping to the Columbia River, the road slices steep, rocky hillsides where wild head winds batter.

When Lewis and Clark explored the Columbia, their namesake road, also called Route 14, didn't exist. Paralleling the river, it lacks the heavy traffic of Oregon's I–84 freeway and offers a wide shoulder, but also includes five short basalt tunnels. Before entering each tunnel, press the bike lights to warn drivers. At Drane Lake steelhead seekers drop lines, most leaving with empty hands and full stomachs: A laid-back bunch, they barbecue steaks, drink beer, and chat with cyclists. A historical marker describes the Broughton Log Flume, a 9-mile, water-powered slide, perched precariously above. Until 1986 it was the last working log flume in the United States.

The Gorge is synonymous with premier windsurfing. On Route 14 bicycle- and board-bedecked cars cram the shoulders. Experts head to the Spring Creek Fish Hatchery. Nicknamed "Swell City" and "The Fishery," the whitecaps require top-notch water-starts. As boarders catch the wind, their grace mesmerizes you. Locals love boarders (and their cash).

Across from the hatchery Broughton Lumber Company crumbles in disuse. Located on the site named for British explorer Lt. William Broughton, the spot served, during the late 1700s and early 1800s, as a major trading post for beads, liquor, and sundry goodies for sea otter and beaver pelts. Thrown in, at bargain rates, were smallpox and other diseases that killed half the local Native American population.

End by touring historical Bingen. The 1909 Bingen School functions as an Inn and Hostel—pretty basic. Nearby, the 1911 Methodist Church houses the Gorge Heritage Museum. Restored 1905 Victorian homes of Theodore Suksdorf (founder of Bingen) and Wilhelm Suksdorf (renowned botanist) are must-sees.

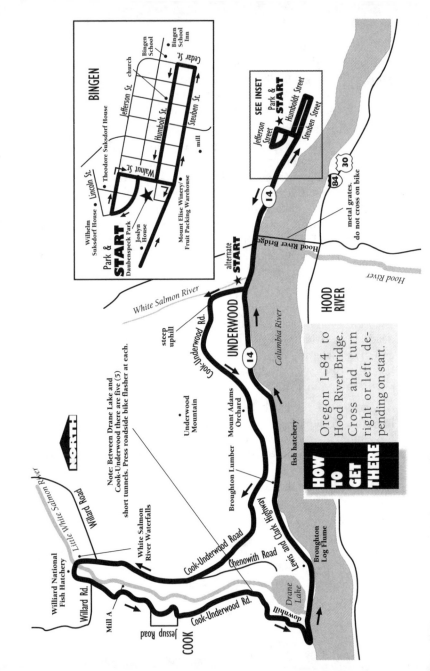

NORTH

BINGEN

Bingen School
Bingen School Inn
Cedar St.
church
Jefferson St.
Bingen School
Humboldt St.
Steuben St.
Theodore Suksdorf House
Wilhelm Suksdorf House
Lincoln St.
Walnut St.
mill
Joslyn House
Mount Elise Winery/ Fruit Packing Warehouse
Park & **START**
Daubenspeck Park

SEE INSET
Park & **START**
Humboldt Street
Jefferson Street
Steuben Street

84 30

14

Hood River Bridge
metal grates. do not cross on bike

HOOD RIVER

Hood River

Columbia River

alternate **START**

White Salmon River

steep uphill

Cook-Underwood Rd.

UNDERWOOD

14

Note: Between Drane Lake and Cook-Underwood there are five (5) short tunnels. Press roadside bike flasher at each.

Underwood Mountain

Mount Adams Orchard

fish hatchery

HOW TO GET THERE

Oregon I–84 to Hood River Bridge. Cross and turn right or left, depending on start.

Willard National Fish Hatchery

Little White Salmon River

Willard Road

Willard Rd.

White Salmon River Waterfalls

Mill A

Jessup Road

COOK

Cook-Underwood Rd.

Drane Lake

downhill

Broughton Lumber

Lewis and Clark Highway

Broughton Log Flume

Cook-Underwood Road

Chenowith Road

0.0 Right onto Route 14 from Walnut Street. Bingen Bakery.

2.7 Cross the White Salmon River. Right to Cook-Underwood Road. Uphill.

5.0 Whistling Ridge Trail.

5.6 Milepost 11.3. Viewpoint. Pear orchards and vineyards.

6.4 Crest. Gorge headwinds. Windy Place Drive. Mount Adams Orchard.

9.5 Right curve. Pass Chenowith Road.

11.0 Veer left on Cook Underwood Road at Y-intersection.

11.8 Little White Salmon River. Willard National Fish Hatchery.

12.5 Mill A. Left curve passing Jessup Road. Cook.

13.3 Left curve. Evergreen Grocery. Downhill.

17.0 Left onto Route 14. Columbia River, Drane Lake, Broughton Log Flume.

18.0 First of five tunnels. Press bike lights.

22.3 Broughton Lumber Company. Spring Creek Fish Hatchery.

24.5 White Salmon River bridge. End shorter ride.

27.2 Left onto Walnut to Daubenspeck Park or straight for historical tour. See inset map.

Multnomah County, Oregon
Columbia River Gorge: Hood River Valley

Distance & Rating:	16.4 miles; heavy-duty hills
Surface & Traffic:	Paved; light to moderate
Highlights:	Views, views, views. Mount Adams, Mount Hood, the Hood River and Valley, orchards, Blossom Festival (April), Harvest Fest (October), High Wind Classic (June)
Eats:	Holstein's Coffee Co., Carolyn's, Mesquitery, Pasquale's, Crazy Pepper, Full Sail Brewing, 6th St. Bistro, Mike's Ice Cream, Brian's Pourhouse
Sleeps:	Hood River Chamber of Commerce/Visitors Center (800) 366–3530, Roomfinder, (541) 386–6767, Gorge Central Reservations (877) 386–6109, Gorge Getaways (509) 493–4216; Oak Street Hotel, Hood River Hotel, Hood River Inn, State Street Inn, Inn at the Gorge, Panorama Lodge, Love's Riverview Lodge, B&B listings at www.bbchannel.com
Etc.:	Discover Bicycles, Waucoma Books, Columbia Art Gallery (305 Gallery); on-line reservations for accommodations and windsurfing, www.gorgeres.com; general information, www.lovesriverview.com

For this ride you need a camera and eyes in the back of your head. Stock up with film and water for this thigh-burner. Spring blossoms and the fall harvest accompany ideal weather, but RVs abound. Summers get hot. Pick your poison. You might (or perhaps not if you hate crowds) coordinate your trip with events such as the High Wind Classic, Harvest Fest, or Blossom Festival. While visiting, expand your horizons: Check out the Historical Museum or sample windsurfing, hiking, rock climbing, or mountain-biking forest trails.

Begin this scenic tour from the riverfront Visitors Center. Climb to the City of Hood River, first occupied by white settlers in the 1850s, when anyone willing to erect a building received free land. There was one catch—the deed included a "prohibitory whiskey" clause that excluded saloons. Nowadays, that doesn't hold. Hood River serves as the hot spot for windsurfers to wet their whistles. Windsurfing shops proliferate like pollinated blossoms. Sporting-gear offshoots stock a dazzling array of bicycles, clothing, hiking equipment, and books.

Pickups, four-wheel-drive trucks, and cars stand loaded to the gills with boards for varying wind speeds and mountain bikes. Stickers announce: FUKITZNUKIN, I'D RATHER BE WINDSURFING and PRAY FOR WIND. Just as football players have a look, windsurfers sport like characteristics; lean, muscular bodies; sun-bleached hair styled in the "flip it out of your eyes" cut; baggy shorts; the requisite Teva sandals and windsurfing T-shirts. These wind addicts gather in late mornings (winds pick up in the afternoon) at the funky, newspaper-strewn Holstein's Coffee Co. on Oak Street. Joining the local crowd for fruit-granola-yogurt "wake-me-ups" and chewy whole-grain waffles, they await the wind report. Don't miss the scene.

In this historic district the elegantly restored 1913 Hood River Hotel does a booming business. Graceful nineteenth-century Victorian homes, such as the immaculate State Street Inn or the 1903 Dutch Colonial Hackett House B&B, include porticoes, balconies, and gingerbread trim. Some suffer from neglect while others are meticulously restored; all it takes is money. A mile uphill, the less well-heeled Heights business section and Spanish neighborhood appear more down-home. Still, they offer superb Mount Adams and Mount Hood views. Consider dining here at the Mesquitery—their grill and rotisserie cook up delectable, moist fish, chicken, and meats at reasonable prices.

As 13th Street becomes Tucker Road, don't despair—this four-lane commercial strip is but a tiny blight. Escaping to Brookside Drive, you fly past pear orchards bespeckled with smudge pots. Friendly workers wave, shouting, "*Buenos días.*" Pastures and orchards stretch upward to Hood River Valley High School's hilltop setting. It's tough to imagine anyone dropping out of this idyllic place. It's not as though this is a grim urban school adjacent to a clattering elevated train—these kids peer at Mount Hood.

A breathtaking, mile-long glide ends across the Hood River, a silty mountain stream tumbling over a rocky bottom. On its bank the River Bend Country Store (rest rooms) overflows with organic fruits and jam, chutney, cheese, and honey and syrup goodies. Cold apple cider hits the spot—and feeds your muscles for the granny-gear uphill ahead (don't groan).

At the crest sprawling orchards and Mount Hood views pay you back. In your bliss don't roll on to Odell. Watch for the angled, unmarked, rural road (8.8 miles) that traverses splendid high-plain orchards. Stacked crates, picturesque farms, and sheep pastures await. Grassy foothills belie past logging and display the transition to Washington's drier side. Farmhouse floral and rose gardens radiate like rainbows.

Across Highway 35 a tortilla factory's aromas announce its presence. Above, at the hilltop cemetery, it's a Mount Hood photo op. Below, an unpretentious white church (intricate steeple and bell) and an old-fashioned schoolhouse (Pine Grove Elementary) recall a vanishing era. Bilingual signs serve the Mexican farm-labor families who live in orchard shacks. Gentlemen farms boast manicured gardens. A brilliant-red barn clings precariously to a steep hillside.

Clumps of scraggly oaks mark the climb to Panorama Point and its blow-you-away views. Pictorial maps detail logged and reforested areas, imparting a sense of the valley's virginal state. Roy Webster, the Point's original owner, donated it for a perpetual park, feeling it took "an hour to visit, a lifetime to remember." You won't forget it.

The steep, winding grade to town "separates the men from the boys"; soaring speed depends on nerve. Beware the sharp curves. It's a white-knuckle, brake-grabbing, bicyclist's "chicken." Cool off downtown with an iced espresso at Holstein's. You deserve it.

DIRECTIONS
FOR
THE RIDE

0.0 Right from Visitors Center, under I–84. (Farmers market on Saturdays)

1.1 Right at the T-intersection over RR tracks to Routes 30, 35, City of Hood River.

1.6 Right onto Front Street. Candy Store.

1.7 Left curve onto Oak Street. Holstein's Coffee Co. Hood River Hotel.

2.4 Left up 9th Avenue. Steep.

2.5 Right onto State Street. State Street Inn.

2.9 Left onto 13th Street. City park.

3.1 Heights business section. Latino neighborhood. Views.

3.3 Left and right curves. Becomes Tucker Road. Commercial strip. Caution!

4.0 Right onto Brookside Drive before cemetery. Orchards.

4.5 Left onto Indian Creek Road at the T-intersection.

5.0 Curves to high school. Indian Creek Road becomes Tucker Road.

5.5 Hood River Airport. Downhill.

6.7 Hood River. Cross bridge. River Bend Country Store (rest rooms). Uphill.

7.1 Left up Odell Highway at the Y-intersection for 0.6 mile.

8.7 Angle left onto unmarked road. Sewage Treatment Plant. Do not continue to Odell.

9.5 Orchards. Right curve downhill. Pass Wickerson Road.

10.2 Left onto Highway 35 at the T-intersection to Hood River. Pippen Apple Orchards.

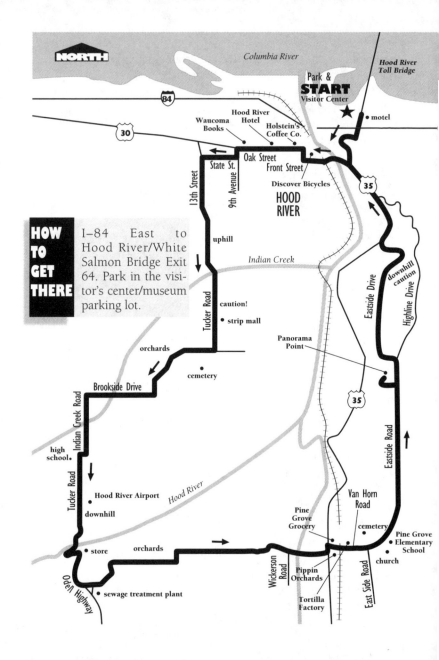

10.5 Right onto Van Horn Road before Pine Grove Grocery.

10.7 Fire department and tortilla factory. Cross RR tracks. Uphill.

11.5 Crest. Cemetery. Mount Hood photo op.

11.8 Pass Eastside Road on right. White frame church.

12.0 Left curve onto Eastside Road. School. Ignore Hood River signs.

14.0 Left up to Panorama Point. Views!

14.5 Left onto Eastside Road from Panorama Point.

16.0 Right onto unmarked Route 35 at the T-intersection. Go under I–84 or to town.

16.4 Left into Visitors Center.

Canada: Vancouver, B.C.
Downtown Neighborhoods Exploration

Distance & Rating:	16.5 miles; mostly flat and easy
Surface & Traffic:	Paved; none to heavy traffic
Highlights:	Downtown Vancouver, Stanley Park, Granville Island & Public Market, Yaletown, Chinatown, Gastown
Eats:	Downtown area: La Casa Gelato, Vancouver Art Gallery Café, Quilicaum, Caper's Market & Café (natural foods), Le Crocodile; Granville Island: plentiful eateries; Chinatown: Phnom Penh; Yaletown: Yaletown Brewing, Villa del Lupo; Kitislano: Star Anise, Terra Breads, Ecco Il Pano (breads and café)
Sleeps:	British Columbia Reservation Service/free (800) 663–6000, Travel Guide (800) 667–3306; Downtown: Hotel Georgia, Hotel Vancouver; English Bay: Sylvia Hotel, Yaletown: YWCA Hotel, Rosedale on Robson, Georgian Court Hotel
Bikes:	Main Station Bikes (604) 669–BIKE, Bicycle Sports Pacific (604) 682–4537, Reckless (604) 731–2420, Stanley Park Rentals (604) 608–1908
Etc.:	Tourist InfoCentre (604) 683–2000; www.tourism-vancouver.org, TicketMaster (604) 280–4444

Oh, what a cosmopolitan treat! Every possible assault on the senses: gorgeous Stanley Park, seaside bike paths, Granville Island Market, Chinatown, developing Yaletown, and Gastown. This tour is truly urban riding at its best. Vancouver's diverse populations and neighborhoods entice you to explore, using a bicycle as transportation. This is not meant to be purely a workout.

Start at Robson and Thurlow Streets, heading toward Stanley Park and Lost Lagoon. Set your mind for a casual, tourist ride. Bicycle paths lace the park, but if you have only one trip to do, go for the seawall. An underpass leads to the seawall, totems, and a string of memorial benches. Bicyclists travel counterclockwise in the park and share the path with joggers, in-line skaters, and casual walkers. At several short spots you must walk your bike ($75 infraction!), but for sheer beauty, this can't be beat.

Commercial and luxury liners cruise the harbor. Fog rolls in and out, abundant waterfowl preen, and people fish. At low tide dogs cavort on the sand below the seawall, chasing sticks into the water. The cast-bronze *Girl in a Wetsuit*, appearing to ponder the meaning of life, rises from the water. Stanley Park's lush forests give way to English Bay's sandy beaches. A short cycle on Beach Avenue leads to the bay path at Bidwell Street, where a stone sculpture graces a point. Cutting through waterfront condo and shopping areas, follow the bike signs past Alexandria Park and Sunset Beach. Slide under three bridges and through the Plaza of Nations, a popular outdoor music-festival site.

Along False Creek the bike path wends through barren and developing land. Years after Expo, the acres are turning into an architectural mix of urban towers and townhouses that sell out before ground is broken. Be prepared to take detours as development heats up. B.C. Place Stadium and GM Place loom on the left as the route circles False Creek's end past B. C .Science World.

The wood walkway will eventually lead to the bike path to Granville Island. Construction of segments is underway, but for now bicyclists take West 1st Avenue, following the bike signs under Cambie Bridge and right onto Spyglass Street to the waterfront bike path.

Granville Island and Public Market are a delight for locals and visitors alike: artist studios, outdoor gear, adventure-travel agencies, Granville Island Brewing, a kids' mall, and restaurants. Without a doubt the superb Public Market tops all lists of places to explore. Performers entertain outdoors on the plaza. Fruits and vegetables, especially those from local farmers, are picture-perfect. Hearty and nutty wild rice from Manitoba beckons. Fish and organic meats beat any supermarket fare. Cheese and pasta shops make you drool. An incredible array of prepared gourmet soups, salads, baked goods, coffee, and juices complicate choices for lunch. Wander a bit before deciding. Remember, you cannot take fruit or produce back across the border. Instead, take a cooler to bring home the mushroom or butternut ravioli—with a touch of butter, parmesan, and sage, you're in heaven.

From Granville Island hop on the Cyquabus (flat boat for bikes) or Aquabus ($2.00) across False Creek to the Yaletown stop. Head up to Pacific Boulevard. Cross onto Davie Street, making a quick right onto Homer Street to Yaletown. Transformed from an industrial and warehouse district (and red-light area), Yaletown is finding new life as home to lofts, brew pubs, gourmet eateries, trendy clothing shops, art galleries, and Euro-style furniture and bath shops. Flocking here are the creative folk: clothing designers, architects, chefs, and actors. Yaletown is growing rapidly—amid the noise and dirt of massive construction. Located in the new Sports and Entertainment District, Yaletown satisfies all hungers. Mangiamo dapples well in Northern Italian. Yaletown Brewing provides good, hearty fare for tourists and sports fans. The young and restless imbibe, hang out, and play pool at BarNun. In the spring of 1996, Starbucks moved in—a sure sign of success. Stroll the streets and enjoy.

Just before Georgia Street note Israeli-Canadian architect Moshe Safdie's spectacular $26-million Ford Theater for the Performing Arts, inaugurated in 1995 with the revival of *Showboat*. Excellent design and acoustics are drawing critical acclaim and top entertainment. Across the street Safdie's Vancouver Public Library (1995) mixes an archaeological coliseum facade with stark modern facilities within.

Vancouver's Chinatown may beat San Francisco's as the largest North American Chinese enclave. For an intriguing lunch and walk, try Dim Sum and check the fish and veggie shops. Visit Dr. Sun Yat-Sen Classical Chinese Garden at Carrall Street, a serene interlude from this noisy street of babble. Close by, old-world Gastown deals in new-world T-shirts, ethnic items, ecology, and trinkets. Known for its late-1800s architecture, brick paving, period lighting, and Steam Clock, Gastown is in danger of losing its charm through an invasion of tacky shops. One holdout, the Spirit Wrestler Gallery, stocks museum-quality Inuit and Northwest Coast art.

Exiting Gastown, Burrard Inlet catapults you to a world of high-quality shopping malls and classy hotels that beckon to the sleek cruise ships and tankers below. Put in some gawking time before racing to Starbucks for an iced latte.

0.0 Robson and Thurlow Streets at Starbucks Coffee. Head toward Stanley Park.

0.9 Veer left onto Lagoon Drive.

1.0 Veer right onto driveway/park path after tennis courts.

1.3 Right along Lost Lagoon and fence.

1.5 Tunnel under West Georgia Street. Veer right and left onto Seawall Promenade. At several points you must walk your bike briefly.

3.9 Veer left as bike path enters woods. Return to Seawall.

4.2 Pass under Lyons Gate Bridge.

7.0 Veer right onto Beach Avenue, exiting Stanley Park.

7.1 Right after Bidwell Street, returning to Seaside Bike Path at English Bay Beach. Stone sculpture.

7.9 False Creek Ferry stop. Circle clockwise around False Creek, at times riding through waterfront condo and shopping areas.

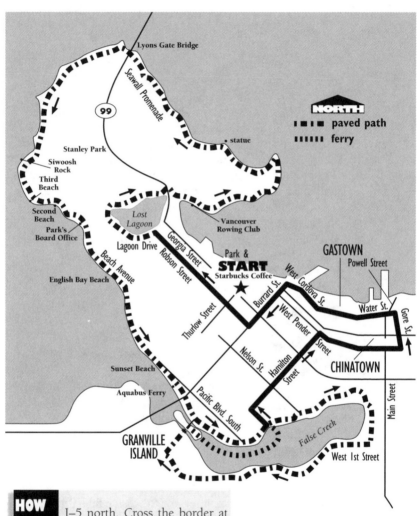

Lyons Gate Bridge

Seawall Promenade

(99)

Stanley Park

Siwoosh Rock

Third Beach

• statue

NORTH

■ ▪ ■ ▪ paved path

▪▪▪▪▪ ferry

Second Beach

Park's Board Office

Lost Lagoon

Vancouver Rowing Club

GASTOWN

Powell Street

Lagoon Drive

Georgia Street

Park & **START**

Starbucks Coffee

Robson Street

West Cordova St.

Water St.

Beach Avenue

English Bay Beach

Burrard St.

West Pender

Gore St.

Thurlow Street

Nelson St.

Hamilton Street

Street

CHINATOWN

Sunset Beach

Aquabus Ferry

Pacific Blvd. South

False Creek

Main Street

GRANVILLE ISLAND

West 1st Street

HOW TO GET THERE
I–5 north. Cross the border at Blaine and stop at Tourist Information for a Vancouver map. Follow Route 99 into downtown Vancouver.

7.6 Stay on bike path, passing condos, shopping, and bridges.

8.2 Hornby Ferry stop. Turn left 0.25 block and right onto Seaside Bike Path.

9.6 Ride through Plaza of Nations, picking up bike path at the end. BC Place Stadium to left.

10.1 Veer right around False Creek. BC Science World. Wood walkway.

10.4 Right onto West 1st Avenue, following bike signs.

11.0 Go under bridge and right onto Spyglass Street 1 block to Seawall Bike Path.

12.5 Granville Island and Public Market. Explore.

False Creek Crossing via Cyquabus

0.0 Reset odometer. Leave Granville Island via the Cyquabus or Aquabus Ferry ($2.00) behind the Public Market. Get off at the Yaletown stop.

0.5 Take path to Pacific Boulevard and cross to Davie Street. Area under massive development.

0.7 Right onto Homer Street into Yaletown.

1.4 Cross West Georgia Street after the Ford Theater and Vancouver Public Library.

1.6 Right onto West Pender Street, downhill.

2.0 Enter Chinatown. Lock bike and walk near Main Street.

2.3 Left onto Gore Street.

2.5 Left onto Powell Street.

2.7 Enter Gastown, veering slightly right onto Water Street.

3.1 Leave Gastown, veering right onto West Cordova Street.

3.4 Left at the T-intersection onto Burrard Street.

3.9 Right onto Robson Street.

4.0 End at Thurlow Street at Starbucks Coffee.

Canada: Vancouver, B.C.
False Bay and Pacific Spirit Regional Park Loop

Distance & Rating:	20.1 miles; easy to moderate, one long hill
Surface & Traffic:	Paved road, paved and packed gravel paths; none to heavy
Highlights:	Downtown Vancouver, Vancouver Museum and Planetarium, waterfront parks, Spanish Banks, Totem Pole Park and the Museum of Anthropology, University Endowment Lands, Pacific Spirit Regional Park
Eats, Sleeps, Bikes:	See Ride 57

Vancouver. The most cosmopolitan of Northwest Coast cities. Spectacular scenery, fine dining, terrific bike paths, a mouthwatering market place, and top shopping (the U.S. dollar exchange rate buys lots for your bucks) combine for an incredibly rich experience.

In a stroke of genius, Vancouver halted suburban flight by banning in-city freeways and encouraging apartment and townhouse construction. The plan worked, making Vancouver densely populated and alive—a real city. The recent influx of wealthy Hong Kong Chinese has brought a new culture to the mix as well as a boom to the economy. Visiting via bicycle allows you to garner the city's worldly ambience. Established bike trails keep you out of traffic, though short sprints on main roads require an "attitude" about your right to ride.

Begin riding from your hotel—ideally downtown. (Stash your car in the hotel garage and forget it.) This ride begins arbitrarily from Thurlow and Robson Streets, complete with not one, but two

Starbucks Coffees, each with its own devotees. A morning cappuccino will perk you up for Thurlow's uphill toward the Burrard Bridge.

Crossing the bridge takes you to the Kitislano neighborhood. Residential Chestnut Street (quick first right from bridge) leads to the popular Vancouver Museum, Planetarium, and Vanier Park on English Bay. At the St. Roch Historic Site, an intricate totem speaks of native influences. Upscale homes, townhouses, and condos are an urban architect's dream. This is city living at its best.

The adjacent Kitislano Park, with its pool, tennis courts, and crowds, skirts the bay. On its far side Point Grey Road is flanked by massive old homes and seaside stone row houses that appear lifted from a country lane in England. At Cornwall Avenue don't get confused. Press the bicycle light, go *straight* across, and climb Trafalgar Street (do not follow Cornwall right). Bike signs lead to Jericho Park, site of the Summer Folk Festival. The park's packed gravel path edges the bay, a hot spot for windsurfing, sailing, and kayaking. At the Sailing and Kayaking Center, the path veers from the water.

Bicycle bypass signs are meant for racers. Stay with the packed gravel path for a delightful jaunt along the Spanish Banks waterfront. The gorgeous sand beach may tempt you to wade. As the beach narrows the path ends, becoming an uphill bike lane on forested Marine Drive (mountain bikers can use dirt path) until the sidewalk resumes at the University Endowment Lands and Pacific Spirit Regional Park. Watch for nesting bald eagles. As the climb ends, rest up at the historic marker and enjoy terrific views. The university is ahead on the left.

Watch for the next right off Marine Drive, marked CECIL GREEN PARK and UBC ALUMNI—SCHOOL OF SOCIAL WORK. At the cul-de-sac continue through the parking lot, past the chain gate, and onto a dirt path to Totem Park and the Museum of Anthropology. Powerful Haida sculptures humanize the stark glass-and-concrete museum. A single-track, wooded dirt path continues to Marine Drive. Visit the museum by going left 0.1 mile.

Downhill, the charming English-style Botanical Gardens are worth visiting. Another historical marker, at a stunning viewpoint, describes the Fraser River exploration. Simon Fraser and John Stewart, under the misconception that this was the Columbia, headed out twice, once in 1793 and again in 1808. After gliding downhill be careful to make a sharp backward left onto Camuson Street at the 41st Avenue and Marine Drive stoplight. Check the University Endowment Lands/Pacific Spirit Regional Park map there, which details the park's mountain-bike trails. Signage on the trails is confusing, but try to exit on 29th Street to pick up the route. Detailed maps are available by mail from the park office (telephone (604) 224–5739).

Use caution crossing the four-lane W 16th Street (no light) toward the bay. Awesome city views highlight the water and mountain setting and portray the extent of city development. On this Kitislano side spectacular Tudor, stucco, and sleek modern homes peer across to city life in glass towers, low-rise town homes, lofts, and row houses—a model for cities under redevelopment.

From Point Grey Road's turn left at the bike light retrace the ride's early miles to Vanier Park. Here, you can turn right onto Chestnut Street or go left into the park to Granville Island Market—not to be missed if you have no other riding day. After the market cycle around False Bay or backtrack to Burrard Bridge. Use extreme caution turning left onto Cornwall Street and in heading toward Burrard Bridge. Head back to Starbucks and wander Robson's plethora of unique shops and food stops—a vast array of ethnic eats, delectable gelato, clothing from conservative to leather and chains, Doc Marten's, and, for persons with a shoe fetish, well-priced Eurostyle shoes at Simard.

DIRECTIONS

FOR

THE RIDE

0.0 Thurlow and Robson Streets at Starbucks Coffee. Climb Thurlow Street.

0.9 Left onto Pacific Street toward the Burrard Bridge. Use the sidewalk.

1.0 Right across the bridge on sidewalk.

1.7 Right onto Chestnut Street. Vanier Park. Vancouver Museum.

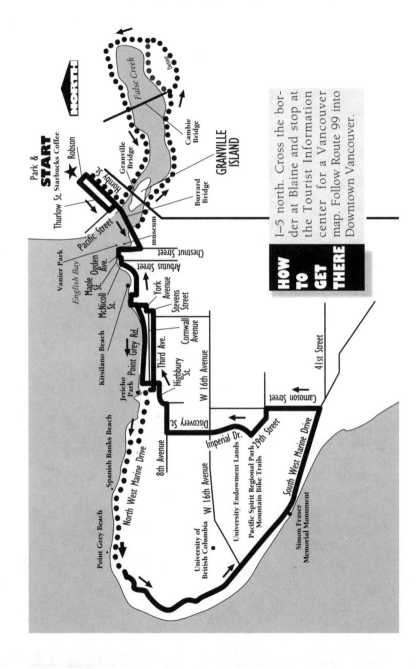

NORTH

Park &
START

Thurlow St. Starbucks Coffee

Robson

Hornby St.

False Creek

Granville Bridge

Cambie Bridge

GRANVILLE ISLAND

Burrard Bridge

Pacific Street

museum

Vanier Park

English Bay

Chestnut Street

Ogden Ave.

Maple St.

Arbutus Street

McNicoll St.

York Avenue

Stevens Street

Kitsilano Beach

Point Grey Rd.

Jericho Park

Third Ave.

Cornwall Avenue

Highbury St.

W 16th Avenue

Discovery St.

Spanish Banks Beach

North West Marine Drive

8th Avenue

Imperial Dr.

Camosun Street

South West Marine Drive

Point Grey Beach

University Endowment Lands

W 16th Avenue

29th Street

Pacific Spirit Regional Park
Mountain Bike Trails

41st Street

University of
British Columbia

Simon Fraser
Memorial Monument

HOW TO GET THERE

I-5 north. Cross the border at Blaine and stop at the Tourist Information center for a Vancouver map. Follow Route 99 into Downtown Vancouver.

1.9 Left onto Ogden Avenue. Maritime Museum. Totem pole. Bike signs.

2.0 Left as the road turns to Maple Street.

2.1 Right onto McNicoll Avenue and left curve onto Arbutus Street.

2.4 Right into the parking lot, following bike signs through park.

2.7 Right at the end of the park onto Point Grey Road.

2.8 Seaside Bikeride sign.

3.0 Cornwall Avenue. Press bicycle light. Straight onto Trafalgar Street.

3.1 Right onto 1st Avenue.

3.2 Left onto Stephens Street.

3.3 Right onto 3rd Avenue, following the bike signs.

4.8 Right onto Wallace Street; quick left onto 2nd Avenue.

4.9 Right into parking lot and Jericho Park. Gravel path.

5.0 Veer left after Jericho Sailing and Kayak Center.

5.5 Ignore BICYCLE BYPASS, USE ROADWAY sign. Use path on Spanish Banks waterfront.

6.8 Exit path, climbing the wooded road.

7.0 Pass parking lot, return to sidewalk. Pacific Spirit Regional Park.

7.3 University Endowment Lands.

7.9 Historical marker. University of British Columbia.

8.0 Right at sign for Cecil Green Park. UBC Alumni: School of Social Work.

8.2 Go through the parking lot. Pass chain gate onto a dirt trail.

8.3 Totem Park and the Museum of Anthropology.

8.4 Continue on dirt path through woods.

8.5 Right onto Marine Drive.

9.6 Botanical Gardens on right.

11.2 Historical marker and viewpoint. Downhill.

12.7 Sharp left onto Camuson Street before the 41st and Marine Drive stoplight. Pacific Spirit Regional Park map. Uphill.

13.1 Left onto 29th Avenue at the crest.

13.5 Curve right as 29th Avenue becomes (unmarked) Imperial Drive. Camosun Bog.

14.2 Cross four-lane W 16th Avenue. Caution! Imperial Drive becomes Discovery Street.

14.7 Right at T-intersection to 8th Avenue. Downhill.

15.1 Veer left following 8th Avenue downhill. Wallace Street on right.

15.4 Left onto Highbury Street. Do not follow bike sign straight ahead.

15.6 Walk across 4th Avenue. Caution!

15.9 Right onto Point Grey Road at the T-intersection and yacht club. Heavier traffic.

16.9 Follow Point Grey Road left as it turns at the stoplight. Trafalgar Street on right.

17.2 Left onto Kitsilano Park's bike path; go through parking lot.

17.6 Left from lot onto Arbutus Street and bike route.

17.8 Veer right to McNicoll Avenue and quick left onto Maple Street.

17.9 Right onto Ogden Street.

18.1 Right onto Chestnut Street. Or see Granville Island Option.

18.3 Right onto Greer Street, following bike signs to Burrard Bridge.

18.4 Left onto Cypress Street.

18.5 Left at light onto Cornwall Avenue. Caution, heavy traffic to bridge.

18.7 Cross bridge on sidewalk. Continue uphill on Burrard Street.

20.0 Left onto Robson Street.

20.1 Return to beginning at Thurlow Street.

Option: Granville Island (begins at 18.1-mile point)

0.0   Left into Vanier Park. Veer right onto bike path along seawall.

0.5   Go under Burrard Bridge. Veer left to seawall. Granville sign.

1.0   Left under bridge onto Anderson Street and Granville Island. *Lock up and explore the market. Mileage restarts from this point.*

0.0   Continue along Island Park Walk seawall.

1.4   Right under bridge following bike route signs.

1.5   Left onto Spyglass Street at bridge. Continuation of route in progress.

1.6   Left onto 1st Avenue.

2.2   Left onto Ontario Street before stoplight.

2.3   Bear right and left around B.C. Science Center and end of False Creek.

2.6   Bear left following False Creek. Dome ahead.

2.8   Bear left into Plaza of Nations. Follow bike signs.

4.3   Go under bridge, following bike path between buildings.

4.5   Right onto Hornby Street toward downtown.

5.2   Left onto Robson Street.

5.4   Return to beginning at Thurlow Street.

About the Author

Judy Wagonfeld, a former nurse and health educator, is a freelance writer and outdoor enthusiast. Over the last eighteen years, she has cycled thousands of miles around Puget Sound, the United States, and abroad, both for recreation and as her basic daily transportation. Daughters Temira and Ariella, avid cyclists also, commute by bicycle, and Temira has put her bike to work by developing a mountain bike unit for Pierce County Search and Rescue.

Please feel free to send comments and suggestions to Judy care of The Globe Pequot Press, P.O. Box 480, Guilford, Connecticut 06437.

Overview of the Rides

		Trail, Bike Lane or Shoulder	Rural or Isolated
1	Birch Bay: Semi-ah-moo Point & Birch Bay Loop	●	●
2	Bellingham: Interurban Trail, Larrabee State Park, Historic Fairhaven	●	●
3	Bellingham: Railroad Trail/Lake Whatcom Loop	●	●
4	Bellingham: Lake Padden Park	●	
5	Orcas Island: East Orcas, West Orcas Loops		●
6	San Juan Island: American Camp and Roche Harbor Loops		●
7	Whidbey Island: Keystone/Ebey's Landing Loop		●
8	La Conner: Fir Island Loop		●
9	Bow: Valley Loop		●
10	Bow: Padilla Bay Shore Trail	●	
11	Snohomish: Centennial Trail	●	●
12	Everett: Smith Island Loop	●	
13	Quimper Peninsula: Marrowstone Island		●
14	Quimper Peninsula: Fort Worden/Port Townsend		●
15	Peninsula: Chief Sealth (a.k.a. Chief Seattle) Poulsbo Loop		●
16	Islands: Bainbridge Island Loop		
17	Seattle: Elliott Bay Trail & Pier 91 Bike Path	●	
18	Seattle: Magnolia Loop		●
19	Seattle: Discovery Park	●	●
20	Seattle: Green Lake Loop	●	
21	Seattle: Seward Park Loop and Lake Washington Boulevard	●	
22	Seattle: Burke Gilman/Sammamish River Trails	●	
23	Maple Valley: Soos Creek Trail	●	●
24	Maple Valley: Lake Youngs Loop	●	●
25	Bellevue: Phantom Lake Loop and Lake Hills Greenbelt	●	
26	Pacific/Tukwila: Interurban and Christensen–Green River Trail	●	
27	Kent: Cedar River Trail—Lake Wilderness to Landsburg Park	●	●
28	Enumclaw: Enumclaw/Black Diamond Loop		●
29	Vashon Island Loop		●
30	Gig Harbor: City Park/Ollala Loop		●
31	Gig Harbor: Three-Loop Option		●
32	Key Peninsula: Home/Longbranch Loop		●
33	Tacoma: Point Defiance Loop		
34	Tacoma: Ruston Way Path	●	
35	Tacoma: Historical Loop		
36	Steilacoom: Steilacoom, Lakewood, and DuPont	●	
37	Dupont: Northwest Landing and Dupont	●	
38	Steilacoom: Fort Steilacoom Park and Waughop Lake	●	

Safest for Children	Difficult Traffic	Romantic Sleeps	Tasty Eats	Scenic Views	Cool Stuff, Historic	Easy to Moderate	Challenging Terrain	
	●	●	●	●	●	●		**1**
●	●	●	●	●	●			**2**
●	●			●	●	●		**3**
●				●	●	●		**4**
		●	●	●	●		●	**5**
	●	●	●	●	●		●	**6**
	●	●	●	●	●		●	**7**
		●	●	●	●	●		**8**
			●	●	●	●		**9**
●				●	●	●		**10**
●	●	●		●	●	●		**11**
●	●			●	●	●		**12**
●		●		●	●	●		**13**
	●	●	●	●	●		●	**14**
	●	●	●	●	●		●	**15**
	●	●	●	●	●		●	**16**
●		●		●	●	●		**17**
			●	●	●	●	●	**18**
●				●	●	●	●	**19**
●			●	●	●	●		**20**
●			●	●	●		●	**21**
●			●	●	●	●		**22**
●	●			●	●	●		**23**
●	●			●	●	●		**24**
●				●	●	●		**25**
●	●			●	●	●		**26**
				●	●	●	●	**27**
	●	●	●	●	●		●	**28**
●	●	●	●	●	●		●	**29**
		●	●	●	●	●	●	**30**
		●	●	●	●	●	●	**31**
	●			●	●	●	●	**32**
								33
●		●	●	●	●	●		**34**
								35
	●		●	●	●	●	●	**36**
●	●			●	●	●	●	**37**
●			●	●	●	●		**38**

Overview of the Rides, continued

		Trail, Bike Lane or Shoulder	Rural or Isolated
39	Tacoma: Wapato Park/Puyallup Loop		
40	Puyallup: Puyallup Valley Tour de Pierce		•
41	Orting: Daffodil Classic—Orting, Kapowsin, Eatonville, Ohop Loops		•
42	Olympia: Priest Point Park, Boston Harbor, Historic Olympia		•
43	Olympia: Chehalis Railroad/Woodard Bay Trail	•	•
44	Millersylvania: Olympia, Mounds, Wolves, and Sandstone		•
45	Chehalis: Historical Lewis County Loop		•
46	Woodland: Covered Bridge and Cedar Creek Grist Mill		•
47	Woodland: Columbia River Delta		
48	Long Beach Peninsula: Historic North Peninsula/Leadbetter Point		•
49	Long Beach Peninsula: South Peninsula/Lewis and Clark's Loop		•
50	Long Beach Peninsula: Ilwaco/Fort Columbia Loop		•
51	Grays River: Grays River Covered Bridge		•
52	Ellensburg: Wild West Weekend		•
53	Yakima: Donald and Zillah Orchard and Wine Loop		•
54	Sunnyside/Prosser Wine Loop	•	•
55	Columbia River Gorge: White Salmon Loop		•
56	Columbia River Gorge: Hood River Valley		•
57	Vancouver, B.C.: Downtown Neighborhoods Exploration	•	
58	Vancouver, B.C.: False Bay and Pacific Spirit Regional Park Loop	•	

Safest for Children	Difficult Traffic	Romantic Sleeps	Tasty Eats	Scenic Views	Cool Stuff, Historic	Easy to Moderate	Challenging Terrain	
								39
				●	●	●	●	40
	●	●		●	●		●	41
		●		●	●		●	42
●				●	●	●		43
				●	●	●	●	44
		●		●	●	●	●	45
	●	●	●	●	●	●	●	46
			●	●	●	●		47
●		●	●	●	●	●		48
	●	●	●	●	●	●	●	49
		●	●	●	●	●	●	50
				●	●	●		51
	●	●	●	●	●		●	52
	●	●	●	●	●	●	●	53
	●	●	●	●	●	●	●	54
	●	●		●	●		●	55
	●	●	●	●	●		●	56
●	●	●	●	●	●	●	●	57
●	●	●	●	●	●	●	●	58

Appendix

Bicycling

Bicycle Alliance of Washington, (206) 224–9252,
www.bicyclealliance.org

Bicycle Paper (information and calendar on bicycling in Washington
State), (425) 438–9031, www.bicyclepaper.com

Bicycle Washington(cross state tour), (877) 224–9252 (toll free),
www.bicyclealliance.org

Blazing Saddles Bicycle Rental, 1230 Western Ave., Downtown
Seattle, (206) 341–9994, www.blazingsaddles.com

Cascade Bicycle Club (Seattle), (206) 522–BIKE, www.cascade.org

League of American Bicyclists (LAB), (202) 822–1333 or (800)
288–BIKE, www.bikeleague.org

Tacoma Wheelman Bicycle, (253) 759–1816, www.twbc.org

Transportation

Washington State Ferry System & Washington State Department of
Transportation, (800) 542–7052 or (800) 542–0810,
www.wsdot.wa.gov

WA State Park Reservations, (800) 452–5687

San Juan Island Shuttle Express (passenger only), (360) 671–1137